The **MIRROR LIED**

Library of Congress Cataloging in Publication Data

———————————

———————————

———————————

Published by STAY WITH US PUBLICATIONS.

Contact Information:
STAY WITH US PUBLICATIONS
5 Sunrise Plaza
Suite # 202
Valley Stream, NY 11580
(516) 825-5005
ZimmerMitgang@AOL.com

ISBN: 1439257027
EAN-13: 9781439257029
LCCN: 2009909100

The MIRROR LIED

━━⧟⧟⧟━━

Based on a true story

Marc A. Zimmer, Ph.D. & N.R. Mitgang

With a Foreword by Ira M. Sacker, M.D.

Dedications

For Hillary, Matthew, Justin, Brittany, and Sherlock, "The Gang."

The utmost of appreciation and gratitude is extended to my family, especially my wife, Hillary, friends, and many patients who have all shared, supported, and inspired the writing of this book.

Without such devotion, this publication would not have been possible.

Marc A. Zimmer, Ph.D.

If you have a brother like mine, Jeffrey Mitgang, an angel has touched your life.

N.R. Mitgang

Table of Contents

Foreword

Dr. Ira M. Sacker

What you are about to read is a biography as told to the authors. Additional scenes and dialogue were added to completely unfold the story. The main character, Jessica, is a real person. For many years, she has been a patient of Dr. Marc A. Zimmer, my colleague and friend for close to thirty years, who specializes in treating people with anorexia, bulimia, and other forms of eating disorders.

Where the stories took place and the names of the characters have been changed to protect the anonymity and privacy of those patients who were so graciously willing to share their narratives with the outside world.

Jessica suffered through many years of depression and social withdrawal brought about by this debilitating disorder. *The Mirror Lied* delves deeply into Jessica's inner thoughts and psyche. Through Jessica's own words, which were obtained through numerous in-depth interviews, you will experience the lifestyle of a person with eating disorders, and you will gain a better understanding of the acute struggle to fight for recovery.

I commend the authors for making a deliberate effort to convey the serious consequences brought about by this disorder. Anyone whose life has been touched by a person with an eating disorder can empathize with Jessica, her husband, children, family, and friends.

More must be done to prevent this disorder. Why? The answer is simple. Once an eating disorder begins, especially if it is left unchecked or improperly treated, it can kill its victim.

* * *

DR. IRA M. SACKER is the co-author of *Dying to Be Thin: Understanding and Defeating Anorexia Nervosa and Bulimia–A Practical, Lifesaving Guide* (Ira M. Sacker, M.D., & Marc A. Zimmer, Ph.D.) and *Regaining Your Self: Breaking Free From The Eating Disorder Identity: A Bold New Approach* (Ira M. Sacker, M.D., & Sheila Buff). Dr. Sacker is a clinical assistant professor of pediatrics, New York University Medical Center and Bellevue Hospital Medical Center, and he maintains a private practice specializing in eating disorders in Manhattan and Long Island. Dr. Sacker is nationally and internationally renowned and frequently appears in print and on radio and television.

* * *

Chapter One

Deadly Déjà Vu

There are two types of people with eating disorders: those who live and those who die. My name is Jessica Gordon. My maiden name was Devoe. For half of my life, I suffered from anorexia and bulimia. I am a forty-six-year-old former medical technician, and I am at a fork in my life's journey. One path leads to life, while the other may take me on an excursion into the afterlife.

Over the past twenty years, I've seen the faces of the starving and walking dead. Their drawn faces and emaciated bodies didn't look much different from mine. That's what scares me. Those deceased women passed me in hospital corridors. They spoke of their lack of medical problems in group therapy sessions, and they denied any concern for their psychological or medical future. Some of those women thought they would live forever. Others wished for death or even attempted suicide. I pray those women who died eventually found peace in the hereafter. That's not what I seek. I pray for peace in the here and now, but it's a goal that seems unattainable for me.

Today my loyal and loving husband, Jack, is driving stoically and silently over the same route from Long Island to New Jersey that we have taken multiple times before. At the end of the journey he'll hand me over to the professionals he hopes will save my life. The truth is, they can't save me. The only person who can save me is me.

Today, as he did in the past, Jack will sign the insurance forms and ask me to sign the self-admitting inpatient consent forms. Once again, he'll carry my small suitcase to the elevator door that will take me up to my voluntary prison walls. He'll kiss me goodbye. I'll go up the elevator, sit on my bed, and cry for two hours as I've always done in the past. I'll chastise and condemn myself for having gotten myself into this situation, then I'll cry again because of the guilt and worthlessness I feel inside.

I don't want to go where I'm going. I don't believe I need to go where I'm going. I feel fine. I hate, more than anything, to be away from my sixteen-year-old daughter and twelve-year-old son. Maybe my kids can handle the separation from me because they will be with their father, but I can't handle being away from them. I'm their mother. I belong with them. I don't belong in a hospital sharing a room with a perfect stranger and being told what to eat, how to behave, and how to exist over the next several weeks. I can take care of myself.

We're minutes away from the hospital. Though it's freezing outside, my window is open to keep me from choking on the suffocating anxiety, anguish, and feelings of failure stuck in my throat. I know this routine all too well. I hate it. I hate myself for putting myself into this potentially deadly and self-inflicted condition. I'm a mother about to abandon my children, again.

God, please, let this be the last journey of this kind, or let me just die and finally find peace in your sanctuary.

* * *

Chapter Two

Recollections of a Messed-Up Childhood

U nlike some other life-threatening and catastrophic health problems, to date, no one is born with a gene that predetermines them for an eating disorder. However, there are certain personality types that are predisposed to an eating disorder, and events in one's childhood or adulthood can trigger that terrible mental disorder into existence. Some get lucky and beat their fated tragedy. I didn't get lucky. At least not in that regard. From birth to age twenty-three, I was on a rocket ride heading straight into a brick wall. Perhaps if I had started therapy when I was five I could have avoided that gruesome crash, but I didn't. Instead, I crashed into that wall at full throttle.

About the only time I can remember living normally was from birth to age five. Why? That's because I have almost no memories prior to age five. I'm sure if I went through successful regressive hypnotherapy, I'd find some nonsense that hit the fan during those years, but I've been through enough garbage since that time and don't have to seek out any more painful memories. Lord knows I have experienced enough tragedy in my life.

Recalling my early years isn't easy at this point. It's not that my mind isn't sharp and full of details, it's just that pain and the effects of depression and repression have set in. Now it's difficult to recall those recollections I do not wish to relive.

I was born in 1960. My brother, Mitch, was born in 1956. Those were the *Ozzie and Harriet*, *Donna Reed,* and *Father Knows Best* years. The family image that we saw on television taught us that all parents knew how to raise, love, and nurture their kids. Well, either my parents didn't watch those shows, or they just didn't get it. For whatever reason, my parents missed that course called "Parenting 101." I did not desire "super-parents." All I wanted were parents who showed me a small part of the kind of love I saw on television, or the kind of love I saw many other kids get from their parents. I wanted simple things like a hug to show me they cared. I didn't get them. I wanted to be able to tell Mom or Dad jokes my friends told me, but they didn't have the time or the desire to listen. I wanted parents who would kiss me when I fell and scraped my knee, instead of scolding me for not taking care of myself properly. No, I didn't have nurturing parents or "super-parents." Instead, I had parents who dragged me into a world I never should have experienced.

My first of what seems like an endless stream of catastrophes hit at age five. It was a typical Saturday morning. My brother and I were eating Rice Krispies and bananas in the kitchen in our home in Green Acres, Valley Stream, New York, a suburban area filled with single-family homes just minutes away from the New York City borough of Queens. We lived in a three-bedroom, split-level house, one-and-a-half bathrooms, dining room, living room, a downstairs family room, and a single-car garage. I loved my room. It was simply decorated with beige walls, a wooden floor with a small green area rug, my four-drawer dresser, a toy chest filled with all my games, and my bed, which was filled with various stuffed animals. Of course, I had a favorite. It was a small white puppy I named Queenie. She was the best puppy a little girl could have, especially since Mom and Dad would never allow me to have a real pet.

By some standards, we were living well. Providing for the family was one thing my parents knew how to do. We never lacked the material things we needed because Mom worked as a secretary and Dad was a banker. Back then, it was unusual for most women to work. Most women stayed home as housewives, a term we don't use too often today. However, the two salaries made it easier for my parents to buy the house, pay the mortgage, and have enough to pay for all of life's expenses. We were not rich by any means, but we never lacked the necessities and a few extra nonnecessities.

As a kid, I thought everything about my parents was normal. With few exceptions, they looked like every other set of parents I knew. Mom was about five foot two, auburn hair, brown eyes, and maybe 5 or 10 pounds overweight. Dad was about five foot eight, also with brown eyes and hair, and clean shaven. It was frowned upon back then for a banker to have a mustache or beard. It didn't look proper. About the only unusual thing I recall about them or their marriage, as I learned later, was that Mom was about seven years older than Dad.

The morning started as most other Saturday mornings. My mom, Helen, was washing the dishes, dressed in her red housecoat and wearing one of her countless aprons. She always wore an apron because she was concerned about dirt on her clothes. "Appreciate what we have and take care of what we have," Mom told me a million times. "Jessica," she said on those rare occasions that we had a mother-daughter talk, "people who don't take care of themselves or their things are not worth knowing. They're shameless and irresponsible."

Saturday morning was my favorite time of the week. Mitch would be out of the house playing basketball in one of his friends' backyards, or he would play baseball in the school yard with the other neighborhood boys. That meant there would not be any fights about which shows to watch. I'd keep Queenie on my lap and sit on the plastic-covered couch to watch our new nineteen-inch, black-and-white television. My favorite shows were *Captain Kangaroo*, *Atom Ant*, *The Flintstones*, *The Beatles*, *Casper*, *Bugs Bunny*, and *Magilla Gorilla*.

It was spring and Dad usually worked in the yard on Saturday, so I was a little surprised when I saw him standing in the kitchen doorway wearing his good clothes. He paused to take a breath before he walked into the kitchen.

"Good morning, Daddy."

"Yes, Jessica," he said as he walked past me, touched Mom on her shoulder and said, "Good morning."

"Coffee's on the stove, Ed. It's still hot. I have my beauty parlor appointment at ten."

"Helen, do you mind if I get the kids out for the day?"

Mom looked at Dad with astonishment. "You? That's unusual."

"Yeah, it's going to be a beautiful day, and I thought I'd take a ride with the kids to Central Park."

"Sorry I can't join you, Ed."

"Don't worry about it, dear."

"What's that I smell, Ed?"

"What do you mean?"

"Is that a new aftershave?"

"Yeah. I thought I'd try something new for a change. I was getting bored with my Old Spice."

"What time will you be home?"

"Not too late. Kids, I took out clothes for each of you. Finish breakfast and let's get going."

"Daddy, I want Mommy to come with us. Mommy always goes places with us."

"Another time, Jessica. Be a good girl. Get dressed, and don't take an hour to do it. If you need help from Mommy, ask for it. I don't want you to do what you did last week." The week before, we were going to my aunt's house for lunch, and I argued with Mom about what to wear. Because of the argument, we were all late.

"OK, Daddy."

"And Mitch, well . . ." Daddy just gave Mitch one of those looks that meant, "Don't give me any trouble, kid." Mitch had seen it a million times before and knew exactly what it meant. "Both of you make sure to wash and brush up. Got it?"

Suddenly, Mitch started screaming, "I'm not going! I'm not going!"

Dad never had patience. This time was no different. "Boy, don't start with me."

Mitch's face turned red as he continued screaming. "I'm not going! I'm not going! I'm not going!"

Mom spoke softly, "Mitch, calm down. Take a deep breath and . . ."

"Shut up!" Mitch screamed at Mom.

"Don't you talk to her like . . ."

"You shut up, too! Shut up! Shut up! Shut up!"

"Young man, this is the wrong day for that nonsense," Dad said as he grabbed Mitch's hand and led him out of the room. "Be ready in fifteen minutes," Dad yelled before he slammed Mitch's bedroom door.

Mom came over to clear the table. "You're always a good little girl, Jessica. You know your brother doesn't mean any harm by all that yelling. It's just . . . well . . . be a good little girl and get ready."

"Yes, Mommy." I went to my room to get dressed. Dad had taken out one of my extra-nice dresses and black patent leather shoes. I remember that clearly because I was surprised he chose nice clothes to wear to a park where I'd run around and play. I thought of my brother when I washed up. His screaming always made me afraid. I loved my brother, but I didn't like being afraid of him when he screamed like that.

I got ready as quickly as I could. Mom came up and helped me get my things on. A few minutes later I saw my dad and Mitch outside waiting for me by the car.

"Hey, Dad, how about some Cracker Jacks and hot dogs at the park?" Mitch said as though nothing had happened before.

"Sure, Mitch."

Mom came out to see us off. Dad patted her back before he got into the car. He started the engine, waved goodbye, and backed out the driveway. Dad and Mitch sat up front. I was glad I sat in the back. I felt safe back there. Mitch turned on the radio to "Musicradio 77 WABC." Dan Ingrum was the DJ. He was playing the top ten countdown. Even at that young age, I loved to listen to music and I had my favorite songs. As we drove along the Belt Parkway, I remember hearing "Help Me Rhonda," "Ticket to Ride," "Game of Love," and "Mrs. Brown, You've Got a Lovely Daughter," which was very special to me because I always thought of myself as that lovely daughter.

It took about an hour to get to Central Park in the city. It was my first time there. The place was big and had lots of trees, but it was not the kind of park with slides and swings that I expected. I was disappointed, but didn't say anything.

"You both want Cracker Jacks?"

"Yes, Daddy."

"I'll take two," Dad said to the man selling all different sorts of candies from a cart. Dad gave him a dollar, got his change, and said, "Kids, we're going to walk to that lake over there." The lake was pretty. There were large, flat rocks all along the water's edge instead of sand or dirt. Behind the trees that surrounded the lake were huge buildings high above the tall trees. There were many birds around, and some of them were just floating on the lake. I'd never seen birds do that before. Then again, this was the first time I had seen a lake. I wondered how the birds stayed afloat without sinking. "How do the birds stay on top of the water, Daddy?"

"Not now, Jessica. You two sit here. Don't move or go anywhere."

Dad walked a few feet away. Although there were big bushes between us and him, I could still see him go over to a pretty lady, hug her, and kiss her on the lips. I remember she was tall compared to my mother, extremely thin with huge breasts, long, wavy red hair, and blue eyes that sparkled like the sky. At first, the woman didn't look too happy. Dad said something to her, she said something back, and then the two approached us. "Kids, this is my, ah, friend, Rachel. Rachel, this is Mitch, and this is Jessica."

"Nice to meet you, Mitch and Jessica. Your father has told me a lot about you two."

Rachel shook my hand, then she shook Mitch's hand.

"Kids," Dad said, "we're all going to take a walk. Here, you can have some Cracker Jacks now. Go ahead, kids. You walk in front of us so we can keep an eye on you."

Mitch and I walked ahead of Dad and Rachel. Every once in a while, I turned back just to make sure they were still there. Dad held Rachel's hand. That seemed unusual to me because I could not remember him ever holding Mom's hand.

The four of us must have walked around the big lake for about two hours. I was getting tired. I was also upset because I saw many little marks on my shoes. I was afraid Mom would be angry with me for not taking care of my shoes. Along the way we stopped for Dad to get us some hot dogs and sodas. We sat down to eat. Dad and Rachel stayed several feet away so we couldn't hear what they were talking about. When we finished eating, we started walking again. After about an hour, we got back to the place where we started. Rachel came over to us and said goodbye. Dad gave her a kiss on the cheek and said something about calling her. I remember him watching her walk away until she was out of sight.

"C'mon, kids. Let's get back to the car."

I don't remember much of the drive home because I slept almost the entire time. I do remember what happened later that night. I'll never forget it because of how it frightened me.

All of a sudden, I heard Mom screaming at Dad, "How could you do this to me? How stupid could you be to have the kids with you? You can't do this to me! I won't tolerate this! What kind of stupid moron are you?"

I saw Mom go into the bathroom and slam the door, but the door swung open again. Mom was sitting on the edge of the bathtub and crying. I went inside and stood in front of her. The tears were flowing down her face like when I cried after I hurt myself. I put my hand on her knee to make nice to her and said, "Mommy, don't cry. I love you. Mommy, please don't cry."

"Jessica, please! Not now!" she said in an angry tone.

Mom gently pushed me away from her. I sat on the floor just outside the bathroom door and started to cry because Mom was so unhappy. This must have lasted for at least thirty minutes. Mitch stayed in his room the entire time. His door was closed. Finally, Mom got up, blew her nose, wiped her eyes, went to the closet, got two suitcases, packed some clothes, and headed to my room with the other suitcase. I followed her in.

"We're leaving now," Mom said abruptly.

"Mommy, where are we going? Is Daddy coming with us?"

"Jessica, be a good little girl and don't ask questions." Within minutes she had most of my clothes packed. When Mom finished in my room, she went into Mitch's room and did the same thing.

"Mitch, come here. Put these suitcases into the car. Jessica, go to the car with your brother."

My father approached Mom. "Helen, don't leave." He tried to touch her shoulder.

"Don't touch me! Don't you dare try to stop me. This is the cruelest thing anyone has ever done to me. I'm leaving. I'm taking the kids."

"Helen, don't be crazy." He tried to take her hand. I actually saw Mom slap Dad's face.

"Get out of my way, you fool." Then Mom turned to Mitch and yelled, "I told you to get those damn suitcases into the car. Kids, move."

Mitch and I were in the car when Mom walked out of the house.

Dad stood at the front door. "Helen, don't be crazy. Get back in here!"

Mom got into the car, slammed the door, locked the locks, and started the engine. Dad approached and screamed to Mom through her closed window. "Helen, turn off the damn car."

Mom backed out of the driveway and kept going.

I started to cry again. "Mommy, where are we going? Why are you and Daddy fighting?"

"Kids, I need quiet now. We're going to my sister's house. I don't know if we're ever coming back. Don't either of you dare call or speak to your father. Is that understood?"

My Aunt Anna and Uncle Dan lived in Freeport, Long Island, only a few minutes away from our home. Aunt Anna was a two-year-older, spitting image of my mother. Uncle Dan sported a crew cut. He was six foot four, a gentle giant with a bushy mustache, but he probably intimidated people with his looks. I say that only because that's how I sometimes felt about him.

I felt upset and started to shake as Mom turned the corner of our block and kept driving. I was too young to understand what had just happened. All I understood was that I might never see my father or my home again. I was afraid to say anything. I just cried silently because I was afraid of making Mom angrier.

Tears were still coming down my face when we parked at Aunt Anna and Uncle Dan's house, but I didn't say a word. After we got inside, Mom went with Aunt Anna into another room. I went into the kitchen with Uncle Dan and Mitch. Uncle Dan made us some tuna fish sandwiches with potato chips. I couldn't eat. Mitch ate his sandwich and mine. After about an hour, Mom came into the kitchen, took me upstairs, got me into my pajamas, and put me into bed.

"Mommy, I'm afraid. I don't want to live here."

"Jessica, don't act like a baby. Be a good little girl and go to sleep." Mom shut the light and closed the door behind her. I don't think she ever heard me call out, "Mommy, please leave the light on. I'm afraid."

No kid should ever feel the way I felt that night. I was alone in a dark, strange room. I had lost my home and my father. It was the first night I could remember going to sleep without Queenie to hug against my face. I felt unbearably uncomfortable and scared in this different environment. I think I was still crying when I finally fell asleep.

I remember how I woke up the next morning. Before I opened my eyes, I prayed it was all a nightmare. But when I opened my eyes, I saw the nightmare was real. I was devastated. Again, I started to cry.

* * *

Mom, Mitch, and I spent the summer at Aunt Anna's house. Mom didn't spend much time with me. She always seemed to be talking with Aunt Anna and Uncle Dan about the situation with Dad, or she was busy trying to calm Mitch down after those times he suddenly exploded with fury.

I was on my own almost all the time. I felt out of place and miserable. I missed my room, my bed, my toys, Queenie, and everything else that I left behind at my real home. Nothing seemed normal. Nothing seemed right. Even Mitch's outbursts were more unbearable because I did not have my real room to hide away in to protect myself from his craziness. Each night, in the darkness and loneliness of my foreign bedroom, I prayed my nightmares would end, that Mom and Dad would be friends again, and that we'd all be back together again.

That summer, I started learning how to be independent and to take care of myself out of necessity. That experience also set me on a path toward perfectionism. It seemed like the only time Mom paid attention to me was when I did something very bad or very good. Luckily, I found that doing the right thing came naturally. It felt good on those rare occasions when Mom took a moment to say, "Jessica, you're a good little girl."

I spent day after day playing by myself in the backyard because I didn't have any of my regular neighborhood friends to play with, and there weren't any kids my age in my aunt's neighborhood. A few times Mitch came out to play a game with me. He's my brother and I'll always love him, but he terrified me each time we'd be playing and he'd suddenly start screaming for no good reason. Whenever that happened I'd run into the house and hide in a closet to protect myself. I hated that closet. It was dark. The blackest dark I ever saw. And once, when I was already terrified because of my brother, I sat there for fifteen minutes until suddenly I felt something crawling up my leg. I opened the door and ran out screaming hysterically. Uncle Dan stopped me. "Quit that screaming. Calm down!" he shouted.

"There's a bug crawling on me. Kill it! Kill it!"

The bug suddenly dropped from my leg and onto the floor. Uncle Dan stepped on it.

"Jessica, go wash your face and calm down."

I did as I was told. God, I hated living there.

July crept by, as did August. I was beginning to believe I'd live out the rest of my life in my aunt's house. Then, just before the last day of August, Mom came into the kitchen as Mitch and I ate lunch. She sat down and took our hands. Something felt different. I thought she had more terrible news for us.

"Kids, I'm going to pack our suitcases."

"Oh, no," I thought to myself. "Where are we going now?"

Mom looked at each of us slowly. "We're going home today."

I remember smiling. Neither Mitch nor I said anything.

"Your father and I have worked things out. We'll leave as soon as everything is packed."

The night we first drove away from home, there were silent tears streaming down my face. During the short drive back home from Freeport, I must have been the happiest little girl in the world.

"Kids, when we get home, I want you to treat your father like you always did before. What happened was just between your father and me. Understood?"

Dad was waiting for us outside when we pulled up on the driveway. I went to hug and kiss Dad because I hadn't seen him for so long. Dad just got the suitcases and took them inside.

I walked into the house. I felt safe and comfortable again.

Words can't describe the magnificent feelings I had that first night when I got into my bed and was once again surrounded by my toys and stuffed animals. I remember how I kissed all of my stuffed animals goodnight before I tucked myself under my blanket. I remember how great it was to hug and kiss Queenie again. I remember thinking that it was just a few days before the start of the school year and my first day in first grade. Before I fell asleep, I remember how I promised myself that I would be the most perfect first-grader that school ever saw.

Mitch took me to school on the first day and put me on the line with the rest of the kids in my class. All the other kids had their mom and dad there.

All the parents were taking pictures of their kids. My parents weren't there. They went to work that morning. It didn't bother me. Well, maybe it bothered me just a little. Suddenly I heard whistles blowing. Everyone got quiet. I turned to face the front of the line and saw a woman about my mom's age. She was my teacher, Mrs. McHugh. She looked like a nice person. She had a somewhat pretty face, stood about five foot five, thin, and she had the cutest, waviest hair I ever saw.

At that moment, I made another promise to myself. I decided to try to please my teacher as much as I tried to please my mom when we lived at Aunt Anna's house.

Within a very short time, I was my teacher's pet. It felt wonderful each time my teacher said, "Jessica, you're a good little girl."

Looking back now as an adult and married woman with two kids, I wonder if I would have made the same decision Mom made about getting back with Dad. I would always wonder if I could trust my husband after he had an affair. Thank God, after more than twenty years of marriage, I have never been in that position. Having my husband cheat on me seems like one of the few crises that I was able to avoid. I love my husband more now than when we first got married. I trust him with my life. I could not have picked a better guy to love and to have as the father of my children.

* * *

Chapter Three

Prelude to Disaster

My years in elementary school were a pleasure. I made friends easily and I got along with all of my teachers. I did whatever I was supposed to do or was told to do, and I was always the good kid. I was constantly ready to please anyone who met me, whether it was a fellow student or teacher. That was my style and I was comfortable with it. My job was to keep up with my work and be as perfect as I could be at all times.

I did my homework religiously. I can't remember my parents ever knowing if I studied or when I had a test. I just did what I was expected to do. I can't remember my parents ever asking me, "Did you do your homework?" or anything like that. In fact, I can't remember them doing anything more than signing my quarterly report card. My grades were consistently good. No, I'll correct that. My grades were very good. I guess my parents just figured I would always do the right thing. I can't remember them ever attending any PTA meetings or parent-teacher conferences. From their point of view, there was no need to attend things like that. Why bother to go? They were tired at night because they worked all day. Besides, they knew what they were going to hear.

I didn't feel like I missed out on anything by my parents not being involved in my life. In a way, I actually preferred it, because I was pretty much on my own, and I was free to do whatever I wanted to do. My parents had no reason for concern with me. Mitch was the one who always took up their attention, concern, and time. Simply put, I was left to grow up on my own. Consequently, there was a sincere lack of parent-child bonding. It's not that I wanted it that way. It's just the way it was. But there was one time, in fact one of the most important times in my life, when my mother let me down at a time when we should have bonded. What could or should have been one of the best nurturing, mother-daughter experiences in my life turned out to be just another time I was on my own to take care of myself.

I had just turned twelve and entered the seventh grade. The first few days at my new junior high school made me a little anxious. Almost all of my old girlfriends from my elementary school were there, but there were many new people surrounding me from other elementary schools in the district. In gym, the cafeteria, the playground, and other places where just the girls hung out together, the conversations were changing from which TV shows we saw or which dolls we played with. Now, some of the girls talked about boyfriends. Some even talked about that big secret subject–their period.

Ginny said, "When it comes, make sure you wear dark-colored clothing."

Pam said, "Yeah, and keep a change of clothes in your locker, plus additional pads. God, I was ready to die when it happened to me. There I was in class and my pants had this big red spot."

Mary said, "You don't go from girl to woman in one day. My moods were going nuts, and it drove my parents crazy. My mother told me to always have three things with me: pads for the bleeding, Tylenol for the cramps, and chocolate, just to make me feel better."

I listened intently any time the other girls talked about their first period. I learned to expect a widening of the hips, an increase in the production of sweat, which will start to have an odor, moodiness, anxiety, headaches, backaches, pimples, nausea, food cravings, and depression. They said it lasted a couple of days and to expect it about every twenty-eight to thirty days once it started, although sometimes it could be a longer time from period to period. They also talked about the pain from cramps. I had no idea what they meant, but the pain women suffered from cramps didn't sound good. I wondered to myself, "Why did God make woman have periods that would cause such misery? Did God hate women?" No wonder the girls usually called the period "a monthly curse." I started to think of periods like a prison sentence. I was only twelve. The girls said we could expect to have a period until we were in our fifties.

By Thanksgiving I felt like all the other girls had gotten their first period except me. Being the last one of your friends to go through what everyone else had already gone through was frustrating. I felt like something was wrong with me. I wondered if it was ever going to happen to me. Then again, I did see changes on my body. I saw hair under my arms and on my legs, outside of my vagina, and my nipples were changing. By Christmas, I actually had small breasts. That amazed me. It made me think about what type of body I would have as a woman. I remember Gladys said, "I don't want big boobs. I want just enough for Johnny to hold in his hand. You know, just enough to fill up the size of a champagne glass." The thought of anyone touching my breasts repulsed me. No one had seen me naked since I could remember, and the only time I touched myself was to wash myself in the shower.

As the days passed, I wondered if I was prepared for what was about to happen to me. I noticed Mom looking at me each day at breakfast and dinner. I wanted to ask what was bothering her but didn't because I was afraid I might have done something wrong without knowing it, and I wanted to stay out of trouble.

Then, to my surprise, I found a sealed beige envelope under Queenie on my bed. I opened it to find a brochure entitled "What We Need to Know About Menstruation." It's interesting that I hadn't heard that word before, but I quickly understood it was a brochure about having a period.

The first thing I read about was how some mothers couldn't discuss the subject with their daughters. I said to myself, "That's my mom." The brochure also said, "Older generations believed that menstruation was a subject to be hidden behind closed doors. It was a secret that was not to be discussed, even between mothers and daughters. However, menstruation is a part of life, and not talking with your daughter about this subject may only heighten her belief in myths and cause your daughter to think that menstruation is something dirty and shameful. Talk with your daughter. Let her know there is no shame involved in this natural part of womanhood."

I must have spent several hours that night devouring every word and trying to understand the process. One section scared me. It was about showers and bathing during the period. It said, "Keep yourself clean to fight off any odors that may occur." I wondered if I was going to walk around smelling from a period, and all the other girls, and boys, would know about it. I couldn't imagine anything more embarrassing or humiliating.

When I read the section about feminine products, I remembered what my friend Francine said one day in the locker room. She said, "I'm going to stick with pads. I don't want to take the chance of breaking my hymen if I put a tampon into my vagina the wrong way." It amazed me how freely Francine was talking about this subject. It repulsed, disgusted, and grossed me out to think that anyone could put something into their vagina. But Francine really got to me when she said, "I don't want my future husband to think I'm not a virgin because I broke my hymen. The first time we have sex, he'll expect to find blood all over the sheets when he breaks me, and I don't want to let him down." At that time, I had no idea what she was talking about. Sex, boyfriends, and husbands were the last thing on my mind.

After reading the brochure, I finally understood what Francine was talking about. The hymen, a thin membrane that covered most of the vagina, was a part of my body I had no idea I had. I never looked inside myself or touched myself in that way. In my mind, that would be too vulgar.

The most encouraging thing I read was that the more physically active you are, the less likely you are to have cramps. That part made me feel good because I was extremely active in gym at school and at the park with my friends. We were always playing games that kept me running around. One of last things I read was to expect a few spots of bright red blood or a brown, sticky stain that would show up on my underpants. Finally, it closed by saying, "Mother Nature took care of her girls. Your first period is usually so little that we may have an accident, but it won't seep through to our outer clothes."

From what I discussed with my friends about their first period, and from what I learned from the brochure, it seemed like I made myself into a small expert. The next day I got some of my allowance money and a coupon I cut from the Sunday paper and went to the drugstore to buy some pads. I was determined to be ready. I was determined not to let my first period be an embarrassing or humiliating experience at school or at home. What I didn't anticipate was my brother, Mitch, and what he did when he noticed my approaching womanhood.

Dad, Mom, Mitch, and I were having dinner. I was wearing a slightly tight shirt and suddenly he said, "Are those little bumps breasts?" God, was that embarrassing. Mom said, "Mitch, you're through eating. Go finish your homework." Mitch left the room. "Ed," she said to my father, "you can take out the garbage now." I thought she had dismissed my brother and father so she and I could have a woman-to-woman talk. I was so excited. I thought Mom was actually going to have a bonding experience with me. I was thrilled. Then Mom turned toward the sink with her back toward me and started washing the dishes. She didn't say a word to me. I just looked at her in her housecoat and apron, felt tears coming into my eyes, went up to my room to listen to some records, and cried for an hour. Two days later I found a brown bag on my bed. It had a training bra and a box of feminine pads. Evidently she knew what was going on but would not or could not discuss it with me.

The next Saturday I was feeling a little down, although I didn't know why. Mitch was out playing with his friends. I laid down on the couch in the family room to watch my usual morning television shows. I remember feeling fat. I remember my breasts, as small as they were, felt tender and sore when I put on my new training bra and my shirt. Within an hour, it felt like my underwear was wet. I looked and found my underwear stained with blood. Then I looked on the couch and found blood on the plastic. I went to change my underwear and get something to clean the couch before Mom saw it. When I got back, I saw I was too late. Mom was already there with her cleaning fluids and cleaning rag. Mitch and Dad had returned in the interim and were close by. She just looked at me and, in a clear and loud voice, she said, "The irresponsibility. I expected better of you. I gave you what you needed to avoid this mess."

All I could do was go to my room. Mom and I said nothing to each other for the rest of the day. She had humiliated me in front of my father and Mitch. She was upset and angry. So was I. For the rest of the day all I could do was cry. What should have been a bonding experience between the two of us turned out to be one of the disasters I would remember for the rest of my life. There was no nurturing. There were no lessons learned in a mother-daughter way, but there should have been.

My first period was over in two days. The humiliation I felt never went away.

* * *

While all this feminine stuff was going on, I still had school to contend with, and I was doing a good job. Most of my grades on my tests and papers were in the mid- to high nineties. Most would say I was an exemplary kid. I was in a special seventh-grade program and, because I did so well, I was allowed to skip eighth grade and go directly into ninth grade when I was thirteen years old. At that time, there were no major negative issues in my life except for one—Mitch.

There was something not right with Mitch from the beginning of his life. He was the cause of all the drama in the house, and he created havoc in my life. A lot of what I think was the problem was that it was so difficult to diagnose what was wrong with him. Doctors didn't know what to do. It's really a weird existence to grow up with someone like him, because he could flare up at any moment and just turn totally crazy. Flaring up at any given moment was an extremely stressful situation for me. His countless problems became my problem, and it definitely had an impact on my life.

My parents had no other choice but to give Mitch all of their attention. They were always tying to figure out what was wrong and what to do, but the doctors they went to couldn't find a solution to stop his crazy behavior. I went the other way for attention. I made myself into the perfect student and good little daughter. I won a million awards, which was a positive thing. Infrequently, I got praise for my accomplishments from my parents. When I didn't get praise I felt like I let myself down—no one else, just me.

By the time Mitch was seventeen, he was addicted to drugs and he had severe problems with school. His long and unkempt hair atop his six foot, two inch frame made him easy to spot from a distance, and most students and faculty made it a point to stay clear of him. At that age, he had already been placed into several special-education programs and was thrown out of all of them. I resented my brother. It was a definite love-hate relationship with him. He was the one person who could always get me totally angry at the drop of a hat. On the other hand, I loved him because he was my brother. Mitch was out of control. I remember something that happened late autumn of 1974 when I was fourteen, in the tenth grade, and a sophomore in high school.

One of my girlfriends, Susan, came over. She was the kind of girl every guy in school was after. She had gorgeous, straight blonde hair, perfect teeth, perfect eyes and nose, very full breasts, and the most perfect tush. I think she hung around with me to make sure she never had any boy competition when we hung out together at school or elsewhere.

Susan and I were in my room practicing makeup on each other and listening to the radio. We heard Barry White's "Can't Get Enough of Your Love, Babe," Andy Kim's "Rock Me Gently," Olivia Newton-John's "I Honestly Love You," Billy Preston's "Nothing from Nothing," and John Lennon's "Whatever Gets You Thru the Night."

The horror started when we went to the kitchen for some soda and chips. Suddenly we heard a scream. It came from Mitch, who was standing buck naked in the kitchen doorway with a huge carving knife in his hand. The two of us froze until he lunged toward us. We got around him and out of the kitchen. Mitch screamed as he chased us, "I'm gonna kill you bitches! You bitches are dead!" We both ran to the closest room that had a door so we could lock ourselves inside for protection from his threatening insanity. Once inside the family room, I threw my body against the door to keep it closed, then I yelled to Susan to open the window for us to escape from the house.

Mitch just kept screaming, "You bitches are dead!" and trying to push the door in from the outside. I kept yelling, "Mitch, stop this! Stop it!" He didn't. The situation was out of control.

By some miracle, we were able to get out of the window and into my neighbor's house, where we called 911. Thank God, Mitch didn't follow us. Several minutes later I saw a police car stop in front of my house. Two big policemen got out of the car, walked up to the door with their hands on their guns, and rang the bell. Within seconds, Mitch came out dressed and spoke rationally with them for a few minutes. Then they came and talked with Susan and me. They told us that Mitch denied the entire incident. Since no one was hurt, they told me there was nothing they could do. I could not comprehend them doing nothing. I was almost killed by my own brother, and they just drove away as if nothing had happened.

I would say that ranks as one of the worst times when Mitch was totally out of control and incoherent. It was just the scariest thing you can imagine. Without a doubt, I thought we were about to die.

That moment and that event marked the turning point in my life. Nothing was normal from then on. The next day at school, I remember being in my math class and, for no apparent reason, I started to cry hysterically. I remember my teacher tried to calm me down. She couldn't. I remember my teacher tenderly holding me and taking me to see Mrs. Lucy Powers, our guidance counselor.

That was kind of the environment I lived in from when I was just entering my teens until I left the house when I was a little bit older. I really didn't have an eating disorder per se at that time. I would go through binges of eating, but there was no anorexia. There was no bulimia. There was nothing like that going on at that time. What I didn't realize is that my whole psychological makeup was primed for disaster. The events that had taken place previously in my life were getting me ready for an eating disorder. I was falling into its clutches. No, I was subconsciously and willingly diving headfirst into that fatal pit of desperation.

* * *

From late autumn until the end of the school year, Mrs. Powers and I met weekly in her office during my lunch period. At that time, it was the closest thing I had to therapy. She was a gentle, sensitive, and mentally strong woman in her late twenties who attended graduate school for her second master's degree in psychology. I admired and respected her because she was accomplishing so much with her life. After a few months, it seemed like we were growing closer. The counselor-student relationship evolved slowly into more of a mentor-student relationship. The more we spoke, the more she comforted me through my problems at home. Each session allowed me to vent my frustrations, which enabled me to focus on my schoolwork and continue my near-perfect academic performance. I was grateful for her help, friendship, guidance, and nurturing, things I never had at home.

Her demure looks–she was about five foot five, 120 pounds, with hazel eyes, blonde hair down to her shoulders which was always well groomed, perfect manicures, and somewhat voluptuous figure–made her a woman most men would desire. She sometimes spoke freely of her private life. She was married for about four years, and pictures of her husband decorated her always-tidy desk.

The more we learned about each other, the more I wanted to emulate her, with the exception that I didn't want to date yet, nor did I want to be desired by the boys. My school accomplishments and hanging out with my friends were still primary. Besides, the boys I knew from school still seemed too immature, and I knew I had plenty of time in the future to get into the dating scene.

That June I was probably the only student sorry to see summer arrive, because it meant the end of the school year and my meetings with Mrs. Powers. It also meant Mitch and I would be home together for two months. I dreaded his outbursts directed at my parents or me, especially since I would not have Mrs. Powers near me to guide me out of my emotional stupor. I remember how, one week after school ended, my mother asked Mitch to take out the garbage. Without a moment's hesitation, he started pounding the kitchen table and screaming in a deranged fashion. I was frozen with fear in my seat across from him. His sounds and actions gave credence and validity to my fantasies that eventually he would inflict violent and grave harm on either my parents or me.

Each day I found myself getting out of the house to find sanctuary and to diminish the chances of being attacked physically or verbally by Mitch. I was too young to drive, but not too young to get on my bike and ride to one of my friends' houses, or to meet them at the county park pool. Those times I couldn't get out of the house, I stayed in my room with the door locked, reading or listening to the stereo with headphones on so the noise wouldn't attract Mitch in my direction.

Eventually the summer passed and I was back in school, and back to my weekly meetings with Mrs. Powers. Much to my surprise, I learned that Mrs. Powers and her husband had separated during the summer. His pictures were gone from her desk. Although she never told me the reasons for the separation, I was amazed that any man would be willing to give up such a magnificent woman.

The start of my junior year in high school went well. My new teachers were no problem at all. They all quickly recognized my diligent work inside and outside the classroom. They all had the same look on their face when they returned my tests with grades ranging from 97 to 100 percent, or when they handed back my reports with the same high scores. My relationships with the other girls at school were also good. I was popular. I was the one who tutored those girls who were having difficulty picking up the math, language, history, or English assignments or test preparations. Little did they know that the more I helped them, the more I got out of my house and away from Mitch. Everyone had a good opinion about me. That was important to me. I relied on their opinion of me as far as how I thought of myself. Simply put, what I thought of myself was based on what other people saw in me. No matter what I did, I threw myself into it and did it perfectly. There was no room for error.

I was pleased with the image I had created for myself. I was the perfect young woman who pleased almost all those around me. I say "almost all" because my parents remained consistent. They still had no clue what was going on in my life or in my mind. As usual, they were preoccupied with Mitch, who was out of school and spending time getting high on pot in his room, or hanging out with his other drug-addicted, do-nothing, go-nowhere, worthless friends.

By November, my weekly meetings with Mrs. Powers turned into meetings on Monday, Wednesday, and Friday. Although Mitch and my parents were usually the main topics of discussion, we expanded our conversations into other areas of my life and her life. Without mentioning any names, she told me how she had started dating other people. She asked why I hadn't started dating, and I always answered, "I don't have the time or need for boys in my life now. That will happen later."

Christmas and New Year's Eve rolled around without fanfare. For the most part, I just considered the vacation as time away from school, time away from my therapy sessions with Mrs. Powers, and time close to Mitch because of the extreme cold that prevented me from getting out of the house.

It seemed like the weather was the main topic of everyone's conversations. It was the year of the El Niño and La Niña effect, where cooler-than-normal sea-surface temperatures in the tropical Pacific Ocean influenced global weather patterns. The Northwest, Great Lakes, and Ohio Valley areas experienced extended rain, which caused widespread flooding, and there was abnormal dryness in the Southwest. In the South, parts of Tennessee, Arkansas, and Mississippi experienced eighty-six tornadoes in a seven-day period. In New York, we were living through extreme and extended sub-zero temperatures.

One Sunday afternoon it got so cold that Dad put some heaters by the front window because the pipes had frozen. He thought the heaters could defrost the pipes, so he tucked the drapes back and let the heaters do their thing. Within an hour, the drapes came loose from where Dad had tucked them in, and they caught fire. We were lucky we were awake at the time and had fire extinguishers to temporarily fight the blaze until the fire department arrived. The firefighters broke the windows to let out the smoke, and damaged the walls in the living room and dining room areas to look for residual hot spots. It's amazing how the fire damage was so extensive when you consider that the firemen arrived only a few short minutes after we called 911.

That night I still smelled the smoke from the downstairs part of the house. I held Queenie extra tight and went to sleep thinking that we couldn't live long in the house under these terrible conditions. All the fears and painful memories of living in my aunt's house after my father's affair resurfaced. I remember crying as I fell asleep.

The next morning I woke and shivered as I dressed for school. Mom gave me a small breakfast and warned me that we would probably have to move out of the house temporarily until the damaged parts of the house were repaired.

It was Monday, and I had my scheduled session with Mrs. Powers. When she heard about the blaze and that my parents intended to move out of the neighborhood during the reconstruction, she got on the phone immediately with my mother and insisted she and Dad attend a meeting with her the next morning. In fact, she didn't give my mother a choice. She said, "I will see you and your husband here promptly at 8:30 a.m. Do not be late. I have a very tight schedule tomorrow." That was all she said, except for, "At this time of crisis, Mrs. Devoe, you must think of what is best for your daughter and do the right thing immediately. Thank you for your cooperation."

Ironically, it took this catastrophic situation and Mrs. Powers' insistence for my parents to finally show up at one of my schools. I was already in her office when my folks walked in. My dad opened the conversation, "Mrs. Powers, nice to meet you. We all have busy schedules, so let's get right to it."

"Mr. and Mrs. Devoe, thank you for being here, and I agree, let's get right down to why we're here. We're all concerned for Jessica's safety and well-being. I'm very sorry for what happened to your home. It must be a devastating feeling. Jessica has informed me that there is a possibility of her moving out of this school district for an extended period of time."

"Well," Mom interjected, "we haven't finalized any plans yet, but there is that possibility. We may have to move into my sister's house for a few months."

"And your sister's house is outside this district. Isn't it?"

"Yes, she lives in Freeport."

"Would you be willing to take Jessica back and forth to school here each day?"

"That's impossible," Dad said. "We both work, and transporting Jessica back and forth to school is out of the question. She'd have to attend school in Freeport temporarily."

"You're probably talking about several months. Possibly until the end of the school year, from the way Jessica described the damage to the house and the necessary reconstruction."

"That's very likely. But she's a smart and good kid. She can get along wherever she goes to school," Dad said.

"With all due respect, I beg to disagree, Mr. Devoe. Taking Jessica out of her regular school might be the worst thing you can do. I have been counseling her for the past year now. I know, from personal knowledge, that she is one of this school's best pupils. Leaving this school at this time could be extremely traumatic and result in incredibly negative consequences. I know about your son, Mitch, and under the stress of relocation, he may have more frequent and violent outbursts. For the sake of your daughter's safety and mental health, I suggest she find a place to stay in this neighborhood so she can remain in her natural environment."

Dad didn't look very pleased. "Mrs. Powers, what are you suggesting? We have no place to stay in this neighborhood and, as I said, we cannot transport her to this school from where we might have to live."

"Mr. and Mrs. Devoe, I have a possible solution. My apartment is only a few blocks from this school. I live alone and I have a guest bedroom. I can provide Jessica with a safe environment, at no cost to you, for as long as the house is under reconstruction. I urge you to immediately accept my offer for the mental health and physical safety of your daughter."

"Live with you? Well, that's an unusual offer," Dad said.

"These are unusual circumstances, sir. Please understand. The only thing I desire is to provide what is best for your daughter. Here is my home phone number." Mrs. Powers handed my dad one of her business cards. "Please call me tonight with your decision."

There was a long moment of silence. I was in shock over Mrs. Powers' offer. My first instinct was to say it was a phenomenal idea. My parents weren't as quick to see the idea's merit.

That night, Mom, Dad, and I had dinner at Nathan's in Oceanside because it was too cold for Mom to make dinner in the house. Mitch was out with his friends. At first, I just listened to Mom and Dad discuss their workday, the cost of reconstruction, the insurance problems they faced, and their plans to move in with Aunt Anna and Uncle Dan. Mitch would have to sleep on their convertible couch, but Mom and Dad would occupy their guest bedroom. The sleeping arrangements finally brought the conversation around to where I was going to stay. The fact that there wasn't any additional space for me became a factor. Dad mentioned his brother's place in New Jersey, or my mother's aunt in Brooklyn. I hardly knew either of those people and dreaded the thought of living with them.

"What about Mrs. Powers' suggestion?" I said.

Dad quickly answered, "Jessica, except for meeting her this morning, we don't know this woman."

"But I do. We've been having meetings for the past year now."

"You never told me about this."

I wanted to scream to Dad that he never asked about anything in my life, but I maintained my calm. "Dad, she's a guidance counselor in my school. You can ask the principal about her."

"Ed, we don't have many choices. If you hadn't been so irresponsible . . ."

"It was an accident."

"Those heaters were a half-witted thing to do. You're the moron to blame for this mess we're all in. That stupid idea you had will cost thousands of dollars and months of misery. I don't trust your brother, and my aunt is too old to take care of Jessica."

"But . . ."

"But what?"

Dad got quiet. I said nothing.

"Then it's decided," Mom said with a tone of total authority. "Jessica will stay with that guidance counselor. Call her when we get home before she changes her mind. Can you handle that, or do you want me to take care of it the way I take care of everything else?"

Dad looked like a whipped dog. "I'll call her tonight."

"Tell her we'll have Jessica's bags packed tonight. You'll deliver them to school in the morning."

I couldn't believe what I just heard. By tomorrow, I was going to be out of the house and away from Mitch. God, it was like a miracle. Unlike the last time I moved out of my house, this time I looked forward to being someplace other than my home.

The drive back from Oceanside to our house filled my head with thoughts about tomorrow and the months ahead. I didn't fear the situation. I welcomed it. For the first time in as long as I could remember, I felt I was going to be safe and out of harm's way. What a magnificent feeling! When we got home, I immediately started to get all of my things together. Even Mom was impressed with how little she had to do to pack my bags. All I left out were the pajamas I was going to sleep in, my clothes for tomorrow at school, and Queenie. Yes, this time Queenie wasn't going to be left behind.

I'm sure there was a smile on my face as I hugged Queenie and fell asleep for the last time in my own bed. Tomorrow starts my new life. "It may only last for a few weeks or months, but it's something I look forward to," I thought to myself.

* * *

I woke up that Tuesday knowing my life was about to change. I said goodbye to Mom and Mitch. Dad and I left the house earlier than usual to make sure we got to Mrs. Powers' office before school started.

As expected, Mrs. Powers was in her office waiting for us. She put my bags out of sight in her closet, then shook Dad's hand. "Mr. Devoe, don't worry about your daughter. You made the right decision."

"Yeah, well, thanks for your help, Mrs. Powers. Jessica, you be a good little girl."

Dad just stood there looking at me. I actually went to him and hugged him. "Dad, I know it was just an accident. Thanks for your help."

Dad never put his arms around me. He patted my head.

"Dad, I'll call you tonight."

"Sure, kid."

Dad turned and left.

"Jessica . . ."

"Yes, Mrs. Powers."

"Young lady, it looks like we're going to be living together for a while, so perhaps you can stop calling me Mrs. Powers and call me by my first name, Lucy."

"Sure. Whatever you say." She was the first teacher I knew who insisted I call her by her first name. I felt so grown up.

"We'll stick to Mrs. Powers when we're in school, but otherwise Lucy will be just fine."

"Sure."

"Oh, and I wouldn't talk about us staying together when you talk with your friends, especially those who attend school here. The less said the better. If someone asks where you're staying, just tell them you're staying with one of your parents' friends."

"Sure."

"Meet me in my office after school this afternoon. We'll talk here for a while, find out what you'll need at my place, and then I'll take you home and help you settle in."

"Sounds fine." Actually, what she just said sounded incredible. I couldn't remember feeling so happy. Tonight I'll be away from Mitch, and safe. I was never religious, but I just looked up to the sky and silently said, "Thank you, God. This is the best thing that ever happened to me."

That Tuesday was one of those days you want to pass quickly, but the time just kept dragging on. Finally, after what felt like years of waiting, the day was over, the kids left school, and I was in *Lucy's* office. I sat without saying a word as she finished some paperwork. It must have been at least an hour. By then, the entire school was empty.

"Well, young lady, are you ready to see your new home?"

"Yes."

"It's just a basement apartment that I used to share with my husband, but I think you'll find it comfortable."

"I'm sure I will."

"Good." She opened her closet and took out my two suitcases. "You get one, I'll get the other. Let's go home, Roomie."

We left school, got to her car, put the suitcases into the trunk, and drove just a few blocks to her apartment. There was a door in the front of the building. It led to the upstairs living quarters. A second door, on the side of the building, led directly to her apartment. Lucy took the key to the front door off her key ring and handed it to me. "You'll need this when you walk here alone after school."

I felt tingles throughout my body when she said that. She opened the door. Everything inside was decorated in a modern fashion. It was so different from what I was used to. Lucy entered, went to a close door, opened it and said, "This is your new room."

At first, I just stood there looking inside without entering the room.

"Go ahead. Get comfortable. The bathroom is out here on your right. Over there is the kitchen. Make yourself at home. I'm going to change and get comfortable. You get your homework started, and I'll get dinner ready. Just let me know whatever you need from the supermarket and I'll get it before coming home tomorrow."

"Sure. I don't need much."

"There are hangers in the closet. That dresser is yours. I left the address and telephone number to this place on a piece of paper for you on top of the dresser. I know you won't discuss it with your friends. Well, again, welcome."

"Thanks for everything."

"You're a great young lady. I'm glad I can help."

Lucy turned and opened the second door, which was directly opposite mine. I could see inside her room. It was modern like the rest of the apartment. I opened my suitcases, kicked off my shoes, took out Queenie, and hugged her as I sat with my feet up on the bed in amazement. The sun coming in from my window to the left of the bed made me feel comfortable and welcome. Within a few seconds, I heard the radio playing in Lucy's room. The first song seemed like a phenomenal omen. It was John Denver's "Sunshine on My Shoulders." That song was followed by Elton John's version of "Lucy in the Sky with Diamonds," and Barry Manilow's "Mandy." Besides those being some of my favorite songs, it was great to listen to music again without headphones for fear of Mitch coming into my room.

I couldn't move. I just sat hugging Queenie, staring around at my new room and out the door into Lucy's room. Then suddenly, I saw something that I thought I'd never see. There was Lucy, standing with a towel in her hand and wearing nothing but her white bra and white bikini panties. In my wildest dreams, I never thought I'd see one of my teachers in her underwear. She put the towel down on her bed, released the clasp on her bra, took it off, and then slipped off her panties. She turned to face me and called out, "I'm going in for a fast shower, Roomie."

"No problem." I think that's what I said. I was in such shock, I'm not sure I got the words out of my mouth. Ten minutes later Lucy appeared at my door. She was wearing a pair of panties and a T-shirt. It was apparent she wasn't wearing a bra. She noticed I was in the same position as when she left me for the shower.

"You've got unpacking and homework to do, Roomie. Let's get going. I'll fix dinner. Do you want hamburgers or chicken tonight?"

"Doesn't matter."

"Good. I see we'll get along just fine. Hamburgers tonight. Chicken tomorrow. Let me know if you need help with your homework."

It only took me a few minutes to unpack my stuff into the closet and dresser. There was a table to the right of the bed with a desk lamp for me to do my homework. At first, I found it a little difficult to concentrate on my work, but then I got into it and finished what I had to do, just as Lucy appeared to say, "Dinner is ready, Roomie."

I wasn't much of a conversationalist that night. The phone rang a few times. Most of the calls were from Lucy's friends. One, however, was her husband. All she said was, "Listen, Joe, tell your lawyer I don't give a sh ... I don't care." She hung up, turned to me, and said, "Roomie, think twice about ever getting married. All men are dirtbags."

What she said took me back to the last time I slept outside my house, when my father got caught having an affair. I thought about what she said and about my father but didn't say anything.

"The television is in the living room. Help yourself. I'll clean up here."

I went into the living room and turned on the television. The 6:30 evening network news was still on. They were still talking about John Mitchell, H. R. Haldeman and John Ehrlichman being found guilty of the Watergate cover-up and what that would mean to the future of this country. They also talked about Ella Grasso becoming the governor of Connecticut, and how she was the first woman to serve as a governor in the United States who did not succeed her husband. The last two stories were about OPEC raising crude oil prices by 10 percent, and President Gerald Ford appointing Vice President Nelson Rockefeller to head a special commission looking into alleged domestic abuses by the CIA.

"Smart girl," Lucy said as she entered the living room. "It's good to keep up on what's going on in the world."

The two of us talked for an hour about how I felt being out of the house. She was glad to know I felt comfortable. In a way, it felt like one of our sessions in her office during my lunch period. The big difference was that we were sitting together on her couch. I felt relaxed. I felt safe. I felt comfortable in my new surroundings, and not the least bit afraid that Mitch was suddenly going to come into the room and explode in my face.

"How about some popcorn?"

"Sure."

"Let's see what we have to watch tonight." Lucy picked up the newspaper, flipped to the television section, and said, "OK. For 8:00 it looks like a choice between 'Happy Days' and 'Maude.' Any preference?"

"I like the Fonz."

"Me, too. How about 'M*A*S*H' at 8:30?"

"Fine."

"You OK with 'Hawaii Five-O' at 9:00?"

"Yes, Lucy."

"You can pick the 10:00 show. We have 'Marcus Welby, M.D.,' 'Barnaby Jones' and 'Police Story.'"

"I'm not much on the police or detective stuff," I told her. "I think James Brolin as Dr. Steven Kiley is so cute."

"Roomie, I agree. Sorry I didn't get a doctor like him instead of . . . never mind. We're going to get along just fine."

That night, after we finished watching television and I was in bed hugging Queenie, I couldn't believe how wonderful and different I felt. That night I felt guilty that I prayed to God that the house would take years instead of months to fix. Then again, I felt like I never meant that much to my parents. I doubted if they would miss me while I was away.

* * *

I woke up Wednesday morning to the sound of Lucy's voice, "Good morning, Roomie. Breakfast will be on the table in five minutes. Remember, we both have school today."

"Lucy, thank you for everything."

"Don't worry about it."

"What about our regular Wednesday meeting?"

"Good point. Let's skip the lunch-hour meetings while you're here. You can talk with me about anything when we're home. Is that OK?"

"Sure."

"And one last reminder . . . nothing about this to your friends. OK?"

"No problem."

If that's what Lucy wanted, that's what she got. The way I felt that first morning, I wasn't going to do anything to upset this heaven I was living in.

"You know, it just dawned on me. I never saw you eat lunch during any of our meetings. Did you buy lunch at school or bring it from home?"

"I don't eat lunch."

"Really. Don't you get hungry?"

"No."

"Interesting. I'm always starving for lunch. Then again, it seems like I'm always hungry."

"With your figure, it looks like you never eat."

"And that means?"

"You have a thin and gorgeous figure."

"Thank you. Oh, you just made my day. It's a shame that schmuck of a husband didn't appreciate my figure as much as you do. Then again, he was too busy playing with his girlfriend's body to think about mine. Like I said, 'All guys are dirtbags.' Well, enough of that stuff. We have school."

"Yes." That was the first time I understood why Lucy and her husband were separated. Unlike my mom and dad, she and her husband started divorce proceedings. In one way, I felt sorry she lost her husband. How could her husband have been so stupid? Lucy, at least in my eyes, was a gorgeous, intelligent, and successful woman. She could probably have had any man she desired. Then I asked myself, "Could I live with a husband who cheated on me?" I had no answer, and it didn't matter. I was years away from marriage or any kind of relationship, so the question was moot.

Later that day I saw Lucy in the school hallway. Our eyes made contact but I just kept on going without saying a word to her. She just smiled at me and nodded her head as if to say, "Good girl. That was perfect."

The first weeks we lived together passed like seconds. Each day after school we had long talks about how things used to be at home. The more I verbalized about Mitch and Mom and Dad, the more I was glad I was with Lucy. Each night I went to sleep hugging Queenie with a smile on my face. As good as I was in school before, I was doing even better. Each of my teachers saw the improvement and commented on it.

On the third Saturday together, Lucy came into my room to let me know she was going to the Peninsula Shopping Center supermarket and that she would be out for a while.

"No problem. I have homework and reading to do."

"Good girl. Always doing the right thing. Help yourself to anything."

"Sure, Lucy."

As soon as Lucy was gone, I had breakfast, did my dishes, and then I got comfortable on the couch in my pajamas to do my history homework. I had three chapters to read and questions to answer, and I wanted to get them out of the way. Before I knew it, two hours had passed. My history homework was finished, and Lucy was home. I put on my heavy robe to help her get the groceries out of the car and into the kitchen. Once all the bags were in the house, Lucy went into her room, stripped down to her bra and panties, and returned to the kitchen to put the groceries away. I found it a little bit unusual for her to dress that way, but I didn't mind it. Evidently, she felt comfortable. I couldn't do it. I think the last time anyone saw me walking around in my underwear was when I was three or four. Since then, especially since I had an older brother, I walked around fully dressed as though I was prepared for a stranger or one of Mitch's friends to walk into the house. This place, however, had only girls, and I guess it was a natural thing for her.

Lucy sat down to have a salad for lunch once the kitchen was straightened away. She offered me the same and a few other things, but I didn't eat. I just sat at the table to talk with her and keep her company. She asked me if I felt less afraid since I put distance between Mitch and myself. "Are you kidding? There is no comparison between how I feel now and how I felt then. I owe you so much."

"Don't think about it. You've helped me, too. I'm glad you feel better here. I enjoy your company. You're special."

I just looked into her eyes and paused after she said that. I didn't know how to react. I couldn't remember hearing someone say something like that to me before. I wanted to ask her what made me "special," but I savored the moment and just let it go as something nice to hear.

"Roomie, do you have any plans with your friends this afternoon?"

"No. I guess the reading made me sleepy. I think I'll just take a nap and figure out what to do later."

"Go ahead. Sleep good. I'll see you when you wake up."

"OK." I got into bed, hugged Queenie after I tucked myself in, and heard Lucy's voice in my mind repeatedly, saying, "You're special." Moments later I was asleep.

I don't know how long I slept. The room was a little dark because the curtains were drawn, which was curious because I usually kept them open to let the sun stream into the room. Lucy was sitting on my right side of the bed wearing just a T-shirt and panties. As usual, she wasn't wearing a bra.

"Hey, Roomie, how do you feel?"

"Glad I slept."

"You had a smile on your face when you were sleeping. Any good sexy dreams you want to tell me about?" Lucy said as she slipped her left hand under my pajama top and rubbed my stomach.

"No. It was nothing like that."

"Ever think about sex?"

"No, not really." I could feel Lucy's hand inch up my stomach.

"It's a wonderful thing. It's something very special that brings two people closer together."

"Don't know too much about that."

"It's a feeling unlike any other in the world. I could teach you about it."

Lucy's hand was suddenly gently cupping my breast. Her thumb and index finger softly rubbed my nipple. Absolutely no one had ever touched me that way before. I was in shock and unable to move or speak. Lucy then put her right hand on my stomach and slowly inched it into my underwear. She rested her hand on my pubic hair.

"We can be closer, Roomie. We can share sensations and feelings that will bring us closer together," she said as she touched the lips of my vagina.

I looked into her eyes but I couldn't move. "Lucy, I don't know if I'm comfortable with this."

"Everything's OK. There's nothing wrong with this."

"Really?"

"You know you can trust me."

Lucy's middle finger touched a spot on my vagina that sent an electrical charge throughout my body.

"See what I mean about new sensations. It feels good. Doesn't it?"

I didn't answer. Actually, I felt horrified. What was she doing to me? Why was she doing this? I didn't feel like I could stop her, even as she unbuttoned my pajama top and slipped off my underwear and pajama pants. I was naked on the bed and unable to stop her. I thought to myself, "I've always trusted her. She says what she's doing is OK. She has done so much for me. Is this her repayment? If I stop her, will she make me move out and back to Mitch?"

"Relax, Roomie. Enjoy the new sensations. Let me teach you how to be a woman."

Lucy kept gently massaging that sensitive spot on my vagina. With her other hand she took my hand and she placed it under her shirt and on her breast. "God," I thought to myself, "what am I doing?"

This went on for a while, then Lucy stood, put Queenie on the desk, took off her shirt and panties, laid on the bed with her legs open, held my head gently, and guided it toward her vagina. "Kiss me," she said. "Kiss me there."

I complied with her wishes but understood that the situation was out of control. All I could think was, "Here this woman saved me from my out-of-control brother. I owe this to her. I have to do this for her. How can I say no when she came through and saved me from being in that household where I didn't want to be?"

Several minutes passed like this. Suddenly Lucy's body was writhing in a way I never saw a person move before. Then she moaned through deep, exhaling breaths. She let go of my head and, for a few moments, she just laid there. I thought it was all over. I was wrong. "Lay down, Roomie. Relax. Open your legs."

Lucy's face approached my vagina. She started kissing me. I felt her tongue inside me. The entire situation was confusing. On some levels, I was feeling pleasure and enjoying these new sensations. I asked myself, "Is this what it's like to feel like a woman?" At the same time, I cringed and felt so uncomfortable and so dirty because of what we were doing. She kissed me for quite some time before she stood, wiped her lips with her hand, kissed my forehead, and said, "I guess you're not ready to finish yet. Don't worry. Just give it time. Wait. It's the most wonderful feeling you'll ever experience. I can still remember my first time." Her eyes looked like she was recalling that moment. "I'm going in for a shower. Relax. You did great, Roomie."

As soon as she was out of sight I got up, got dressed, and took Queenie with me into the living room. I sat on the couch, cuddling Queenie and thinking about what had happened. Lucy used guilt to make me do what we did. It seemed like I left one hell just to enter another. I knew I couldn't discuss this with my friends, and I certainly didn't feel I could discuss this with my parents. The whole thing was so loathsome, and yet I didn't feel angry. I was, however, resentful that she took advantage of me. I kept silently repeating, "I trust her. She's a counselor at my school. She's the woman who rescued me from a disastrous situation. She doesn't want to hurt me. At least I don't think so. How can she be doing this? How could it be wrong if she's someone I trust? Why didn't I resist her? I'm ashamed of myself. This was my fault. How could I have agreed to do that?"

It took hours before I started to pull myself together again. That night at dinner, I hardly touched my food. Lucy talked as though nothing had happened that afternoon, and I just listened and nodded my head at the appropriate times. Although I had skipped lunch, there was a sad feeling inside of me that kept me from getting hungry and eating.

I spent Sunday working on schoolwork and preparing for my upcoming second round of SAT tests. My PSAT test scores from last year were pretty good, but nowhere near perfect. Last June's SAT tests were also pretty good. Again, they were nowhere near perfect. I felt like the March SATs had to be phenomenal, so I got every possible practice test, took them, and religiously studied each question I got wrong and why I got it wrong.

Throughout those weeks of preparation, Lucy and I seemed to be back in the pattern we had been in before that Saturday encounter. Neither of us ever discussed it. After a while, it was almost as though it never happened. My schoolwork remained nearly perfect. In fact, that desire to do everything perfectly increased and dominated my personality. I didn't resist it.

Things changed again after the SATs. Every few weeks we would go through another sexual encounter. After about the third time, I had my first orgasm. Lucy was right. It was a feeling I never could have imagined. The difference between her and me is that I didn't want to remember it.

My feelings were mixed. I was totally confused. On one hand, I enjoyed the sexual sensations. On the other hand, I was ashamed at what I was doing with her and repeatedly expressed that feeling to her. It didn't stop anything. From then on, she continued having sex with me. Sometimes weeks would go by and nothing would happen. I thought, "This is OK. This is something I can deal with." Then it would happen again.

At one point, she actually set me up with a guy named Richard, who was about five foot eleven, stunning looking with an impeccably shaped nose, gorgeous white teeth, and a Kirk Douglas type cleft in his chin. Why such a gorgeous guy would go out with a relatively flat-chested, plain Jane like me always remained a mystery. He could have had, at least in my mind, any girl he wanted just by looking her way.

I had no sexual activity with Richard. He didn't even try to kiss me. Actually, I think he was gay. I wasn't sure. I think Lucy set it up just to appease me and make me feel normal. It was strange. Other guys followed. None of them meant anything to me, and I never felt normal out on dates.

All the times Lucy and I had sex–I would never call it making love– seemed the same except one. Lucy's hand was massaging the outside of my vagina when suddenly I felt a sharp pain from her finger entering me. Then I had the feeling of liquid flowing down my thigh. It was blood, and it got on the sheets. "Roomie, didn't any of those guys make love to you? I thought you lost your virginity long ago."

"What a fool," I said to myself. Lucy had no idea that I felt like I lost my virginity the day she told me to open my legs. I suddenly flashed back to what my friend, Francine, said years ago, "I don't want my future husband to think I'm not a virgin because I broke my hymen. The first time we have sex, he'll expect to find blood all over the sheets when he breaks me, and I don't want to let him down." Back then, I had no idea what Francine was talking about. Now, as I held my hand over my vagina and ran to the shower, I knew exactly what she meant.

I never actually thought of what was happening between Lucy and me as an abusive relationship at all. It was just something that happened. I actually thought of it more in terms of being involved in a lesbian kind of relationship. And yet she would continue to set me up with guys to go out with as she continued having sex with me. It was really a very confusing time for me.

What I understood most was that the woman I trusted more than anyone else in the world was raping me, and I allowed it to continue. The woman who I wanted to be with to protect me, the woman who helped me to escape that environment with my brother, was also the woman doing the most harm to me, and I allowed it to happen. So often I let her know that I was not happy and I asked her to stop, but she would just tell me, "It's OK." It was not "OK," but I allowed it to happen. It was my fault because I didn't stop it. Each time it happened, it felt like I was there, but it was like an out-of-body experience. Each time I just waited for it to be over. Then, once it was over, I could just forget it happened.

I felt I owed those things to her. I thought, "How can I say no to her when she did all this for me?" But this was one hell of a price to pay.

I thought I was in control and that I was making a conscious decision to do this. I felt very ashamed. I felt violated. I hated the fact that she was my first sexual encounter. I hated the fact that the person who was supposed to protect me, raped me. The one sensation I didn't feel at that time was feeling like a victim. At that time, I couldn't. I had allowed it to happen. That victimized feeling didn't surface until decades later when I was in therapy. Some protective part of my psyche buried and repressed that feeling deep into my subconscious.

By the time my junior year ended, my applications to college were already in. The house was finally finished at the end of July, and my parents, who had called me occasionally over the past months, told me it was time to return home. I told them I was staying with Lucy because I couldn't tolerate being near Mitch. I didn't tell them it was Lucy's suggestion, almost insistence, that I remain with her.

My senior year in high school, what should have been one of the happiest years of my life, went by like a blur. Perhaps that is because I didn't want to remember it. I didn't go to the prom, nor did I date much. I just stuck to my work and consumed myself with always doing things as perfectly as I could. Having always been the perfect little girl in school with nearly perfect grades, I was able to pick and choose which college to attend, and I chose to accept New York University because of its pre-med program. My parents were glad with my choice and had no problem telling me they would back me with part of the tuition. I took out student loans for the rest. My parents never had a problem with giving me financial aid or material things; they just never learned how to support me emotionally. But even that was changing. It seems they knew how to get along with adults much better than with kids and, as I was about to enter college, their image of and attitude toward me were improving. We were getting along better and talking more on the phone. I liked the idea that I could now talk with them as friends. Why? Because the friend

I was living with was a constant source of consternation, humiliation, and grief.

I entered NYU with high expectations and my usual "Miss Perfect" demeanor. By the end of my first college year, however, I understood that my expectations and aspirations had no validity. I was failing out of NYU. For the first time in my life, I was far, very far, from perfect. Lucy's constant, indignant violations of my mind and body were the cause of my failing. It was time for a change. I was miserable, and I knew Lucy had been the cause of that misery ever since that first sexual encounter. I didn't want to be involved with that anymore. I kept repeating inwardly, "Enough's enough." I used the excuse that I couldn't afford to live out of the house and pay for school. I let her know that I intended to move back with my parents.

Lucy had caused me to lose control of my life, and I wanted that control back regardless of the mental or monetary cost.

* * *

Receiving straight Ds for eighteen credits was probably the catalyst to change my life. Never before did I, Miss Perfect, feel like a failure. Lucy tried to excuse the poor grades as an adjustment from high school to college, but I didn't buy it. I was no longer the fifteen-year-old who had moved in with her out of desperation. Now, I was the almost eighteen-year-old who had to move away from her out of desperation, even if it meant being close to Mitch again.

I called Dad to tell him I was moving back home and, for a change, he supported me. He could have given me a hard time for wasting the tuition, but he didn't. I was glad about that. I didn't need any more condemnation in my life. I was supplying enough condemnation of myself each time I looked in the mirror and questioned how I let myself become such a low-life fool.

Lucy stood in the doorway of my room and watched me pack. I tried not to look into her eyes. I was afraid her power over me would change my mind. A few times she simply said, "Roomie, are you sure about this? I can help you get through this temporary situation."

Hearing her suggestion to help me made me remember how her "help" got me into this condition. I kept on getting my things together until Queenie was the last thing I had to pack. Dad's timing was perfect. The doorbell rang,

Dad came in, helped me get my stuff into the car, and then waited there for me to say goodbye to Lucy. There were tears in my eyes. Lucy misinterpreted them.

"Don't worry, Roomie. We'll see each other again soon."

I felt like saying, "Bitch, get out of my life." I restrained myself. Instead, I simply said, "Thanks for what you've done," and then got into the car with Dad. It seems like traveling in a car, either to or from my home, had affected me since the day my mother dragged Mitch and me out of our home to live with Aunt Anna and Uncle Dan when I was five. Those feelings resurfaced as Dad drove closer to the house I used to live in. No, I didn't want to call it "home." Home, as they say, is where the heart is. Home, as they say, is where you return to feel safe. Returning to the house where Mitch lived made me feel anything but safe, but I was a different person now. I was stronger, even in my fragile state of mind.

Mom, who I hadn't seen for months, actually greeted me at the door when I got home. She kissed my cheek. "Welcome home, Jess. It's good to see you. Everything is ready for you."

"Thanks. I'm sorry . . ."

Mom gently put her fingers on my lips to stop me. "You have nothing to be sorry about. Knowing you, you're going to turn this situation around and come out a winner. You've always been such a good little girl. You always knew the right thing to do."

Those words touched me more than she ever could have imagined. She had never said anything like that to me. I started to cry. She actually hugged me. I asked myself, "Why couldn't it have always been like this before?"

Dad came over to us. He actually kissed my cheek. "Welcome home, Jess."

My room hadn't changed, except for the songs I heard since the last time I was there: Manfred Mann's Earth Band's "Blinded by the Light," The Eagles' "New Kid in Town," David Soul's "Don't Give Up on Us," Thelma Houston's "Don't Leave Me This Way," and Bill Conti's "Gonna Fly Now," the theme from *Rocky*. One other thing changed. It must have been a force of habit to reach for the headphones to listen to my stereo, but something stopped me. I said to myself, "No. No more living in fear of Lucy, or Mitch." I turned up the volume and let the music's inspirational messages fill my heart with renewed strength. Jessica was back. "Roomie" was a dead-and-buried thing of the past.

That summer I searched for a new direction in my life and found it quickly. I wanted to remain in the medical field, although I knew I wasn't destined to be a doctor. There was a school in the city for lab technicians. I applied and immediately got accepted for the yearlong program, and Mom and Dad were willing to help with the tuition. The school sent me the required syllabus and, throughout the remainder of July and August, I sat alone with my books on the beach, digesting every phrase and word with a renewed hunger for learning. By the time I sat in my first class, all the books were read and practically memorized. I was Jessica again. I was that perfect young woman, getting perfect grades, and pleasing everyone around me, including myself.

The first half of the program passed without incident. My grades were straight As, and academically I was the student to chase after. I spent Christmas and New Year's with Mom and Dad and actually enjoyed myself, especially since Mitch had taken a trip with his friends for two weeks.

The second half of the program also started positively. Once again, over the previous vacation, I had read and digested every word and phrase of the required syllabus. Also over the vacation, I had renewed my friendships with some of my high school girlfriends. We attended parties together, and on a few occasions guys asked me to dance or invited themselves for a chance to talk with me. Marijuana, pot, was the rage of those days, and parties usually meant me smoking some to be sociable. It was no big deal. A beer and a joint were common forms of entertainment, but that didn't make me a drug addict.

Some of my girlfriends brought up Lucy. They suspected something. They felt free to say they didn't trust her, but I always quickly dismissed the conversation. I had become the social queen with my old friends and enjoyed the position. Even at school, the new girls I met invited me to parties with other students who attended the technical school. The other girls, and boys for that matter, weren't jealous of my academic standing because, as it was in the past, I was always the first to offer help to anyone who felt they were falling behind or didn't understand something taught in class that day.

It was at one of those parties that my life changed again. Debby Boone's big song, "You Light Up My Life," was playing. Someone tapped me on my shoulder from behind me and said, "You could light up my life, but I'd rather you help me light this joint."

I turned and saw a cute guy. He was a few inches taller than me, nicely dressed, and he had a smile on his face that turned me on like never before.

"Excuse me," I replied.

"Seriously. I'll share the joint if you have a light. I'll share it even if you don't have a light."

I didn't smoke cigarettes at that time, but I always carried a lighter for just such an occasion. I lit him up. He took a few tokes and then passed it to me. He was holding his breath to keep the smoke inside his lungs, but still managed to say, "I'm Jack. Nice to meet you."

"I'm Jessica," I said, took a toke, and just stared into his brown eyes.

He finally let the smoke out and said, "I've seen you in the school library, but you always had your head buried in a book. I didn't want to disturb you."

"Good idea. I take this school seriously."

"I just started a few weeks ago. You're lucky you're halfway through it already. Any advice to a rookie?"

"Do your homework."

"Any other words of wisdom?"

"Yeah, get a roach clip."

"Smart woman. I see you don't like to get burned."

"I got burned once. It won't happen again."

"Was it a guy, or a joint?"

"Neither."

"Sure, keep me guessing."

"It'll add to my intrigue."

Jack turned to a guy next to him. "Sam, take care of this," he said, handing Sam what was left of the joint. The Bee Gees' "How Deep Is Your Love" was playing in the background. "Care to dance?"

"Can I trust you?"

"With your life."

"That's a lot of trust."

"That's the kind of guy I am."

"How can I believe you?"

"Give me enough time, I'll prove it with actions. In the meantime, how about a dance?"

"Jack, huh? Is that short for John?"

"Nope, just plain Jack. Jack Gordon."

"Jessica. Jessica Devoe."

Jack took my hand to lead me to where the others were dancing. I felt something when he touched me. I had never had that feeling before, and I liked it. I liked him.

That's how it started between us. After that night, we'd meet in the library to study together. It was nice to see that he was as serious about school as I was. Six months later I had my certification and moved onto my internship. Six months after that, Jack got his certification and got his internship in the same hospital as me.

Our personalities were very similar. We would do things very spontaneously. I could talk with him about anything, almost anything. Not once did I ever mention what happened between Lucy and me. That was in my past, and I was determined to keep it locked in my subconscious and away from the world. That was my private hell, and I didn't need to inflict it upon the man I was falling in love with.

Jack had become a fresh and welcome part of my life. I remember how we used to get stoned together after work and go back to my parent's house to eat all of their snacks. They were clueless about our condition. Actually, on a few occasions, we smoked pot together at the hospital when things were desolately still. The people there were also clueless.

By the time I finished my year of internship, I started to chart a new course for my life because things were going so well for me. I had a man who loved me. I loved him. I was hardly ever home, so Mitch wasn't an issue. Even when Mitch and I were home together and he'd go nuts, I was able to tolerate it better. I was strong again. Even more important, I was happy with myself and in love with a man who wanted to marry me.

I felt I had the strength to return to college and did. Neither of us thought it was the right time to get married. We decided it would be better to wait.

In 1979, college was different for me. No more Ds. Instead, I ran a 3.4-3.5 grade point average my first year. Not perfect, but far from failing. The next few years passed quickly. Before either of us knew what hit us, it was 1983 and our wedding was set for September.

I remember looking at myself in the mirror one day while shopping for my bridal gown. I thought it would be great if I lost some weight so my dress would fit better. At the time, I weighed about 135 pounds. At five foot five, I didn't look fat, but what bride doesn't want to look great for the most important day in her life? Besides, there was enough time to go on a diet and lose 10 pounds or so without using much willpower. All I had to do was cut out the garbage and sugar. So I made up my mind to reach my newly desired weight goal and started watching what I put into my mouth. Ever so slowly and gradually, the weight started coming off. I felt great. The 10 pounds came off effortlessly, so I just continued with the same eating pattern.

My weight was down to 120 by the time our wedding day arrived. The wedding was beautiful, and Jack was my handsome knight in shining armor. I remember how, after we kissed in the ceremony, I looked up and said silently, "God, thank you for all you've done for me."

When we arrived at our honeymoon suite, I remember I remarked to Jack when he carried me over the threshold, "See, I'll do anything for you. I even made it easier for you to carry me over the threshold by losing 15 pounds. I'm the best wife you'll ever have."

"You're the *only* wife I'll ever have," Jack said. "And you're the most beautiful wife any guy could ever ask for."

Jack and I had made love before that night, but the honeymoon night was extra special. With Jack, it wasn't having sex, it was making love. I relished all the pleasures that physical contact and love offer a woman who is committed to the one she loves.

We had already set up our apartment before the marriage. I was never much of a cook back then, so we ate out most of the time. Interestingly, when you eat out a lot, you have a tendency to put on weight. I went the other way and continued to lose weight, although I was willing to eat any healthy food on the menu. What was not clear and obvious to me was that once you start down that weight loss road, it becomes something like an obsession. Losing two dress sizes wasn't good enough. I wanted to lose three dress sizes. Losing 20 pounds wasn't good enough. I wanted to lose more. Put another way, the lower you get, the more you want to go down. People did not discourage me. Everyone kept saying, "Jess, you look great. How'd you do it? What's your secret?" Statements like that only motivated me to lose more weight. It felt great for people to notice how good I looked, but I wasn't satisfied with myself as far as my weight was concerned.

Marriage was great for me. I never considered marriage a big upheaval or drastic change because, in a way, it was like the perfect culmination to all those bad events before. Here I was with someone I loved and someone I trusted with my life, just as Jack had promised when we first met. For me, marriage was only a positive thing.

Slowly and gradually over the next two years I kept losing weight–a pound here and there. It was never anything extravagant. The same people who once told me I looked great now started telling me to hold the line on my weight loss. I thought it was envy and jealously on their part, because most of them were overweight. Then even Jack started saying, "It's too much. Don't lose anymore."

When I looked at myself in a mirror, I thought I looked great. It's amazing. I survived all that past negative history and thought I was OK. I thought I was stable when, in actuality, things were falling apart.

My first three years of college were behind me, and I was headed toward my degree and something I could be proud of, but the pressures of a full-time job and college were getting to me. I was losing strength from the loss of weight, but I never admitted that to anyone. Every time I went to work, people, in passing, would ask, "How are you doing?" I'd smile. "I'm fine." Inside I knew, "I'm not fine. I'm horrible." It was just so two-faced. I couldn't deal with it. I was trying to show the world this face of everything's OK and I'm great, but inside I was so miserable. I just couldn't deal with that. I couldn't deal with people.

Something deep inside my mind was bothering me, but I didn't know what it was. I was happy with Jack, but that wasn't enough. My parents were talking with me more often, but I wasn't satisfied. I smiled less. I laughed less. I made love with Jack less often. I found myself crying more, but I didn't understand why. I took fewer calls from my friends and started to withdraw from those close to me. I isolated myself. I wouldn't leave the house. Before I knew it, I couldn't go back to work. It was awful. I did a lot of crying and felt miserable. I could talk with Jack about anything, but I didn't talk with him about my eating problem. I kept that, and my negative feelings about myself, a secret. I could not and would not discuss it with him. To top things off, my parents, who I had finally gotten close to, decided to move to Florida. I felt like they had abandoned me.

I knew the meaning of "obsessive-compulsive," and I was its living definition. I had never let go of my perfectionist attitude. Everything, at school and at work, had to be perfect, but it wasn't, at least not in my mind. I needed to be in control of my life, but I wasn't. I needed help, but I refused it from all those who offered it. I still needed to be that perfect little girl at school, but I wasn't. I had thrown myself into my work at the hospital and had gotten advances, but that wasn't good enough. Instead, it just meant more pressure. I was desperate for help and didn't get it, not even from Jack. His attitude was, "Just do whatever you want. You know how to do the right thing all the time." He should have recognized that his wife was out of control and needed to be reined back in for a reality check. Even if I didn't understand it consciously, subconsciously I must have begun to resent the fact that everyone–Jack, my parents, my friends and co-workers–all trusted me to do the right thing and thought I could take care of myself, but I couldn't. I went to the doctor, but the fool simply took my blood pressure and blood samples and told me that everything was fine. It wasn't fine.

The weight loss started to consume me and take control of my life because the weight wasn't coming off as fast as it did before. By 1985, my weight had become an obsession. For a person with an obsessive-compulsive and perfectionist personality like mine, that's dangerous. My diet and eating patterns became the most significant part of my life. Whereas before, I ate anything healthy and didn't give it a second thought, now I didn't eat certain foods, and I thought three times before I put anything into my mouth.

Slowly and gradually, I labeled certain foods as "unsafe." At first, it was a small list, but then the list started to grow. I only ate what I called "safe" foods. If I felt too full after a meal, I solved the problem by taking a laxative. The more often this happened, the more laxatives I took. Before I knew it, I was taking twenty laxatives at a time, then thirty, forty, and eventually up to sixty laxatives at one time.

Increasingly, my thoughts about my weight consumed my every waking moment. Unfortunately, I never understood why. Except for Karen Carpenter's death in 1983, eating disorders were not discussed. The words "eating disorder" hadn't gone mainstream yet. Few doctors knew how to recognize the symptoms, and even fewer doctors knew how to treat those symptoms.

I had no idea what was going on with me. I knew I had lost all this weight. I knew I couldn't eat. I was terrified of food. I was terrified of gaining weight. I was abusing laxatives, but there was no name, at least none that I knew of, to put on what was wrong with me.

Gradually, I wouldn't eat anything unless I knew I was going to be abusing laxatives. What I ate and the size of the portion for each meal decreased. What was normal for me would be a third of a portion for anyone else, and that was still too much for me. Each time I ate such a meal, I followed it up with handfuls of laxatives, thinking, "I've got to wash this poison out of my system."

I knew I was consumed with depression. Instead of smoking pot as a social thing, I took it to the extreme. I began smoking in the afternoon and didn't quit until I went to sleep. I had to be high all the time. Jack sometimes smoked with me, but that was infrequently. Through it all, I was lucky enough to finish school and get my degree. A short time after I graduated, I had to take a leave of absence from work because I couldn't deal with seeing people. I just stayed home and constantly cried. I kept asking myself, "What is wrong with me?" I had no answer. I knew I had a problem, but I couldn't fix it on my own. I didn't know if it could ever be fixed by anyone.

Silently, I prayed, "God, please help me because I can't help myself."

* * *

Chapter Four

Misery in Manhattan

The year 1986 was not short on news in the United States and around the world. President Reagan denied exchanging arms for hostages, President Jean-Claude Duvalier fled Haiti, and President Ferdinand Marcos fled the Philippines. It was the year of the Chernobyl disaster and the space shuttle Challenger disaster. It was the year the "Amazin'" New York Mets defeated the Boston Red Sox in the World Series, Nintendo video games were introduced in the United States, and *The Oprah Winfrey Show* came to national television. Those headlines had their famous or infamous places in posterity. The name of Jessica Devoe Gordon, a twenty-six-year-old lab technician from Long Island, New York, never made it to the press, and rightfully so. My life was worthless. My life was not worth the ink my name would waste on paper.

I hated myself and my body disgusted me. As thin as I was, I wasn't thin enough. When I looked in the mirror, all I saw was an awful shape that disgusted me. I couldn't stand my body. I didn't want my husband to look at my body or touch it. I didn't want to see myself naked. I didn't want him to see me with no clothes on because my body was gross.

At three years into our marriage, Jack should have been smart enough to pack his bags, throw me out of his life, and find some normal person to fulfill his destiny. Instead he stuck by me and never let his love waiver. Jack gave me my space. He never pushed me. He handled me with kid gloves. He just kept telling me, this ugly creature imprisoned in my own living hell, that I was beautiful. He was "Mr. Nice Guy," and, as the old expression goes, nice guys finish last. He didn't deserve me. I didn't deserve him.

Suicide was the first thing on my mind in the morning and the last thing on my mind at night. I kept thinking, "I can't live like this anymore." I wanted to end my life. I just didn't know how. I made no attempts, but never stopped contemplating one thought–death is my savior. Death will grant me peace. I kept asking myself, "How far do I have to push my body until I finally die?"

Co-workers from the lab called to see how I was doing during the first few weeks of my leave of absence. I never answered the telephone. I let the phone answering machine take messages, which I never returned. What was I going to do? I was tired of lying to people and telling them things were all right. Things were not all right.

Things went on that way from April to June. No, actually things got worse. I knew it, and Jack knew it. If sexual relationships for a married couple were a thermometer of how they were doing, Jack knew something was definitely wrong because our lovemaking must have decreased by at least 25 percent because of my obsession with my physical self-image.

Losing weight had become a control issue. When I ate, if I ate, and what I ate were the only things I could control in my worthless life. Everything else was out of control. I couldn't work. I couldn't cook for Jack. I couldn't take care of the bare necessities of the house. Everything was crumbling, especially me. The only pillar that kept me standing was my weight control. It was also the issue that was tearing me down. It's not that I was opting not to eat, I just couldn't. I had an intense fear that I might eat something, anything, and I'd gain weight.

Jack spoke about my problem with a few doctors at the hospital. Most tried to dismiss my behavior as premenstrual syndrome, but PMS doesn't last for months at a time. All those doctors did was show their male-dominated, barbaric medical opinion about problems women faced. Jack and I needed a label for my problem. If we could find the label, we could find the right course of action that would finally reverse my suicidal flight.

One Friday Jack got home from work and showed me a pamphlet from a New York hospital. A female doctor from work had given it to him that morning and strongly suggested that Jack and I follow through by investigating their relatively new and unique program. Jack made the appointment for Monday at 10:00 a.m. He managed to get me out of the house that morning, and then he stayed with me as Dr. Jeffrey Winston and I discussed my problem. As the session started, there was something about how Dr. Winston looked that bothered me, and I couldn't figure it out. His hair and facial features were about average to below average. He was short, about five foot three, but that wasn't what was getting to me. Then it hit me. He must have been between 40 and 50 pounds overweight. That's what bothered me.

I finally tuned into what he was saying when he asked, "Mrs. Gordon, when you look in the mirror, what do you see?"

"A fat cow staring back at me."

"Do you often feel depressed?"

"Yes. Always."

"Even suicidal?"

I didn't answer immediately. I had never expressed my suicidal tendencies to Jack. I had to believe Jack's promise to me when we met: "You can trust me with your life."

"Yes, doctor. I have felt . . . I do feel that way." Jack didn't get judgmental. He didn't say anything.

"Have you lost more than 20 percent of your weight in recent times?"

"Yes."

"Do you restrict your food intake?"

"Absolutely."

"Do you regurgitate after a meal or take a large amount of laxatives?"

Jack wasn't aware of my laxative abuse, but I wasn't going to lie to the doctor and decrease my chances of getting help from him. "Yes. I mean I don't throw up, but I'll take handfuls of laxatives at a time if I feel too full from a meal." Jack was kind to me again. He said nothing.

"Has your lovemaking decreased because you're ashamed to let your husband see your body?"

I looked at Jack. He grinned at me as I answered, "Yes."

"I see."

"Doctor, get to the point."

"Mrs. Gordon, you have an addiction."

"Doctor, I smoke pot, but that's not the problem here."

"You have an addiction of the mind that can kill you as assuredly as an addiction to heroin."

Jack and I looked at each other like this doctor was out of his mind and we were wasting our time and money.

"Mrs. Gordon, you have all the classic symptoms. The depression. The emaciated look. Food restriction. Laxative abuse. You probably feel dizzy at times or catatonic. You probably think your life is out of control and the only thing you can control is your weight and your food intake."

I stopped thinking this doctor was a quack, because he had just described me perfectly after knowing me only a few minutes.

"Doctor, we're strangers, but you know me too well. What is my problem, and is there a cure?"

"A cure? Not exactly."

I took Jack's hand and squeezed it.

"There is recovery. I'll explain. Cigarette smokers, alcoholics, and drug addicts are never cured. They can only go into recovery. They can cease their substance abuse, but they'll spend the rest of their lives one drink, one cigarette, or one fix away from a possible recurrence to their addiction. Are you aware of the term anorexia nervosa?"

"No."

"That is your mental addiction, and it can kill unless you take actions to reverse your lifestyle and go into recovery."

"And how do I do that?"

"We have a new program here at the hospital designed exactly for people suffering from depression and eating disorders."

"How long does it take?"

"Two months."

"And what does the program entail?"

"Therapy and behavior modification under strict supervision. In simple terms, we have to teach you how to eat."

"I know how to eat."

"But you don't. Do you?"

"No."

"Mrs. Gordon, *you* have to want to be here. Your husband and I can't force you to help yourself. What happens next is your decision. You are the one who has to take control."

"Control. That's an interesting word at this moment."

The doctor extended his hand and looked at me as though he was looking into the eyes of his own dying daughter.

"Do you have any questions?"

"Yes. No."

"Mrs. Gordon, I urge you not to walk out of this hospital. I urge you to start our inpatient program today."

"Dr. Winston, everything you said makes sense. I need a few minutes to make sense of this in my own mind."

"Understandable."

Jack and I went to the waiting room for me to think about what to do next. Jack didn't push me in any direction. All he said was, "I'm here if you need me. Take as much time as you need."

There was a huge window overlooking the crowded New York City streets. I could see thin women all over the place. I wondered if they shared my disorder.

I spent the next two hours reexamining my conversation with the doctor, who had finally put a label on my problem. I had no choice but to believe what he said because that label fit me so perfectly. I was the definition of anorexia. There was no way I could delude myself and deny his diagnosis. The question I asked myself a million times was, "Now, what do I do about it?"

Jack sat patiently and silently. I paced.

Finally, I sat next to my husband, took his hand and said, "Jack, thanks."

"Jessica, I love you."

"Yes, you do. Yes, you do."

Several moments passed as I stared into Jack's eyes for strength and support. "Jack, I don't want to do this. I don't know if I can stand being away from you."

"It's up to . . ."

"I know it's up to me. I don't want to do this, but if I don't . . ."

At first, I couldn't force the words out of my mouth because it meant facing the realization of my condition. I started crying as I said, "If I don't, I'll die."

Jack took me in his arms. I kissed him.

* * *

Dr. Winston must have known what my decision was going to be. As soon as we walked back into his office, I saw the insurance forms and admittance papers ready for me to sign. Reluctantly, I picked up the pen and put my life into his hands.

Ten minutes after the ink was dry, I was at the elevator door with Dr. Winston and Jack.

"Mr. Gordon, this is where you part company. Your wife will need clothes and toiletries."

"Sure, Dr. Winston. I'll take care of it," Jack said as he looked at me.

"See the nurse at the reception desk when you get back. She'll get the things up to your wife."

Jack hugged me with a greater love than I ever felt before. "Jess, you're going to come out of this better than ever before. Our life is just starting together. I love you."

I kissed Jack goodbye and held myself together as the elevator doors closed. Within moments, we were out of the elevator and approaching the room where I would be living for the next two months. Dr. Winston opened the door and let me enter first. The room with white walls looked sterile. There were two beds, two wooden chairs, and two dressers. The dresser and bed to the left, by the wall, had someone's belongings. The bed on the right near the window was where I'd be sleeping that night. Between the two beds was a sink with a fine metal strainer covering the sinkhole. Dr. Winston must have noticed what I was looking at. "There is no toilet or shower in the room. Those facilities are outside under constant observation by the aides."

I didn't understand what he said, but didn't question it.

"The other women," Dr. Winston said, "are in a group therapy session now. Mrs. Gordon, things will work out if you want them to."

"I hope so."

"You did the right thing," Dr. Winston said, then he left the room and closed the door behind him. I sat on the bed, put my face in my hands, and started crying. "I don't want to be here. I want to be with my husband. I hate this place." Those sentiments screamed in my mind like horrifying devils that wouldn't stop.

I don't know how long it was before the door opened and my room-mate entered. She simply said, "Hi."

"Hi." It was embarrassing to have her see me crying. I went to get a tissue from my purse but remembered that I had to give up my purse to Jack.

"I'm Kylie. Here, use one of mine. I've got boxes of them for the same reason."

"Jessica," I said as I accepted her tissues.

Kylie had a gentle-looking face. Some would call it "the nice girl next door" kind of look. If she had blonde instead of auburn hair, I'd swear she was Doris Day's younger sister. Of course, she was thin.

Kylie sat on her bed. "Your first time here?"

"Yeah."

"My second."

"I don't want to be here."

"None of us *wants* to be here. We *have* to be here."

An aide walked into our room. "Jessica?"

"Yes."

"Your husband brought these things." The aide opened my suitcase and searched it. I felt violated at what she was doing, and the feeling must have been obvious on my face.

"Don't let that bother you," Kylie said. "She's looking for diet pills and laxatives."

"This place feels like a prison," I said to Kylie as the aide left. Kylie just nodded her head. I put the suitcase on top of the dresser without unpacking anything, laid down on the bed, and cried hysterically.

"Jess . . . I . . . I understand what you're feeling now. Let it out."

* * *

I must have fallen asleep. The sound of Kylie's voice woke me. "Meal is in five minutes, Jess." Kylie's statement made me think of movies about prison that I had seen. I pictured the prisoners exiting their cells and marching single file toward the mess hall under the watchful eyes of prison guards toting shotguns. I went to the sink to run cold water over my eyes to reduce the swelling the crying had caused. I stared at myself in the mirror above the sink. I looked and felt awful. I thought to myself, "There's no way I can do what they are going to want me to do. They're going to make me eat and gain weight. I can't deal with that."

Well, there were no prison guards, but there were aides lined up throughout the hall to make sure we all left our rooms and went directly to the dining room. On the way there I saw an opened room with someone sitting on a chair by the window. The woman scared the hell out of me because she looked like a living skeleton. She was about my age. She couldn't have weighed more than 60 pounds. She was wearing a hospital gown, and she was staring out the window with a blank look on her face. There was a tall, metal intravenous stand next to her. It held a bag of liquid. Kylie noticed me looking at her and whispered, "They're feeding her through a tube." I noticed her bare leg. I could actually see the bone under the flesh. It horrified me. I couldn't believe someone could be that thin and still be alive. I was 95 pounds, so I must have had some bones sticking out, but I could never see my own bones.

"Kylie, what's wrong with her?"

"The same thing that's wrong with us, only she's taken this crap further than we have. Her name is Christy. If they didn't intervene she'd be dead in days. Makes you think you did the right thing coming here, even if it's going to be tough."

By the time Kylie and I sat down, all of the women from the eating disorder unit, except for the one in her room, were in the dining room. Suddenly, there was a plate of chicken, potatoes, and string beans placed before me. Ordinarily, as I learned later, we had a choice of three items for each meal. However, since this was my first meal and I didn't have a chance to place a prior order, they chose my meal for me. I started feeling nauseated just looking at the plate.

"Jess, it may be difficult, but you . . ."

"Thank you, Kylie," said one of the short and obese aides standing behind us. "Mrs. Gordon, you are here for a reason. Henceforth, understand that each meal must be finished completely. We can't help you if you don't eat. We have rules here and they must be followed. Break the rules and you lose your privileges. Those privileges consist of outside walks, visitation rights, television rights, and telephone rights. You work with us to help yourself, and we'll work with you. Do we understand each other?"

I didn't respond.

"Jessica, do we understand each other?"

"Yes."

"You're invited to a therapy session following the meal."

I gave no verbal response. Inside I thought, "Invitation, huh? It's not like I have a choice."

Feelings of anger and resentment built up inside me. I picked up my fork, pushed a few pieces of food about the plate, and took my first bite toward my possible recovery. In my mind I quickly calculated, "Sixty more days, 180 meals from now, and I get paroled. I'm not giving into this nonsense without a fight."

Two-thirds of my meal remained on my plate when I stood to walk out. One of the aides angrily started toward me. A second aide stopped her. I could hear her say, "Let her off this time only. It's her first meal. Keep an eye on her at breakfast."

Kylie tugged at my arm saying, "C'mon, Jess. We have therapy now. Don't bother with the bathrooms. They're all locked for the next hour."

"What if I have to go?"

"You'll have to learn to go before the meal, or cross your legs and hold it in. The bathrooms are locked because they don't want any purging."

I had no idea what she was talking about. I just followed Kylie and the other women into the large therapy room. I positioned myself in the corner to isolate myself as much as possible. Kylie sat next to me. There must have been forty of us in there. Some women were thinner than I was. Some women looked like they weighed a little more than me. We all had one thing in common—we all suffered from eating disorders.

Quiet took over the room as Dr. Winston entered at the front. He began immediately. "Ladies, let's welcome Jessica Gordon on her first day here and let's wish her well. Mrs. Gordon, is there anything you would like to share with us?" I shook my head to decline. There was no way in hell they were going to get me to talk. I was not a participant. I was an observer and I was going to remain a silent observer until I decided otherwise.

There was a rush to the bathroom when the session concluded. Aides stood outside each door and went inside after each woman exited the bathroom. "They have to check for purging," Kylie said. I still had no idea what she was talking about and didn't want to ask any questions in ear shot of all the other women for fear of being embarrassed by my ignorance. I didn't have to go, so I headed straight to the room. I was alone for a while and had a chance to admonish myself for getting into this situation and this terrible mental condition. Kylie joined me a few minutes later. I was sitting on the bed with my clothes on. My knees were tucked close to my chest, and my head was buried between my knees.

Over the public address system we heard, "Lights out at 10:00 p.m. It was 9:55. Kylie said, "Better get into your pajamas while there is still light."

There was no barrier separating me and Kylie, and no privacy. We had to undress in front of each other to get on our pajamas. I chalked it up to another form of humiliation. The only consolation was that we were there for the same reason, and our bodies looked the same. It felt different from being undressed in front of Jack.

Kylie turned off the lights and the two of us got into bed.

Darkness and silence took over as soon as Kylie and I were in bed.

"Jess, it'll get better."

"Sorry, Kylie, but I can't see how."

I thought about escaping—just getting the hell out of there. After that I regressed back to the night I was five years old and I had to sleep at my Aunt Anna's house after my mother learned about my father's affair. As happened that night long ago, I cried before I fell asleep. The last time I was without Queenie. On this night, for the first time in three years, I went to sleep without my husband.

* * *

The next morning started with a rush of everyone going to the bathroom. The same short and obese aide told me not to flush before they viewed the contents of the toilet. "Violation of this rule will cost you your privileges," she warned.

Leaving my bowel movement in the toilet for someone else to observe had to be one of the most mortifying experiences, but I did it and went to the showers, which were communal. There we were, three abreast on each side, three of the thinnest naked women you can imagine, all showering together.

At the therapy session the night before, they kept repeating the word "trigger." I learned that a trigger was something you heard or an event you observed that caused you to take a certain action or feel a certain way. For normal people, a trigger can be positive. For instance, you can hear a song that reminds you of your first date with your husband or wife. But for a person with eating disorders, triggers are frequently negative. The sight of such thin women in the shower could trigger an anorexic into thinking, "I have to restrict my diet more to be as thin as them." Fortunately, at this hospital unit, there was no restriction, no laxatives, and no diet pills allowed on our floor. We were simply there for them to fatten us up.

At breakfast, as with my first meal, I lifted my fork and pushed the food around the plate to procrastinate. The evening before, I'd had a chance to pick what I was going to eat for breakfast, but that didn't entice my appetite. All I felt was a huge fear and terror. I thought, "This food is going to make me gain so much weight. Normal people don't eat like this. Normal people don't eat every little thing on their plate. Why do I have to?" Without a doubt, there was still a lot of rebellion going through me. I looked around and saw the aides carefully watching me.

I paused to look around again before I took my first bite. Everyone else was eating and finishing everything on their plate. If I didn't do it, I would stick out. I wanted to be able to call Jack, so I used that thought as an incentive. I used all the mental strength I had to convince my mind to eat. I lifted my fork and took my first bite. I realized that the mind was willing, but the rest of me had other problems.

With advanced anorexia, various organs frequently shut down. The digestive system slows down to a point where it's no longer just a psychological problem. That's what had happened to me. After a few bites, I felt so full. My mind was overwhelmed with fear. It was awful.

I managed to get the meal into me, but I was in incredible pain. When I left the dining room, I complained about the pain to one of the doctors, and

I was instructed to undergo tests to diagnose the cause. They found nothing wrong, but the pain and sick feeling I had were real. Over the next few days, I was constantly weak, dizzy, in pain, and nauseated. The one thing I didn't feel was hunger. My hunger mechanism was messed up and whacked out.

That night Kylie and I walked to dinner together. I was telling her about Jack when we passed Christy's room. I was curious about her condition and hoped she had made some progress. The door was open, but she and the tall metal intravenous stand were gone. "Kylie, where's Christy?"

Kylie put her hand on my shoulder, "You didn't hear?"

"Hear what?"

"She died this afternoon."

"From what?"

"Her eating disorder. Jess, sweetheart, wake up. The final blow could have been a heart attack, but it was surely caused by her ED, her eating disorder. Jess, the problem we all share is deadly."

When Kylie and I were served our meals I found it more difficult than usual to take my first bite. I felt sick to my stomach over Christy's death. An aide approached me, tapped my plate with her pencil, and said, "Better start and finish it all."

I had heard about it before, but I never really believed people actually died from an eating disorder. I took my first forkful of food reluctantly, looked around the room, and wondered if any of the other women in the room would share Christy's deadly fate.

* * *

By the seventh day, I was given my first privilege because I had been a good little girl. I ate my meals, and the staff felt I had reached a certain level of conduct. My privilege was the ability to see my husband. We met in the visiting room at the end of the corridor on the floor below. Civilians, non-eating-disorder people, were not allowed on our floor. We were under constant surveillance by the aides to prevent our visitors from smuggling contraband such as diet pills or laxatives to us. Before I entered the room where Jack was waiting for me, an aide threatened me, saying, "Make no physical contact whatsoever. Do so and this privilege is gone."

The first thing Jack wanted to do when I sat down was hug me. I lurched back. I knew I hurt Jack's feelings, so I was quick to explain. "If I touch you, they won't let me see you again."

"Sorry, Jess."

"No, I'm the one who should apologize. I'm the one who put myself into this position. You're just the one who suffers along with me."

After Jack left I took the elevator back up to my floor. When the elevator opened, an aide instructed me to hold my arms out so she could pat me down and search me. I wanted to scream, but didn't. I just returned to my bed and cried for hours until it was time for the evening meal.

* * *

Eight days and twenty-four meals were behind me. Kylie and I got to know each other and grew close. Kylie was more of a long-term eating-disorder person who actually wanted to recover and save herself. She was about my age, but she had been going through it since her teens. Compared to Kylie and the others I listened to in the therapy sessions, I started pretty late in life.

Two days after I saw Jack, a new woman entered the morning therapy group. Unlike me on my first day, she was willing to open up to the group.

"Well," she began, "my name is Stacey. This is my third time here. I'm twenty-three. I was just released from St. Luke's. I was treated there for a heart attack, which took me totally by surprise. I was transferred from there directly into this program. Why? I don't know. There is nothing wrong with me now. I feel great and don't belong here."

Kylie and I looked at each other. I leaned over and whispered, "She'll be back."

Kylie retorted, "Unless she dies first."

Dr. Winston asked Stacey, "Do you have a child?"

"Yes. A daughter. She's two."

"You're single now. Do you have any family close to you?"

"No."

Dr. Winston didn't come right out and say it, but he was thinking, "Do you want your daughter to be an orphan?"

Back in the room, I talked with Kylie about Stacey. Kylie said, "She's anorexic and bulimic."

"I've heard the word 'bulimic' several times. What does it mean?"

"It means they purge their meal."

"Purge?"

"Hey, Rookie, anorexia isn't the only way to starve yourself to death. Some women can't restrict, so they eat, run to the bathroom, and throw up."

"Do you think her heart attack was related to her eating stuff?"

"Without a doubt. Women don't have heart attacks when they're twenty-three. Her potassium must have gone below the safe zone. Whether it's anorexia or bulimia, they're both nothing more than suicidal lifestyles. You don't know when this eating stuff can turn against you. One minute, you look in the mirror and think you look fat. But you're probably emaciated and on your way to a heart attack, like Stacey. And if that isn't the problem, you're catatonic, your hair falls out, you get osteoporosis, your lungs fail, your liver gets messed up, or your teeth decay from that bulimia crap. This non-eating crap will do one of two things to you–make you look uglier than you are, or just plain kill you."

"You'd think a heart attack would motivate her into a recovery mode."

"Jess, don't you understand? The only thing Stacey says to herself is, 'That's not going to happen to me.' She'll say it until, like Christy, she drops dead from this stuff. She's in denial. She'll just go through the steps just to get out of here. Mark my words. It's like you said in therapy: 'She'll be back.' It's just a matter of time. Jess, how many times have you passed out from your eating disorder?"

"How'd you know?"

"Because it happened to me, dozens of times. We're both alive because it didn't happen when we were driving."

"But . . ."

"C'mon, Jess. A person with an eating disorder is like a heroin junkie. The junkie may wind up in an emergency room near death from an overdose, but the minute after that junkie gets out of the hospital, she'll be looking for a fix."

"On the outside, Stacey looks like she's OK."

"Wake up and smell the roses, Jess, or they'll be planting lilies six feet above your face. Don't be stupid like I was. Get out of here the first time, and stay the hell out of this miserable place."

An aide opened the door and walked into our room. "Jess, you have a call."

"Thanks. Tell Jack to hold on."

"I have a feeling your husband is a great guy," Kylie said with a big grin.

"Oh, yes," I said as I got my slippers on and ran out of the room. I got to the pay phone in the corridor and burst with happiness as I said, "Jack. Thanks so much for calling again."

"Hey, Roomie. What did you do to yourself?"

My happy feeling was instantly gone. "Lucy?"

"I was thinking about you lately so I tried to call your home. Your husband gave me this number."

"That was nice of him."

"Say, let's get together for a drink when you get out."

"Are you serious?"

"Sure. My treat. There's a great new place over on Sunrise Highway."

"Lucy, when we were together, didn't you see anything unhealthy about our relationship?"

"Unhealthy? You were my best buddy."

"I can't believe you're saying that."

"Why?"

"You saw nothing wrong in what we did?"

"No. Everything was fine."

"Lucy, everything was *not* fine."

"Well, if that's the way you feel . . ."

"That's *exactly* how I feel, and it's about time I said it."

"Take care of yourself, Jess."

"That's exactly what I'm doing," I said as I hung up the phone.

I couldn't believe the fury inside me. The unmitigated gall. The audacity. She got away with raping a minor and never faced a single repercussion.

My rage was evident on my face when I got back into the room.

"Have a fight with Jack?" Kylie asked.

"No. That was an old acquaintance. With luck, that was our last conversation."

"Get dressed for the outside."

"What's up, Kylie?"

"It's time to exercise the inmates."

"What?"

Within minutes all of the women were huddled up in the corridor. Aides surrounded us, and at least one rode down in each elevator to where we gathered again in the lobby. As I learned, they wanted us to get outside for fresh air and exercise. I noticed that each patient was dressed in long sleeves and long pants, although the temperature was close to ninety degrees that day. None of us wanted the outside world to see our "fat" bodies. This was my first of many walks to follow. I clearly remember thinking about how I could easily have veered off, gotten lost from the group, gotten onto a train, and gone home. I thought about it, but that's as far as it went.

Seeing so many skinny women walking together must have looked like a freak show to passersby. I was glad no one said anything to us, but we did get strange looks from some of the "normal"-looking pedestrians. Their eyes said, "What is this group?" I definitely felt like a freak. Fortunately, however, in Manhattan, many odd things happen, so we probably didn't stick out as much as my mind imagined we did.

* * *

It bothered me when Kylie reached her sixtieth day and finished meal 180. I was glad for her, but I didn't want to see her go. She had become a friend and confidante. She was someone who I could relate to because we shared the same disorder, and the same recovery goal. We hugged for several minutes before she picked up her suitcase to leave. I walked with her to the elevator. Although I'm not religious, I said a prayer that she would remain in recovery. When she was gone, I sat in my chair, stared at her empty bed and dresser, and wondered who would take her place, and when.

My second roommate, Emma, took over Kylie's place the day after Kylie was paroled. Emma was a sweet, twenty-two-year-old girl with red hair and normal facial features planted on an extremely narrow face. Of course, she too was extremely thin. She suffered from anorexia and bulimia, and this inpatient stay was her third time around. She, like so many others I met, started her problem as a young teenager. The two of us were friendly, but it wasn't the same as with Kylie and me.

By the fifth week and meal 105, I actually felt like I had started to get my appetite back. I hadn't felt that sensation for a long time. I also opened up more during the therapy sessions. I realized that if I spoke about the problems and feelings I had, I could help myself to better understand a way to find recovery.

The sessions were fascinating, and I learned how pervasive and epidemic the disorder was. The more I accepted and embraced the program, the faster the time went by. When Dr. Winston invited me to speak, I talked about Mitch and the anxiety and depression he caused me. I was asked about "the good little girl" syndrome, and I related my stories about my mother and father, my teachers and friends, and anyone else around me, including the staff at the hospital. That part got a laugh from the other women. The aides didn't think it was funny. It didn't matter. I just continued talking.

"Before I entered the hospital, I was taking sixty laxatives."

Dr. Winston asked, "In what period of time?"

"In one shot," I replied. "Yeah. I was crazed."

Dr. Winston asked, "How did you get them down?"

"Very slowly."

"Pills? Chocolates?

"Pills. The little ones. I usually took ten at a time."

Emma patted me on the back and said, "You were a champ, huh?"

"Yeah. I was."

Dr. Winston asked, "How long before those sixty kicked in?"

"I would take them after eating supper. My little supper. The next day they kicked in. The cramps were incredible."

"Did you have any other physical effects?"

"Absolutely. I would get incredibly dehydrated. I passed out in the bathroom a couple of times. I knew something was wrong when I woke up with little square marks on my face from the bathroom floor tiles. But, being in total denial, I thought there was nothing wrong or unusual with this." That got a little chuckle from the crowd. I had a feeling one or two other women passed out and woke up with the same design on their face. Like the old cliché goes, "No truer words are said than those spoken in jest."

The woman who spoke after me shared similar personality and family characteristics with the rest of us in that room. She was twenty-eight, about my height, but much thinner than me. Her arm was in a cast. "My name is Camellia," she said. "My life's been messed up since I was eleven and I heard an explosion come from my twelve-year-old brother's room. I opened the door to see blood splattered on the walls because he blew his brains out with my father's gun. My about-to-be-ex-husband is a charmer. He got his rocks off by insulting everything I did and mentally abusing me. I come from a fairly wealthy family, and my parents put that putz into business. Then that bastard would curse my parents out and demean them behind their backs." Camellia laughed a second. "I'm glad my parents were smart enough to keep the business in their names. It's with great pleasure that I can now report that the putz is out of a job." There was a small round of applause from the rest of us.

Camellia continued, "I had my first heart attack last year. I'm on medication to stay alive. I suffer from osteoporosis. I wish that schmuck of a future ex-husband broke this," she held up her cast, "so I could put him in jail, but he didn't do this. I bumped into a wall. My bones are so weak from my eating disorder that I fractured my arm in two places. This is my third time here. I wish to God I could figure out what's wrong with me so it would be my last time in this godforsaken place. Ah . . . no offense, Dr. Winston."

"No offense taken, Camellia."

One horror story followed another in those sessions. Most husbands or boyfriends were like Camellia's "future ex-husband." That's where I differed. Jack phoned me regularly and visited with me every weekend. That made it easier for me to deal with the pain and misery of missing him.

Acknowledging my problem and accepting the fact that I needed help started to turn me around. It reminds me of the Alcoholics Anonymous program, where people stand, say their name, and say, "I'm an alcoholic."

Standing at one of those sessions and saying, "My name is Jessica and I'm an anorexic," did the same for me. From that point on, I looked forward to the meals and ate every morsel on my plate. Why? Because the food was the medicine that put me on the road to recovery and the possibility of a normal life. I prayed that one day I would look at food again without caring what it was and just eat it because it tasted good and I was hungry. I wanted to eat without thinking about it. I just wanted to be like a normal person again–if that was possible.

It took me time to accept being heavier. I didn't like it. I kept repeating, "I'd rather be alive and fat than dead and thin." Once I reached the point of acknowledging I was sick, the time started going fast, and the scale kept inching to a higher and healthier weight. Before I knew it, it was the end of my sixtieth day and I had finished meal 180. My weight, which started at 95 pounds, was back up to my safe zone with a small cushion.

I had a new outlook on life as Emma escorted me to the elevator. She didn't say so, but she probably said a little prayer for me to continue my recovery. I know I said one for her. I hoped she would never have to endure a fourth stay.

Jack was downstairs to meet me in the lobby. He took my bag and we headed for the car. Being outside, without any hospital personnel escorting us, made me feel like I had a newfound freedom. I relished every second and swore to myself that I would never return. The best armament I had to keep that promise to myself was the belief that Jack would be there to support me, along with my new outpatient program, which meant regular appointments with a therapist. The hospital and I were well aware that a battle against eating disorders could never be won alone. Only with a team of specialists could anyone have a chance of getting through the first critical days, weeks, and months into recovery.

A few things, besides my weight, had changed since I first entered the hospital. My depression was under control because of the medication I took. My first appointments with my new psychiatrist, Dr. Roger Becker, and my therapist, Stephen Richards, Ph.D., were already set up, and I intended to get to every appointment. I never wanted to see that place, or any other hospital, again. I was determined to stay in recovery and not fall off the wagon. I was happy, and yet I was scared. I kept asking myself, "What's going to stop me from going back to abusing laxatives and not eating what I don't want to eat and controlling my diet as much as I did before?" I had no answers, only questions.

Weight wasn't the only thing I thought about. Another major issue caused me to have mixed feelings. On the way home, Jack looked longingly at me. I knew that look in his eyes, and it concerned me. The look meant he wanted to make love with me. We hadn't been together for eight weeks, and it was quite a natural desire on his part, but things were different for me. I felt uncomfortable about letting him see my body because I had put on so much weight and thought I looked like an enormous cow. I was afraid he would be disgusted when he saw me.

The first night he didn't say anything. We just snuggled together as we fell asleep. The second night I got my courage up to tell Jack I wanted to be with him. I set the mood with candles and soft music in the bedroom, then he showed me again why I loved him so much. As soon as he saw my body he said, "You look beautiful. I like you better this way than the way you were before the hospital. You're gorgeous. I love you more now than I've ever loved you before in my life." I felt comfortable. I felt like I had passed through another level of my healing process. The only emotions I felt were how much I missed him and wanted to be with him. On that level, we never, no, I never had that problem again.

After the hospital, I continued eating correctly and gaining weight. My sessions with my psychiatrist and therapist were helpful. If there was something negative inside me, they helped me understand it, cope with it, and relieve whatever stress I felt about it. Things went on that way for at least a year. I was back at work and remained on my antidepressant, which helped tremendously. Finally, I felt comfortable enough to tell my therapist that I no longer needed the sessions. He agreed. The same held true for my doctor. Except for appointments to renew my medication, my visits with him were over.

About the same time I stopped seeing my therapists, I called my "unofficial therapist," Kylie, who turned out to be a great friend and unexpected benefit of my inpatient stay. Ever since we were both paroled from the hospital, we remained in touch and frequently called each other to share whatever feelings we had about our problems and to support each other's continuing recovery. I could discuss things with Kylie about my eating disorder because, unlike Jack, she shared my disorder. She knew exactly what I meant when we talked about what we had been through. I remember one night when we got together for dinner in Manhattan. One particular sentence we said to each other summed up how close we had become. At the end of that dinner, we noticed that we hadn't finished everything on our plates. Both of us grinned as we looked around the room expecting to find the food police. Then we both laughed as we simultaneously said, "Looks like we'll lose our privileges."

* * *

Chapter Five

"I'm Not Going Back!"

Jack and I finally reached that point in a loving marriage where we decided we wanted to try to have a child. I put away my sponge and we started having sex without protection with the hopes that I would get pregnant. I was glad that I had never taken birth control pills because I didn't have to be concerned with any hormonal imbalance the birth control pills might have caused.

After the ordeal I had put my body through, there was only question that scared me: Could I still get pregnant? I had always been "Miss Regular Period" throughout my eating disorder problem, but I never went to a doctor to completely remove my female medical trepidation. I didn't think anything bad medically had happened to me in that way. I just wasn't positive.

Some women go overboard to get pregnant and treat it like a science with thermometers and charts. I didn't. Jack and I weren't in a rush, and we didn't want to push it or put any pressure on that situation. We just figured that it would happen when it happened. Jack was always a great lover and, I have to admit, I cherished making love with Jack more often.

Eleven months after we started having unprotected sex, I missed my first period. That day at the lab, I did my own pregnancy test. Sure enough, the rabbit died, but I felt like I was reborn. That night over dinner, I gave Jack the news. He was ecstatic. So was I. Jack hugged and kissed me a hundred times, ran out of the house, and came back in twenty minutes with roses, pickles, and ice cream. I told him he was crazy. I told him I loved him. I told him our child couldn't ask for a better father.

That night we also decided we wanted to raise our child in a house, instead of the apartment we lived in. Four months later we moved into a great colonial house in Lynbrook, Long Island, not far from our apartment, and not far from Jefferson General Hospital in Valley Stream, where Jack worked. The house had four bedrooms, a large, modern kitchen, two-and-a-half baths, living room, dining room, den, and two-car garage. The cost of the house, plus the cost of the additional furniture and decorating, was expensive, so I decided to keep working as long as it didn't interfere with my health. I was actually glad that I kept working because it kept me busy, it brought in the extra money we needed, and it gave me a sense of satisfaction that our child would grow up in a beautiful home and neighborhood.

My first trimester went smoothly, except for the usual morning sickness, a few headaches, and an occasional mood swing. I religiously took my prenatal vitamins, plus the folic acid and calcium my obstetrician prescribed. My eating habits were strong and normal. I remember saying to myself, "This little kid is not going to go hungry."

My second trimester began uneventfully, which is a good thing. I started having cravings for sweet, starchy foods, and I started putting on weight, which was a perfectly normal thing, according to my doctor. We also moved into the house at that time. Jack and I did all the work to get the house fixed up and decorated. He's great with things like that, and he got phenomenal satisfaction from the happiness I constantly exuded. One of my fondest memories happened when I was painting the living room. I was about eighteen weeks pregnant. I thought I had felt that feeling before, but excused it as nothing special. I was wrong. It was one of the most wonderful feelings a woman can experience. It felt like a fluttering. It was my child alive inside me. I sat down and cried. Jack immediately came to hug and comfort me and to find out what was wrong.

"There's nothing wrong, my love. Just the opposite. Everything is right in this world. I can feel the baby. Our little boy or girl is alive and well." Later that day Jack went out and surprised me with two dozen pink roses.

"Jess, my precious, I love you," he told me with tears welled up in his eyes. "I hope you don't mind, but I hope the baby is a girl."

"Why?"

"Because then I'll have two gorgeous women in my life."

"Well, as long as you're picking the sex, did you also choose a name?"

"Actually . . ."

"You didn't . . ."

"What about Megan? I looked it up. It means 'child of light, strong and capable.'"

"Strong and capable. I like it."

"Jess, my precious, I'm crazy in love with you. You're the best thing that's ever happened to me. You still light up my life."

Again, I started crying.

"Jess, what's wrong?"

"Nothing. Absolutely nothing. Put your arms around me and hug me, you big lug."

"My pleasure."

From that day on, I was a different and better person. I no longer lived for my husband or myself. I lived to protect, nurture, and love the helpless little being within me–my child–the blood of my blood, and the product of the love I shared with my husband. For the first time, I was ready to sacrifice all within me for the benefit of another. Never again would I risk my health, because it meant I would hurt my child.

* * *

The house was ready by the time I entered my final trimester. The fatigue I felt before was diminishing along with my morning sickness. I felt cramps in my legs. I also felt heartburn and had some indigestion. When I went to my obstetrician for a checkup, he said everything was fine and the feelings I had were normal. He also gave me another ultrasound that day. It was amazing to see the baby moving around inside me. I drove home that day with a renewed sense of determination to do everything possible for that little kid squirming around inside me. Well, perhaps squirming isn't the right word. You see, the fluttering I felt earlier was replaced by vigorous kicking. That night at about 3:00 a.m., I woke to a strong kick in my rib cage. I was sleeping on my right side, as usual, because it meant I faced Jack. One kick was so strong that I called out, "Jack!"

"What? What's the problem?"

"This kicking is becoming unbearable."

Jack put his hand on me. "Wow, I can feel it. Jess, try turning over."

"What?"

"Just try it."

I did. The kicking stopped immediately. "OK, wise guy. How did you know that?"

"One of the guys at the hospital told me about that happening to his wife."

"Well, I like to sleep facing you."

I turned back over. The kicking started again. "Amazing! It looks like *Megan* is telling me which side to sleep on."

"Megan?"

"Yeah. I found out today with the ultrasound. For the past few months, the doctor has been asking me if I wanted to know the baby's sex. I finally gave in today."

"Oh, Jess . . ."

"There goes another one to the rib cage!"

Jack turned me back around again. The kicking stopped. Jack snuggled up behind me, kissed me on the back of my neck, and said, "Let's you, me, and Megan get some sleep."

"Strong and capable. The name fits," were the last words I said as I finally fell asleep again.

My weight was never an issue throughout my pregnancy. All I cared about was Megan. All I kept saying to myself was, "I'm going to protect this baby no matter what. I'm going to do whatever is necessary." I ended up gaining 40 pounds and loved every ounce of it until the last few days. Like every other woman, I couldn't wait for Megan to come out. The weight had started to become uncomfortable, but I didn't feel any more uncomfortable than any other pregnant woman.

I went the full term. In fact, I continued working until two weeks before I gave birth. The joke in the hospital was that I would go from my desk into the delivery room during a coffee break. Everything went fine until the last few moments. Megan went into distress because I had a premature separation of the placenta. They thought about giving me a cesarean. It scared me. At first, I thought it might have had something to do with the eating disorder, but my doctor ruled it out. He saw me constantly during the pregnancy, told me I did everything right, and he was emphatic that I never denied the baby, nor myself, anything. He said I had gained an appropriate amount of weight, if not more. It wound up that I delivered Megan the normal way at 7:12 a.m. on June 2,1989, after twelve hours of labor. When she came out, she was a little blue, but then she recovered very nicely, and everything was fine after that.

* * *

Megan was four months old when I went back to work on a part-time schedule. Jack was always so amazed at how patient I was with her. Shortly after she was born, she got into a habit of waking up at night and crying, although she wasn't hungry and she hadn't dirtied her diaper. It seemed like Megan just wanted to be held. I went to her room, held her until she fell back to sleep, and then I went back to bed for the few remaining minutes I had before the alarm went off for me to get up and get to work. I had always blamed my parents for not being nurturing. I was determined not to repeat their error.

When Megan was two, she became a real handful. At mealtime, she would suddenly start to scream and cry for no apparent reason. Instead of losing my cool and getting frustrated, I found that kissing her face and holding her calmed her down. It made her feel better, and it made me feel great. Megan made me feel needed. Megan made me feel I had a purpose in life beyond just going to work for a paycheck to pay the bills.

I remember one time when Megan was four and she was playing on the floor with her dolls in the den. Kylie had come over to visit with us that day. It was great to see her, and it was great that she was still in recovery, newly married, and happy with her life. Suddenly, Megan started to scream. Kylie had a look on her face that said, "Jesus, I'm never having kids." Again, I maintained my cool and went to hug Megan and to use my magic touch. There was a certain spot on her rib cage that never failed me. This time was no exception. As soon as I touched it, Megan started to laugh. "Who's my little tickle giggle puss?"

"Me, Mommy."

"And who do I love?"

"Me, Mommy."

"And who loves me?"

"Me, Mommy."

I stood and continued to hug Megan. That "never having kids look" disappeared from Kylie's face.

"Jess, you're incredible."

"Kylie, you're 100 percent correct," Jack said as he came home from work and joined us in the den. "How are my two favorite girls?" Jack said as he kissed and hugged us both.

"Who is your favorite girl, Daddy?"

"Both of you. How are you, Kylie? It's great to see you again," Jack said as he kissed her cheek. "Staying for dinner?"

"Not tonight. Dave is taking me out to eat."

"Let's the four of us get together soon. OK?"

"Good idea. I better get going, Jess." Kylie kissed Megan. "See you again soon, giggle puss."

"Bye, Aunt Kylie."

I handed Megan over to Jack and walked Kylie to the door. When we got outside, Kylie hugged me. "Jess, we've come a long way."

"And we're going to stay there."

"Jess, I love you."

"I love you, too. Make sure you finish everything on your plate in the restaurant tonight or I'll get the food police to take away your conjugal privileges."

"We'll talk soon."

Kylie was right. The two of us had returned from the brink of death and put our lives back together. I don't think either of us could have imagined we would be at this point when we first spoke in the hospital.

* * *

In 1992 Jack and I tried for our second child. I got pregnant, but I lost the baby. My doctor reassured me that it had nothing to do with my anorexia. A little over two years later, I was pregnant again. Some people think that if you're pregnant once, you know all you need to know about your second pregnancy. I don't think so. New questions and issues came up. Should we tell Megan? When and how do we tell Megan? Should Megan join us in the delivery room? Why wasn't I experiencing morning sickness the same way as with Megan's pregnancy? Did it mean something was wrong?

Well, all of the questions seemed to work themselves out. We told Megan when she noticed my stomach was getting much bigger. She was thrilled. She kept insisting she wanted to be "Mommy's helper," and I kept promising that she would always be my precious little helper. As for the medical questions, they were all resolved in my frequent visits to my obstetrician. There was always a little nervousness tucked deep in the back of my head because I had lost the second baby. Thank goodness, nothing went wrong. On August 3, 1995, at 6:19 a.m., after seven hours of labor, Jason was born without any complications whatsoever. He was healthy and gorgeous, just like his father. As for his name, this time the name was my idea. I wanted to name our son after his wonderful father. I chose Jason because the name meant "healer," which is what Jack was for me.

By 1995 our family was complete.

Four months after Jason was born, I was back at work on a part-time basis. I was the only part-time manager in the hospital, which was a unique experience. Unfortunately, I was doing a full-time job on a part-time schedule. Once I got home in the afternoon, I took care of the usual cooking and cleaning, plus I took care of the kids. Megan had to be picked up from kindergarten, and I always wanted to spend time playing with her in the afternoon. I didn't want her to feel that just because Jason came I would neglect our wonderful relationship. As an infant, Jason needed a great deal of care and attention. I was always cognizant of the fact that I wanted to nurture him and love him from the moment I first held him in my arms at the hospital. My kids were precious to me, and I wanted to do everything possible to be a great mother. What little time I had left after that, I gave to Jack. What I didn't have was time for myself. I was, in essence, the supermom at home and the superwoman at work.

The one good thought I held dear was that I was still in recovery. During extremely stressful times, I always thought about skipping a meal because I wasn't hungry. Oftentimes, I consciously had to fight the urge to relapse, especially when I learned about one medical problem that was a result of my anorexic condition–constipation. I took laxatives and always remembered how I used to pop sixty at a time. Once or twice I found myself dumping the entire container in my hand, but then I put them back and took only took the manufacturer's recommended dosage. I did not revert. I did not go back to my old ways. Those days were gone. That old me was gone. I was the "new" Jessica, with a loving husband and two incredibly beautiful children. I never thought life could be so wonderful. I truly believed that all my past troubles were gone–forever.

* * *

The year 2000 marked the change of the millennium. More importantly, it marked a significant change in my life–I turned the "Big 4-0." Sophie Tucker's old song "Life Begins at 40" rang through my thoughts, but I disagreed with her. My life wasn't at the beginning. According to various statistics, my tenure in this world was exactly halfway between my birth and death. My mortality loomed through my thoughts, and I despised the fact that death was nearer than farther each new day I awoke. Turning forty also meant the "Big M," menopause, lurked just around the corner, ready to throw me into a world of hot flashes, night sweats and uncontrollable mood swings. Turning forty meant checking my blood pressure and my cholesterol, and the ever-growing closeness of a heart attack. Turning forty meant starting mammograms. I did not relish the idea of putting my little boobs on a cold plate and having them squashed by another cold plate.

No longer did I have an unlimited horizon or future. My days were numbered. All I had to look forward to was unwanted wrinkles, gray hair, and breasts that would sag to my knees. Actually, my breasts were very small, so they wouldn't sag that much. No more bobby socks. It was time for support hose and a cane. Gone were my bikini days. Next summer I'd be wearing some sort of matronly swimsuit to the beach.

I knew that nothing could stop the inevitable. I wish I could have accepted aging calmly and graciously, but I couldn't.

Things were even less enjoyable at work because I was taken out of my usual environment of the lab or my office and, as manager, placed in charge of a new computer system installation. I hated computers. I used them only reluctantly at work. I didn't know anything about them except that they're cold. They're stupid machines that manage to crash and drop dead at the most critical times. When the hospital put me in charge of the upgrade to its complete system and the installation of a new patient database, it got me scared. No. It made me feel terrified. The hospital's computer system contained the health records of thousands of patients. Those patients' lives and safety suddenly became my responsibility. Failing meant they would be in jeopardy. The pressure became instantly enormous. I wanted out. I asked to be relieved of the assignment. They told me that, although I was the part-time manager, it was my duty to see this long-term project through to its conclusion. There was no escape from the 24/7, tension-filled pressure. Like it or not, I had to live with it, deal with it, and cope with it. Little did I realize that these were actually the good times compared to what I was about to face.

* * *

Except for the pressure of the computer assignment at work and the fact that I hated my age, I started the new millennium feeling great and enjoying my kids more than I ever could have imagined.

Jason, now age five, was the most precious, cutest, and brightest young man. He loved his big sister, and she loved him. I was lucky that way. Every time I looked at my two kids, I wished I could have grown up with such a loving feeling for my big brother, instead of the constant anxiety I felt whenever I was near him. I often found it most relaxing just to watch them play in the backyard. It's not as though things were perfect. Occasionally, Megan would flare up at Jason, but it was no where near how Mitch flared up with my folks or me. Jason was great. He always took it in stride. He just looked at his sister with his beautiful big brown eyes, hugged her, kissed her cheek, and always said he was sorry, even though he almost never did anything wrong to cause her behavior. I often thought I was the luckiest mom in the world to have two such wonderful kids. Besides my magnificent husband, they were the greatest treasures in my life. I never took them for granted. I always loved every moment I was near them, and I relentlessly kissed and hugged them.

In June of 2000, when Megan was eleven, Jack, Jason, and I attended her elementary school graduation. It was difficult to believe the years had gone by so quickly. Everything was perfect that day. Well, almost everything was perfect. I noticed the skirt I was wearing felt a little loose around the waist. For the rest of the day I didn't give it a second thought or attach any negative connotation to it.

That night I weighed myself. The scale read 132 pounds. I excused my 3 pound weight loss as a result of the stress I had at work and stopped thinking about it because my eating patterns were normal and healthy.

By the middle of the summer, I was still living with the stress of the computer system installation, but something else started to give me concern—Megan. She wasn't the happy little girl she had always been. She wasn't playing with Jason the way she used to; neither was she playing with her friends as often. A few times I found her just laying on her bed and staring at the ceiling. The change disturbed me, and I spoke with her about it. At first, Megan kept insisting that nothing was wrong. I knew she wasn't telling me what was on her mind, but I gave her time to tell me her feelings when she was ready.

Three weeks before Megan was scheduled to start junior high school, I found her laying face down on her bed and crying. In my mind, there was no more time to wait for her to open up to me on her own. I had to know what was bothering her.

"Megan, honey, Mommy's feeling sad. Mommy needs a hug. Can you help me?"

"Mommies don't get sad or afraid. Just kids do."

"Oh, no, sweetheart. There's always a little kid inside of us no matter how old we get. Mommies get sad too."

"What are you sad about, Mommy?"

"I'm sad because my special little girl is sad. It makes me want to cry."

"Mommy, I'm afraid of . . ."

I kissed Megan's cheek and hugged her with all the passion I had in my heart. I didn't want to press her with questions. She seemed like she would open up on her own, and I felt any questions might close the opportunity for her to express herself.

"Mommy . . . Mommy, I'm afraid of junior high school."

"Thank you for sharing that with me."

"There'll be so many new kids. I hear the work is so hard. I'll have so many new subjects to learn. I'll have so much homework. I won't be able to do it. They tell me so many of the teachers are mean and yell."

"Megan, I love you. You're a smart girl. Everything will be OK."

"No, it won't!" Megan screamed as she broke away from my arms. "No, it won't!"

"Sweetheart . . ."

"Mom, you're smart. I'm not. You do everything perfectly. You never do anything wrong. I'm different."

"Megan, do you trust me?"

"Yes, Mom."

"You'll be OK."

"How do you know? Do you have some magic wand to make everything OK? No! Am I smart enough to do what they'll want me to do? No. I'm stupid! I'm worthless!"

"No, you're not! Don't say that! You're . . ."

"I'm an idiot!"

"Don't say that! Don't think that!" I shouted.

That was the first time I ever lost my cool with Megan. I felt terrible. I felt like I let her down when she needed me the most. "Megan, I'm sorry I shouted at you," I said as I stood up. I realized she needed distance from me, so I headed toward the door. "I have to start dinner. I'll be here to listen when you're ready to talk. Megan . . . Megan . . . I do love you."

Megan shoved her face into her pillow and started crying. I felt helpless. My little girl was in pain, and there was nothing I could think of to help her.

Megan never came to dinner that night, and I didn't force the issue. Jason, Jack, and I didn't talk much. Jason told us about the games he played with his friends that afternoon, but my mind was elsewhere. My thoughts focused on Megan's horror and my helplessness.

After Jack and Jason finished eating, they spent time playing catch in the backyard. I loved when they did that. It was something my father never did with Mitch.

I left the dishes in the sink and started calling the mothers of Megan's friends. Each of the seven or eight women I spoke with told me the same thing. "It's normal. Don't worry about it. There's a big adjustment for some kids between elementary school and junior high school, and Megan will get over it. Just give it time. Everything will turn out fine."

That night I had difficulty falling asleep. That was unusual for me. I usually fell asleep seconds after my head hit the pillow. But that night, Megan's words echoed in my mind: "I'm stupid. I'm worthless. Do you have some magic wand to make everything OK? No!"

Something else scared me. I thought of Mitch at Megan's age. He often acted the same way. Only now, at forty-four, he had finally been diagnosed as being bipolar. I must have asked myself a thousand times, "Is Megan bipolar? Is it a genetic defect that has passed from my family, through me, to my daughter?" I began to shake uncontrollably. I could feel the sweat on my forehead although I knew the room was cool from the air conditioner. It must have been close to 5:00 when I finally fell asleep. When the alarm sounded, I got up without any hesitation, looked into Megan's room, saw her sleeping, and started crying. She looked peaceful for the moment, but I knew all the fear and anxiety would return the moment her eyes opened. I wanted to call in sick that morning, but my professionalism forced me into work because I knew we were testing an important phase of the hospital's computer system and I had to be there. I felt guilty that I put that damn computer system, and the safety of those thousands of patients, before my daughter.

Before I knew it, Labor Day arrived, which meant Megan had to start school. She had shown no signs of improvement over the past few weeks. If anything, her stress level and feelings of depression were on the rise. On several occasions I tried to talk with her about it, but she clammed up or shut me out of her room completely. Jack and I talked about it, but we had no answers. Between the two of us, we just tried to excuse it as the "normal" feelings the other mothers had discussed with me. When I dropped Megan off at school on her first day, I drove away hoping that things would turn around after she met her new classmates and teachers. Unfortunately, when I got out of work and picked her up at school, she gave me an envelope from school. It was a referral note for me to call the school to discuss Megan's behavioral problems.

After the first school day, it seemed like each time I picked Megan up from school, she handed me another one of those envelopes. The school constantly notified me that Megan was disrupting one of her classes, skipping classes entirely, or talking abusively with her teachers or classmates. I couldn't understand it. Megan was not the same lovable little girl I had always known. Something was terribly wrong. Neither Jack nor I could get through to her. After endless hours of talking, Jack and I couldn't find a way to resolve the problem that was constantly getting worse on a daily basis.

We hoped the Christmas and New Year's vacation would give Megan a chance to step back from the problem. We gave Megan extravagant gifts with the hope that it would lift her spirits and give her strength to talk with us and help us find out what was wrong. But there was no improvement. Again, Megan just hid away in her room in a state of strong depression. By Valentine's Day in February, things deteriorated. I'll never forget that day. Megan came into the kitchen when I was preparing dinner.

"Hi, honey, can I get you something?"

"No, thanks."

Megan was wearing a T-shirt. I noticed two parallel scratches on her forearm. "Sweetheart, what are those scratches?"

"I cut myself."

"Did you wash it good?"

"No, Mom. I don't care."

"How did it happen?"

"I cut myself."

"What do you mean?"

"I cut myself. Don't you understand what I'm talking about?"

"No. Please help me."

"It's simple. I took a razor and cut myself."

"Was it an accident?"

"Mom, wake up! I took a razor and cut myself."

I looked at Megan's arm, then looked into her eyes. After a few seconds the gravity of her simple statement of admission finally got through. I was devastated beyond belief. All I could do was ask a stupid question, "Why?"

"Because I'm no good," Megan shouted. "I'm no good. I don't care if I don't wake up tomorrow. I'd rather die than face that school," Megan shouted into my face before walking out of the kitchen.

I was in shock. Suddenly I just dropped to the ground as the realization of my daughter's actions penetrated into my consciousness. For the next twenty minutes, I couldn't find the strength to get up. Then Jason came into the kitchen.

"Mommy, are you OK?"

"Sweetheart, Mommy can use some help to stand."

"Sure, Mommy."

My little five-year-old helped me to get back on my feet. "Good boy, Jason. Mommy's better now."

Jason didn't understand that I was hugging him to prevent myself from falling again. I think a minute or two must have passed before I said, "Go wash up, precious."

"Sure, Mommy. Are you OK now?"

"You're the best little boy in the world. You're always Mommy's little helper," I said as I kissed his head.

That night I didn't know how to break the news to Jack, but I understood he had to know what had happened. It was one of the few times I ever saw Jack cry. We held each other and cried together. The gravity of the situation had gotten to both of us. No parent should ever have to live through that kind of pain.

I never slept that night. At 4:30 a.m. I called Megan's pediatrician, Dr. Ethan Bruno, and left a message to call me at the office or home and said it was urgent. Dr. Bruno was a tall, thin, extremely good-looking man with blond hair. He had that Dr. Kildare look about him, which is probably why I always trusted him with my kids. He had been Megan's doctor since she was born. He knew her, and I hoped he had a miracle cure for our daughter's depression and self-mutilation. It didn't take a genius to understand that this situation was far beyond what Jack and I could handle. Our daughter's life was at stake and, without professional help, we could lose her forever.

* * *

Dr. Bruno called me later that morning. I explained that I was in shock that Megan could have so many problems and be hurting herself. I was blown away by what I had to explain about her behavior over the last several months. No mother will ever find it easy to come to the realization that her child is in such emotional pain. By the end of the phone call, he had set up an emergency appointment for us to see him that afternoon. I was so grateful.

I left Jason with one of his friends so he wouldn't be a part of the doctor's visit, then I picked up Megan from school. Once again, Megan handed me a referral note from one of her teachers. I just put it in my purse without reading it. I had matters a great deal more urgent to deal with.

Dr. Bruno started by examining Megan. He paid particular attention to the cuts. I was pleased that he was extremely calm, patient, and understanding when he spoke to Megan after the examination. Megan explained her feelings toward school. She wasn't the least bit hesitant to tell him about the cutting. He wasn't shocked by what she said, although just hearing Megan talk about it made me feel weak, helpless, and as frightened as I was when I first understood what was happening to her. I said nothing the whole time.

When Dr. Bruno finished talking with Megan, he asked her to sit in the waiting room. Megan agreed, which left the two of us alone to talk about what to do next.

"Jessica, unfortunately, Megan is not the first child to walk into this office with such a severe form of depression. I understand how you feel. All the other parents with children who display Megan's symptoms are incredulous, as you are now. Do not blame yourself. I have known you and Jack for all these years, and I know you're both wonderful, loving parents who would go to the ends of the earth to do anything to help your children."

I kept looking at Dr. Bruno and hearing his words. It was difficult for me to accept that he was talking about my sweet daughter. I kept listening for the part when he would suddenly tell me that all Megan had to do was take a pill or two and everything would be OK, but he never said those words.

"Jessica. Are you OK?"

"No. I mean, yes. I have to stay strong for her, but it's difficult."

"Indeed. We have a problem here, and it's not something I can fix."

I felt tears well up in my eyes when he said that. He must have understood my emotional state.

"Jess, don't misunderstand me. I can't fix this, but I know an excellent doctor who has years of experience with adolescent depression. He's a psychiatrist. His name is Dr. Stephen Willsen. I've known him for twenty years. His results are excellent. Are you willing to see him?"

"Doctor, just tell me what to do to help my daughter." I felt tears start to stream down my face.

Dr. Bruno picked up his phone and dialed a number. "This is Dr. Bruno calling for Dr. Willsen." He paused. "Yes, I'll hold."

There was a pause. I took tissues from my purse to wipe my eyes.

"Steve, it's Ethan. I need your help. I have a patient, twelve, who needs to see you immediately." There was a pause. "Yes, severe depression and cutting." There was another pause. "Good. Her mother is here now. Jess, can you see Dr. Willsen tomorrow afternoon?"

"Yes."

"OK, Steve." There was a pause. "Good. I'll let Mrs. Gordon know. Thanks for your help." There was another pause. "Yeah, the family is great. Take care. I'll see you Friday night."

"OK, Jess. You and Megan have an appointment to see Dr. Willsen at 4:15 tomorrow. Trust me. He is a specialist who knows what he's doing."

"Thank you so much."

"Jess, I'll speak plainly. The wounds are superficial. They were nowhere near life threatening. They were on the upper forearm. They were not near the wrist. That's a good sign."

I was amazed that he spoke so matter-of-factly.

"There are medications for Megan, but I won't prescribe any for her at this time. Dr. Willsen will probably do that tomorrow."

"I understand."

"However, perhaps you or Jack might need something."

"I'll be OK."

"Jess, this won't be a fast process. It will take time, antidepressant medication, and therapy to help Megan."

"I understand."

"I wish you and Jack the best. Please call me immediately if you or Jack have any questions. I promise I'll get back to you as quickly as possible."

"Dr. Bruno, thank you. We didn't know where else to turn."

Dr. Bruno gave me a piece of paper with Dr. Willsen's address and phone number. We shook hands goodbye, then I went to the bathroom to wash my face so Megan wouldn't notice that I was crying.

Neither of us had much to say on the way home.

Later that night, when Jack and I finally got a chance to be alone, I explained everything that had happened that afternoon.

"Jess, you did everything perfectly."

"Jack, what are we going to do?"

"Exactly what Dr. Bruno told us to do. Evidently he has experience in these matters. He highly recommends Dr. Willsen. Let's put our faith in those two and pray they can help Megan."

Jack hugged me and stroked my back. Alone with my husband, I started to cry uncontrollably. Countless times, Jack told me he loved me and wiped away my endless tears.

* * *

There were no miracle cures the first time we saw Dr. Willsen. When we first met, I kept looking at him and thinking he reminded me of someone I knew, or an actor on television. Several minutes into our conversation, it hit me. He looked like Dr. Ben Casey's older mentor, Dr. David Zorba, played by Sam Jaffe, with his receding and wild-looking hair. That appeased me. However, it bothered me that he wanted to see Megan alone. Intellectually, I understood that he wanted Megan to be able to talk without my interference, and without her being afraid to say something about Jack or me. The session lasted for a little over thirty minutes, then Megan and I exchanged places in the office and waiting room and it was my turn to talk in private with Dr. Willsen. He explained what I already knew–Megan was in a deep state of depression with thoughts of suicide. He also explained the cutting. He said that cutting becomes a release of tension. He compared it to the feeling of a drug addict after getting a fix. It gives the person a psychological high when they mutilate themselves and attempt suicide without dying in the process.

The whole time he spoke, I could hear and understand what he was saying. I just couldn't fathom that he was talking about my daughter.

Several minutes went by, and he still hadn't said what I needed to hear. All I wanted to hear was how he was going to fix the problem. Finally, he reached that subject, but it wasn't exactly what I wanted to hear. He told me that he was going to prescribe an antidepressant. He also said that people react differently to the drugs and that we were probably going to try a few antidepressants before we would learn which one was best for Megan. In addition to which drug worked best, we would also have to experiment with the dosage. He also told me that Megan required weekly therapy sessions so he could track her progress and modify the medication accordingly. I should have been satisfied with what he said. I wasn't. It was apparent that Megan was in a condition that was going to take months, if not years, to fix. Understanding the concept of that time frame made me start to shake. I don't know if it was evident to Dr. Willsen, but it was obvious to me, and that was enough. The stress I felt at that moment was like no feeling I had ever had before in my life. I felt like a failure as a mother. I believed, in my deepest feelings, that everything wrong with Megan was my fault. No mother should ever feel that way, but I did.

The next day at work, I had no patience for anything or anyone. Megan was the only thing I wanted to think about, and I was forced to think about my work. So, when Doug, my unkempt and nerdy-looking IT computer specialist, who was never without his pencil pouch in his shirt pocket, came into my office to tell me he had to use my computer for five minutes to fix a bug in the system, I was annoyed. Reluctantly, I let him do it. Fifteen minutes after he began working, I had to voice my frustration and annoyance, "Doug, your five minutes is long over, and you're destroying my schedule for the day. Can't this wait?"

"No, Jess. They said this detail had to be worked out today."

"OK. Get to it and wrap it up."

"Sure, Jess. Just five minutes. Five minutes."

An hour and fifteen minutes later, I asked Doug the same question and he gave me the same "five minute" response.

"Doug, I must be out of here by 2:30 to pick up my daughter. Understand?"

"Sure, Jess. Five more minutes. I just about have it."

At 2:27 I'd had it. "Doug, pack it up!" I said in an unusually authoritative and bossy voice.

"But, Jess, this has to be done today and your terminal is the only one that has access to the part of the system I need."

My voice and anger peaked. "Three hours ago you told me it would take five minutes!"

"But, Jess, our jobs are at stake over this."

"Doug, I don't care. In fact, I ought to fire you for being incompetent. You IT guys have no concept of time. Understand this, mister, three hours don't equal five minutes. Got it? Now, get out!" I screamed as I turned off the computer without shutting it down properly, grabbed my sweater and purse, and marched out of there not caring if I had a job tomorrow. I got into the car knowing I would be late picking up Megan for her weekly session with Dr. Willsen, which made me more annoyed.

Before I knew it, the sessions with Dr. Willsen started mounting up without favorable results. Soon, months had passed. Megan was tested with one medication after another at various dosages. Most of the time, it seemed like nothing helped. Megan's cutting continued. She went from once a week to several times a week. Each time I saw a new wound, it was like a new wound to my heart. They were all superficial and non-life-threatening, but that didn't matter to me. What would happen if her hand slipped and she accidentally cut too deep or hit a vein or artery? I could lose my daughter because she bled to death in her room while I was out shopping or downstairs doing the laundry.

Thoughts like those constantly preyed on my consciousness and horrified me beyond belief. Increasingly, I was becoming incapacitated at home and at work. In short, my psyche started to crumble. Her depression and self-mutilation gave rise to my own deepening depression. Between Megan's problems and the pressure from the computer system installation, I felt like I could crack at any moment. All I wanted was a hole to bury my head in to escape the psychological catastrophe I was living through.

The end of June rolled around with me not noticing that spring had come and gone. My only solace was that Megan was out of school. I hoped that would lessen her stress and help to relieve her depression. It didn't. We still hadn't found the proper medication and dosage.

It was around July Fourth that I looked at myself in the mirror. My face looked tired and drawn. There were dark circles and bags under my eyes. I was thoroughly dissatisfied with the look of my body. I looked disgustingly fat and decided to do something about it. That night I started serving myself smaller portions, and I decided to stay away from any foods with a particularly high calorie count. Furthermore, my constipation seemed to be getting worse so I began to up the laxative dosage to empty myself out to get rid of the bulge I had developed. At first, I only took twice the recommended dosage, but that didn't last long. I kept rationalizing my actions by saying to myself, "At least I'm not popping sixty pills at a time." It wasn't sixty, but I was slowing inching up the count. Before long, I was up to twenty or twenty-five at a time.

Jack was unaware of my dietary changes, and there was no need for him to know. The only thing he noticed and commented on was our sexual relationship. He would want to have sex, and I would be kind of withdrawn and thinking about how awful I looked or how awful I felt about Megan and myself. Sex was the last thing I wanted to be involved in. Infrequently, he commented that we weren't getting together as often as we should. Then Jack came up with the idea of the family visiting my folks in Florida. I had the vacation time coming to me but was at first reluctant to go. What eventually made me agree was Megan's next session with Dr. Willsen. He had good news. It seemed like he finally had found the proper medication and dosage for Megan, and she was feeling its positive effects.

I watched Megan over the next few days and saw that she seemed calmer. Suddenly I realized that getting away to spend time with Jack and the kids, getting away from work, and getting away from all of the pressures I felt in New York sounded like a good idea. I asked Jack to investigate the availability of airline reservations for the fourth or eleventh of August. We would leave on Sunday and get back on the following Sunday in time for me to get back to work. By the next night, Jack told me we had confirmed reservations for the eleventh.

Escaping everything I was living through at home seemed great. Then I started having mixed feelings about where we were going. As an adult, my relationship with my parents was vastly improved from what it was when I was a kid. I hadn't seen them for quite some time, and I missed them even though we frequently spoke on the telephone. What concerned me was the fact that Mitch lived with them. I loved my brother just because he was my brother, but I never forgot how he used to go nuts without warning.

* * *

The flight to Fort Lauderdale was smooth enough for me feel at peace and take a nap. The plan was for my folks to drive down from their community in Delray Beach to pick us up. Most retirees in Delray lived in condominiums, but my folks, since they had the money, decided to buy a three-bedroom house when they retired. They needed one bedroom for themselves, one for Mitch, and a guest room in case we came for a visit, or in case their friends came down for a visit.

We found my folks immediately at the gate, and they were fast to give Jack and me a hug. Interestingly, they didn't hug Megan and Jason. I wasn't surprised. I felt bad for the kids, but I understood that's just the way my parents are. They don't deal well with children, not even my children. They only seem to know how to deal with adults. What pleased me most was that Mitch wasn't with them.

During the drive to Delray, Jack did most of the talking. My mind slipped in and out of the conversation because I found myself thinking back to my relationship with my folks when I was a kid. However, when Mitch's name popped up, I gave the conversation my full attention. It seems that Mitch had gone in and out of different programs to get help. It was in one of those programs that a doctor finally diagnosed his condition. It all made such sense. I always thought, based on the way he acted, that he had typical manifestations of bipolar disorder. When we were growing up, he would have periods where he was manic and hyper. He could go on forever. Then he would plunge into his depressive mode. I think his drug habit also had some influence on those times when he would lose control and become incoherent. The doctor's diagnosis finally put a label on his problem, and the doctor prescribed medication to help him. Even with his medication, however, my parents said he was still verbally abusive with them. They told Jack that Mitch had been arrested for shoplifting, and that they got him out of it by slipping the store manager a few hundred dollars to drop the charges. They also told Jack that he still flared up insanely, but not as often. I didn't comment. I wondered what other disastrous trouble he would get himself into and hoped it wouldn't happen while we were there. Then I thought that one day I'd get a phone call from the Florida police telling me that Mitch finally went off the deep end and killed my folks in a fit of rage.

That evening Mitch showed up just before dinner was ready. He could always tell time by his stomach. Although I felt a little anxious, I went to him and hugged him. I was extremely glad he was calm and that he was friendly to the kids, who hardly knew him. The barbecue in the backyard was fun, and Jack never noticed how little I ate. He was too involved in the conversation and sharing jokes and stories with the kids, my folks, and Mitch. I felt comfortable as just an observer. I kept looking at Jack fitting right in with my family and felt a love for him that I hadn't felt in quite some time. Back in New York, I was so involved with feelings about myself, feelings about Megan's troubles, and the stress from work that I lost sight of just how great a guy I married.

That night we got the kids into bed on the convertible couch in the den. Mitch had his room, my folks had their room, and Jack and I had the guest bedroom. At first, we watched a little television. Then I turned off the television, got into bed, hugged and kissed Jack, and made love with him without any regard about how I felt about my body. I missed being with Jack, and it felt good to be in his arms again.

The vacation went by so quickly. Most of the time the kids, Jack, and I just stayed at the pool, taking in the sun and swimming. I didn't swim. In fact, I never got into a bathing suit because I didn't like how it fit me. Jack couldn't understand how I wore long pants and a loose top, but he was kind enough not to give me a hard time about it. On Saturday, just after I finished packing up to leave the next morning, my dad asked me to drive to town to pick up Mitch. The kids joined me. Jack stayed back to prepare dinner on the barbecue.

Mitch was outside the barber shop at the time we had agreed upon. The kids were in the back seat. He joined me in the front seat for the drive home. Everything was fine until I told Mitch his hair looked really nice. He blew up and went crazy without a moment's hesitation.

Mitch started yelling, "I hate the haircut! It's up to me if it's a good haircut! How the hell do you know if it's a good haircut or not?"

All of my old fears and anxieties were back, only now I was driving and my kids were witnessing Mitch banging the car windows and dashboard. The kids looked terrified because of their crazed uncle. When I was a kid, I had the same look on my face when Mitch pulled one of these incidents. The only thing I could do was to hit the brakes and pull the car over to the curb.

"Mitch, get out of the car!"

"Drive the car, bitch!"

"Mitch, get out of the damn car." He didn't move. For the first time I stared into his glazed eyes instead of looking for a way to escape. "Mitch, I took this from you as a kid. No more. No one in this world will ever terrify my kids. Take your damn medication."

That's when Mitch grabbed my shirt.

"Go ahead, Mitch, hit me. Hit me!" I thought he would. "Touch me and I'll put you in jail for the rest of your life. That's not a threat. That's a promise. Do you understand me?"

My heart pounded as I looked into his eyes and waited for him to throw the first blow. Thank God he didn't. Instead, he actually got out of the car.

"You can tell Mom and Dad I'll stay at my friend's for the next few days," Mitch said before he slammed the door and walked away.

I turned to the kids in the back seat. I could see the fear in their faces. "Kids, everything's OK. Uncle Mitch has a sickness. He can't help acting that way when he doesn't take his medication. I'm sorry you had to see this. I swear, this will never happen to you again."

"Mom," Jason said, "are you OK?"

"I'm fine, sweetheart."

I could see the tears well up in Megan's eyes. "Mom, I never want to see him again."

"I understand, sweetheart. Believe me. I understand."

Until that point, the vacation seemed more like a second honeymoon for Jack and me. But after seeing that violent look in Mitch's eyes, and the terrified look in my kids' eyes, the vacation turned out to be a nightmare I'll never forget or want to relive.

* * *

September came and Megan went back to school with a different attitude. She did better in class, and there were much fewer referrals sent home. However, each day I still had that feeling of "What's it going to be today?" The truth is, her medication was working. We continued the weekly sessions with Dr. Willsen, and he continued to monitor her progress.

By the middle of September, I noticed I had dropped 15 pounds from where I was a year ago. I wasn't satisfied and continued with the same weight-reduction plan. Portions became even smaller and more foods were put on my "unsafe" list. I also found myself starting to withdraw from the rest of the world and to isolate myself from people, even those friends who were close to me, like Kylie. She called one day and I just let the machine take the message. I never returned her call. Subconsciously, I must have felt like I let her down.

At the hospital, I gave the appearance of being OK. I was getting comments like, "Jess, you look terrific. You've got to tell me how you lost that weight."

Jack heard different comments from friends that we knew. "What's wrong with Jess? She doesn't seem to smile much. We don't see or hear from her. Is she feeling well?" At first, Jack just made up polite answers and dismissed the subject. Toward the second week of October, on a Friday night, Jack started to hug and kiss me as we tucked ourselves into bed. "Jack, please, not tonight."

"Jess, you've changed since we got back from Florida."

"Jack, Florida was like fantasy land. We're back in reality land now. I've just got too many things on my mind."

"Is it the computer project?"

"That's part of it."

"Sweetheart, talk to me."

"Jack, give me a little time."

"If something's bothering you, maybe I can help."

"I know you mean well."

"Jess, what's wrong?"

"Everything's fine, honey. I'm just tired."

Jack kissed my cheek and rolled over to his side of the bed. He was turned away from me so I couldn't see his face, but I knew he was disappointed, frustrated, and concerned about me. Conversations like that became more frequent as the next few weeks passed. Eventually, Jack's asking me what's wrong became more like nagging, and there was a tension growing between us.

* * *

Thanksgiving rolled around without much fanfare. Holiday dinner was just for the four of us. While Jack and the kids enjoyed the huge meal I prepared, I just had my two thin slices of turkey and called it quits. Jack noticed what I ate, looked at me with despair, but didn't say anything. He knew it would only bring about more tension.

Sunday night Megan went out with a few girlfriends to a party given by one of the other girls from school. Ever since Megan started going out in the evening, I made it a habit of staying in the den to wait for her to get home. Jack went upstairs to sleep at 10:30.

More often than not, I'd fall asleep on the couch, but I always woke at the sound of the key unlocking the front door. That night I didn't fall asleep. All I could do was think of the list of things that were bothering me. I still hated the fact that I was past forty and that half my life was over. I was bothered by Megan's depression, even though she was showing signs of improvement. Megan was still cutting, but she reduced the frequency from a few times a day on a daily basis to perhaps once every few weeks. The endless computer assignment was coming to a close, but there were the final testing phases we had to pass, and I was nervous about the outcome. Although I had lost weight, I still hated my body image. My food restriction continued, as well as my heavy use of laxatives. Only now, I started taking diet pills I got from the hospital to help speed up the weight loss. Needless to say, there was an ever-growing tension between Jack and me. We were together less and less. It bothered him. It bothered me, but I wasn't willing to do anything to improve the situation. Our marriage and the love we shared for so many years were being tested, and it was all my fault. Jack was doing nothing wrong.

It was about midnight when I heard Megan's key unlock the door. Since I had to go work the next day, I was glad it was finally time to get upstairs to try to get some sleep for the night. I immediately knew something was wrong because Megan was crying as she came in and dashed upstairs to her bedroom. There was no way to ignore the situation. It was one of those times you have to ask what's wrong, even though you're positive you don't want to hear the answer.

Megan's door was closed. I knocked. There was no response. I knocked again, and again there was no response. I opened the door. Megan was dressed and laying on her stomach with her face in the pillow to muffle the sounds of her crying.

"Megan, what's wrong?"

She didn't answer. I sat on the side of her bed and caressed her head.

"Megan, whatever it is, you can tell me."

Megan turned over and I saw red marks on her face. "Sweetheart, what happened to you?"

"Mom," Megan said through her heavy sobs, "I can't tell you."

"Sure you can."

"I can't!"

"Please, sweetheart, you know you can tell me anything."

Megan was hysterical. I took her in my arms and gently rubbed her back to try to soothe her and calm her. For two or three minutes, we said nothing. Then Megan broke the silence.

"Carol, Jenny, and I walked back to the block together. We noticed three older guys leave the party behind us. They weren't at the party, but we saw them hanging outside the house when we left. None of us knew them. We thought things were OK. Carol and Jenny went into their house. Mom, they only live a few houses away. I thought I would be OK. Then the boys suddenly ran up to me. One of them put something over my eyes, forced me to the ground, and held me there. He was too strong. I couldn't get up. I never got a good look at their faces. I don't know them. All I know is that one forced me to open my mouth and . . ."

"And what, Megan?"

"I can't tell you. I'm too ashamed."

"Megan, what happened?"

"He put his thing in my mouth. He kept pushing it in and out and hurting me. Then I felt this sticky stuff in my mouth. That boy stopped, and a second boy did the same thing to me. He was choking me with his thing. Then they just let me go and ran away."

"Oh, my God. Oh, my precious baby. I'm so sorry. I'm so sorry. I'm so sorry."

"Mom, they just left me there on the ground."

I couldn't keep myself from crying. "My poor sweet baby. My sweet baby." I didn't know what to say. I could only hug her as hard as I could and rock her like I did when she was an infant. "How could people be so cruel?" I asked myself. "Why my daughter? Haven't things been tough enough for her?"

The two of us must have stayed embraced for ten or twenty minutes. I needed Megan to hold me as much as I needed to hold her.

"Megan, I have to take you to the emergency room."

"No."

"I'll call the police."

"No. I'm too ashamed! Don't call the police! I'll deny anything happened."

"I'll wake Dad."

"Don't you dare tell him!"

"Megan . . ."

"Mom, I beg you!"

"Wait here. I'll be right back."

"Where are you going? Promise you won't wake Dad."

"I promise."

I went to the bathroom to get some antiseptic mouthwash. I knew it was a futile attempt at helping her, but I felt I had to do something. I returned with the bottle of mouthwash and put her garbage pail next to her bed.

"Rinse your mouth and spit it out into the garbage."

Megan rinsed.

"Again."

Megan complied.

"We're going to Dr. Bruno tomorrow."

"Why?"

"He has to examine you."

"Why?

"Megan, your throat may be injured."

"I don't care."

"Megan, what if one of those boys had AIDS?"

"Mom, I don't care."

"I do!" I yelled. "Honey, forgive me. I love you. We'll tell Dr. Bruno that he's to tell no one else what happened."

"You promise?"

"I swear."

I hugged Megan again and started rocking her again. I thought to myself, "This is all my fault. This is all my fault."

* * *

The next day I called in sick to get Megan to Dr. Bruno. Jack asked what was wrong with her, and I told him she had a sore throat. I didn't call for an appointment. We just went to his office and told the receptionist that it was an emergency. By 9:45 a.m. we were in his office and explaining the horror that had happened the night before. He kept shaking his head in disbelief the whole time and telling us how sorry he was that Megan had to go through such an ordeal.

"Megan, do you feel pain in your throat now?"

"Not really."

"I see. OK."

Dr. Bruno escorted us into the examining room. He took Megan's pulse and blood pressure, listened to her heart and lungs, then examined her eyes, ears, and throat. He spent a particularly long time with her throat.

"Everything looks OK so far. Megan, your mother has to sign this consent form for the AIDS test." He handed me the document and I signed it without reading it. "We'll have the results back in a week."

"What if the results are positive?"

"Then there are procedures we'll have to start. But, let's pray it doesn't go that way. In the meantime, I'm going to call Dr. Willsen . . ."

Megan interrupted anxiously, "Mom, the promise. You forgot the promise."

"Dr. Bruno, this situation . . . Megan doesn't want it to go beyond these four walls."

"Megan, sweetheart, besides the physical effect, you and your mother both have to deal with the psychological effects of this assault on you."

Megan started crying.

"You need his help. Your mother needs his help."

"Do you promise me only you two will know?"

"Megan, those boys should face the consequences for . . ."

Megan started getting hysterical and screamed, "Tell me you promise no one else will know. Say the words! Say the words!"

"I promise you, Megan. I will tell no one about this. Not even my staff will know."

"Thank you, Dr. Bruno," I said as I hugged Megan.

"Is it OK if I call Dr. Willsen now to set the two appointments for tomorrow?"

"Megan . . ."

"OK, Mom."

Dr. Bruno reached his hand out to Megan and said, "Thank you for trusting me, Megan."

"Dr. Bruno," I said, "just tell us when to be there."

"I'll be right back," Dr. Bruno said before leaving the examining room to make the call.

The drive home from Dr. Bruno's office was silent. Megan was still sobbing. All I could do was harp on my question to him, "What if the results are positive?" I was terrified that I could lose my daughter. I felt like I couldn't live if anything happened to her.

Dinner that night was unusually quiet. Afterwards, Jack came to me privately and asked what was wrong.

"Jack, please be patient with me now. Let me answer when I can."

Jack hugged me. "Jess, we're a team. If there's something wrong, I want to help you. Please don't shut me out."

"Jack, I beg you. Give me time. Please."

Jack kissed me. "Tell me when you're ready. But please don't shut me out."

"Thank you, Jack."

The next morning Dr. Willsen got into his office two hours before his first appointment to make time to see Megan and me. I was grateful that he was so considerate and accommodating.

Megan took the first appointment. I tried flipping through a few magazines, but nothing could hold my attention except my concern for Megan. An hour later she came out of his office crying.

"Sweetheart, are you OK?" I asked as I hugged her.

"I'm OK, Mom. Dr. Willsen helped me."

"I'm glad you're here, Mrs. Gordon. Let's talk."

It had been several years since I was in therapy. At first, I was a little anxious.

"Mrs. Gordon . . ."

"Jess."

"OK," he said as he held out his hand to shake mine. We had seen each other countless times before, but the relationship was about to change, and those few seconds comforted me.

"First, I'm terribly sorry about what happened. I pray the results come back negative."

"Thank you."

"How do you feel?"

I looked at him but couldn't say anything. All the negative feelings in my mind were choking me and kept me speechless.

"Jess, take your time."

I closed my eyes and nodded my head to acknowledge what he said and to calm myself. It took me several moments before I finally said, "This is all my fault."

"How so, Jess?"

"I can't explain it. That's just how I feel."

"I see."

I knew he was giving me time to think about what I wanted to tell him and to open up my feelings, which, at that moment, wasn't an easy thing to do. I took a deep breath, paused, and said, "I feel very guilty about my daughter. I feel like I'm the cause of her problems."

"Is there something you've done that makes you think this?"

"I've been under tremendous stress since last year. Megan has me worried. This last incident was horrific."

"Yes, it was."

"Genetically . . . has Megan explained about her uncle, my brother?"

"No. Tell me about him."

"My brother was diagnosed as bipolar. I grew up watching him go through manic and depressive states. I feel like Megan has the same symptoms. At first, I thought her apprehension about junior high school was normal. Then, as we've witnessed, it went much further. She was in an extreme depressive state until you found the right medication and dosage. From depression, she started self-mutilation and self-abuse."

"And you're blaming yourself for this?"

"Yes."

"But I've seen you care for her and try to help her. Where do you think this feeling of guilt comes from?"

"Because, obviously, I'm not a good mother. What happened with those boys . . . I feel like it's my fault."

"Jess, Megan's depression is a chemical imbalance. And from everything she's told me, it is something you couldn't have avoided. Let's look into your past. Is there something that happened to you that is similar in nature to the attack by those boys?"

"No. No boys ever molested me. I was . . ."

"Go on, Jess."

"I was . . ."

All my thoughts were scrambled and senseless. Consciously, I wanted to say something, but my subconscious thoughts seemed buried and repressed to a point where I was speechless.

Dr. Willsen believed he had to hear what I couldn't say. "Perhaps there was an incident . . ."

Suddenly the cloudiness in my mind lifted. "I was . . ." I could feel the thoughts rise to my consciousness. "I was raped by a woman."

Neither of us expected to hear that.

"Jess . . ."

"No, wait. It wasn't the same. I wasn't raped, I . . ." Thoughts about Lucy that had been repressed for decades were suddenly resurfacing to my consciousness. Only now, they took on different perspectives.

"Dr. Willsen, I've never thought about this. I've never talked about this with anyone. Not even my husband knows what happened."

"Tell me what you can remember."

"I was about fifteen. Yesterday, if you had mentioned the term 'guidance counselor,' I would have said, 'Yeah. I knew one.' And yet, now . . ." I suddenly felt nauseated.

"Jess, you're doing the right thing."

"I never thought about it as an abnormal or abusive relationship."

"But now you do?"

"Yes. She was supposed to protect me. She was my school's guidance counselor who got me out of that hell I lived in with my bipolar brother. I always felt grateful to her. What I did was repayment for her having taken me out of that environment. I owed her for the help she gave me. But the person who was supposed to protect me never should have raped me. I thought I was always in control and that it was my conscious decision to be involved with . . . with a lesbian relationship. I felt ashamed about it then as I do now. But before now, I never felt like I was violated. Until this moment, I never felt like I was a victim."

"Jess, you were fifteen. Mentally, you were still a child."

"I thought I knew what I was doing."

"Jess, put yourself in Megan's shoes as if she were involved with that counselor. Do you think that she would be thinking with an adult mind? Do you think she would be making a choice as an adult or as a child?"

Dr. Willsen looked at his watch. I could see on his face that he wanted to continue, but it was obvious the time was up. "Jess, please, make another appointment."

"OK. I can't believe what I just told you. All those memories were so repressed and buried."

"We'll get through this, Jess," Dr. Willsen said as he shook my hand and escorted me back to Megan. I looked at Megan's sweet and innocent face. I hugged her so she wouldn't see me cry.

That night I searched around the bedroom and found a box of old pictures of Lucy and me. I looked so young. Being in that kind of relationship was not a decision I would have made with an adult mind. I looked at Lucy's face and said to myself, "You raped me. You violated my body."

Jack came into the room. "Who is that with you in the picture?"

"She was my guidance counselor." It was difficult to start speaking again. "Jack, hug me. There's something you have to know about me, and Megan."

Jack and I spoke for hours until the sun came up, then we both called in sick.

* * *

Between Megan's tragedy and the revelation of emotions about Lucy, I had become a total mental waste. It took me several days before I had the emotional strength to get back to work. Exactly one week after we saw Dr. Bruno, we received a copy of the lab results. The AIDS test was negative. Megan was almost nonchalant about the news. At least that's how she seemed outwardly. Internally, I think the news hit harder than expected.

The next day I was supposed to see Dr. Willsen. I canceled the appointment and never rescheduled. Instead, I drove the kids to school as though things were fine and normal, but they weren't. I thought about Jason a great deal. I felt guilty about neglecting him. He's such a great little guy and I love him so much, but I wasn't nurturing him. I almost felt like I was treating him the way my parents used to treat me, and I hated that feeling of him being somewhere off in the distance. I was there for him physically, but not mentally. I was in my own little problem-filled world and didn't let him in.

That afternoon after school, Megan came into the kitchen for a snack, and I saw three fresh parallel cuts on her arm. She saw that I noticed them. She looked into my eyes and probably thought I would explode, but I didn't. I wanted to, but I didn't. Instead I hugged her. "Sweetheart, you've gone through a terrible ordeal. I'm sorry. Please don't let this last week set you back."

"I'm sorry, Mom. I needed some kind of release," Megan said before she took her snack up to her room.

I could feel that my stress level had increased and, once again, I blamed myself for Megan having mutilated her body. I had to get rid of the anxiety, but I didn't know how.

Things were quiet that night at dinner. My mind was focused on a question about myself: Am I bipolar? Genetically, it runs in the family. I didn't think I was, but, like Mitch, I had my manic and depressive turns.

How I looked also bothered me. By that time, I had already dropped 30 pounds from where I was over a year ago, and yet I wasn't satisfied with my weight loss or how fast the weight was coming off. Interestingly, instead of cutting back on dinner, I found myself eating more that night and finished the meal with several cookies. I felt like I had to punish myself.

"Why did I do that?" kept running through my mind as I started washing the dishes. Jack and the kids were in the den with the television on. I turned the water off and went up to the bathroom. I got on my knees and stared into the toilet bowl. My mind went back to the inpatient program thirteen years ago, and I remembered another technique some of the patients used for losing weight. Slowly and deliberately, I stuck my finger down my throat. Except for feeling like I was choking myself, nothing happened. Then I looked up and saw my toothbrush. I took hold of it by the bristles and shoved it down my throat. At first, I started to choke, and then I began to sweat from the frustration, nervousness, and anxiety I felt. I had just eaten a much larger than average meal, and I couldn't get it out of me. Desperately, almost with a sense of panic, I kept shoving the toothbrush further down my throat. Finally, some vomit spewed from my mouth and into the bowl. It wasn't the amount I was expecting, but at least it was something. I was reviled by the entire situation. For a moment, I wanted Jack to walk into the bathroom so he could chastise me for my actions. He didn't. I just rinsed my mouth and looked at the vomit with a sense of disgust before flushing the evidence of my actions away.

I went back to the kitchen and finished washing the dishes. I thought about the stories I had heard about bulimia in the hospital therapy sessions. They made it seem like purging was simple. It wasn't, at least not for me. Then again, maybe they had a technique I didn't know about.

Two days later, after dinner, I found myself on my knees again with my face in the toilet. Only this time, I drank a great deal of juice with my meal and had two cups of tea after the meal. I realized that if I put the tooth-brush in a certain position it made me gag more. I also realized that using my finger in a certain position helped me. I was learning what to do, and I was learning quickly. Before I knew it, the entire meal was out of my stomach. This time the experience was pleasurable. I thought to myself, "This is a good way to lose weight. I could have my cake, eat it, and get rid of it." The process was disgusting. The taste of vomit in my mouth was disgusting. The sight of the vomit in the toilet was disgusting. Nevertheless, knowing that I had just emptied my stomach of an entire meal felt satisfying. I felt a certain release of tension. That pleasurable feeling definitely outweighed all the negative sensations. If I were a drug addict, I would say it was my first pleasurable high. In essence, that night I got mentally hooked.

Several weeks passed. My purging continued on a random schedule of twice a week. By February, I increased the cycle up to three times a week and maintained my restrictive diet, except for those evenings I binged. I followed those bingeing meals with cookies, cakes, cereal, or any other sweet and starchy thing we had around the house. I also continued abusing the laxatives, and continued taking diet pills. The scale showed progress, and my weight continued to drop.

By March, my bingeing and purging went from three times a week up to four, then five times a week. All I kept thinking was, "This is the easiest way to lose weight." I denied the fact that it was self-abuse. If I were in my right mind, I would have understood the pressures I was under, and that this new routine was another pressure that should have been avoided, but I wasn't in my right mind. I was in denial. Any therapist would have told me that any form of restriction was a return to my eating disorder with a guaranteed journey's end in the hospital. Any therapist would have said that the additional bulimia pattern was heading me straight back to the deadly position I was in thirteen years ago. But I wasn't seeing a therapist. I was avoiding all therapy because I wasn't willing to let anything get in the way of my self-appointed form of stress management. Each time I binged and purged, the process put me into a trance that was totally involving. It was just the food and me. Nothing and no one else mattered while I was in that other dream world where no problems existed. It was like I was purging out all the bad thoughts and stress. The high I felt never failed to be there, and it never diminished.

By the end of April, I purged on a daily basis.

By the middle of May, I purged a few times a day. Jack didn't know what I was doing, but he wasn't blind to its results. Jack started asking me what was wrong.

"Jack, everything is OK."

"It can't be OK. Look at how much weight you've lost."

"Everything is fine."

"If it's so fine, then why aren't we ever making love anymore?"

"Is that all you ever think about?"

"Sorry if I want to be with the woman I love. Sorry if making love every five or six weeks doesn't seem normal to me. Jess, what's happening here?"

"Nothing. Stop nagging me."

"Is that what you think this is—nagging?"

Jack had every right to feel neglected, but there was nothing I was going to do to improve the situation. I wasn't going to divulge the secrets I kept from him about abusing diet pills, laxatives, restricting and purging. His concern and attempts to resolve the problem only added more stress and frustration. All I could do was increase my purging frequency to escape those negative feelings.

I was great at keeping my secret. There was never a hint of vomit on my breath. Any bathroom I used was always spotless when I left it. I always made sure Jack and the kids were far enough away in the house so they couldn't hear me heaving my guts up.

I was blind to the fact that I was repeating a pattern I had suffered through in the past when I had to deal with negative situations. I would get through them, then collapse and mentally break down.

By the first week of June, I was no longer able to think things out using a rational thought process. Except for the weight loss, all outward appearances made it seem like I was OK. I was going to work and doing my job. I was taking care of the kids. Megan's cutting frequency was declining, and her depression was easing. She continued her sessions with Dr. Willsen, only now I always waited outside for her in the car because I felt a little guilty that I had stopped my sessions with him.

The only other signal that anything was wrong was my decrease in sexual activity with Jack, but only he knew about that. My own mental state, on the other hand, which only I knew about, was a disaster, but I denied it. My own depression was on the rise, even if I wouldn't admit it to anyone, including myself. Suicidal thoughts crept into my mind. I didn't fight them. No, let me rephrase that. I refused to believe those thoughts even existed. As far as I was concerned, everything was fine. It got to a point where I actually believed the lies I kept dishing out to others and myself. However, any therapist would have labeled me a catastrophic bomb prepped for detonation without any way to prevent the inevitable explosion.

There were obvious and serious warnings, but I refused to accept them as anything abnormal. The first happened on the second Saturday in June. I had just gotten into the car to run some errands. Jack and the kids weren't home. I remember starting the engine and feeling that my heart was beating exceptionally fast. Thank goodness, the car was still in park because the next thing I remember was the sound of the horn blasting because my face was pushing it. I had no idea about how long I had passed out. I went into the house, doused my face with cold water, waited a few seconds until my heart calmed down, then got back into the car to do what I had to do.

Later that week I remember I was washing the dishes. Jack and the kids were outside. Again, I felt my heart beating extremely fast. The next thing I remember was my face on the floor with the broken dish in front of my eyes. Incredibly, I still thought there was no need for concern. Jack thought differently as he walked into the kitchen and saw me on the floor.

"Jess, we're going to the emergency room."

"Why?"

"Are you serious?"

"Absolutely."

"I just found you unconscious on the floor."

"So?"

"Jess, two choices: get in the car so I can take you to the emergency room, or I'm calling 911 for an ambulance."

"Jack, let it go."

Jack picked up the phone. I hung up the receiver after he dialed 9-1. "Jack, you're taking this out of . . ."

"Get in the car."

"Fine."

Jack called out to the kids, "We'll be back in a while. I want both of you to stay around the house and off the telephone in case I need to reach you. Got it?"

Megan and Jason both yelled back to say they understood.

We waited around the emergency room for two hours before they saw me. It was pissing me off that we were there, but there was no way in hell Jack would let me leave without being checked out first. Finally, I was taken in for an examination. They listened to my heart and lungs, checked my ears, nose and throat, took my blood pressure, and ran an EKG. Everything looked fine.

Finally, Dr. Short-and-Fat-Something-or-Other—I didn't bother to remember his name because I knew I'd never see him again—emotionlessly explained, "Normally the heart beats between sixty and one hundred times per minute. If your heart rate is very fast, over one hundred beats per minute, this is called tachycardia. Palpitations are often not serious. However, it depends on whether or not the sensations represent an abnormal heart rhythm, which is called an arrhythmia. You are more likely to have an abnormal heart rhythm if you have a known heart disease at the time the palpitations begin, significant risk factors for heart disease, an abnormal heart valve, or an electrolyte abnormality—for example, low potassium."

None of us knew at the time that his last sentence hit the nail on the head. Fortunately, or unfortunately, he failed to take the proper blood test to substantiate my condition.

"So," Jack asked, "what do we do about this?"

"Reducing stress and anxiety can help lessen your heart palpitations. Try breathing exercises or deep relaxation. Also, consider practicing yoga or tai chi on a regular basis to reduce the frequency of your palpitations. Based on the results of all I've seen here today, I don't think this isolated incident is anything to worry about, unless the frequency of heart palpitations increases."

Jack looked at him incredulously. "That's it?"

"Yes, Mr. Gordon, unless you and your wife have any questions. I have other patients waiting for me."

"Do what you have to, doc. We're fine," I said to dismiss him.

I don't know if Jack was more upset with me or the doctor's nonchalant reaction and diagnosis. Either way, he didn't say a word to me as we drove home, neither did he talk with me at dinner. In fact, he didn't say anything to me until the next morning and, even then, the entire conversation consisted of, "Good morning. I've got the list. I'm going food shopping."

Jack's not speaking with me really didn't bother me at that time. His going food shopping was a perfect opportunity for my to have a binge breakfast, purge, and take a nap–and that's exactly what I did.

* * *

Except for this inconsequential heart thing, I thought I had everything under control. I was able to purge several times a day, no one knew it, and the escapes from reality felt wonderful. Then, on June 2, Megan's birthday, my world of secrets got exposed. I was making a birthday cake for dinner that night. I remember bending over to take the cake out of the oven when I suddenly felt a little light-headed. The next thing I remember was seeing the cake on the floor and Jason and Megan both screaming for Jack, who was upstairs getting dressed to go out and do some errands.

Jack got into the kitchen and saw me on the floor unable to stand up. This time, he didn't offer me any choices. He picked up the phone and called 911.

"Yes, she lost consciousness, but she's awake now." There was a pause. "Yes, this has happened before." Another pause. "No, she doesn't have any known heart problems, but she was examined recently for heart palpitations." How I felt didn't bother me. What concerned me was the fact that my secret little world might be exposed. At the time, I gave no concern to the horrified look on my kids' faces. That didn't get to me until they wheeled me out on the gurney and Megan and Jason both asked Jack, "Is Mom going to die?" My family felt threatened, and I was the sole cause.

When I got to the hospital, I didn't get as lucky as last time. The homely, almost ugly, tall, skinny female doctor looked at me and immediately checked me in for a complete physical and medical workup. Just as they started to roll me up to my room, I saw the doctor take Jack out to the hall to talk with him in private. Months later, Jack told me what they talked about.

She said, "Mr. Gordon, I need some information from you that I don't believe your wife will be willing to supply. Do you know what's going on here?"

"Yes, my wife is having these heart palpitations."

"Mr. Gordon, I mean beyond the heart palpitations?"

"What are you talking about?"

"Well, we'll run the standard tests, but I've seen this situation hundreds of times. Perhaps I shouldn't be so blunt, but I'll bet dollars to doughnuts, just based on the obvious physical condition of your wife, that what's happening to her now is directly related to an eating disorder."

"I don't understand. She got over her anorexia over thirteen years ago. She eats meals with us. I see her eat cookies and cake."

"What happens when the meal is over?"

"What?"

"Does she disappear from your sight for a while?"

"No. I mean . . . sometimes. Doctor, what's going on? I beg of you to be as blunt as possible."

* * *

The doctor released me from the hospital the next evening after dinner. Jack drove me home, only this time he wasn't silent. He told me that he spoke with Dr. Willsen, who said he wanted to see both of us because of something to do with Megan, although Jack didn't know what it was all about.

Jack was annoyed with me for not answering him immediately. Then I said, "Can't you handle it on your own?"

"Jess, the doctor said he had to see both of us. Whatever is in your head, put it aside. This is for Megan." Reluctantly I gave in, but only because of my love for Megan.

We got to Dr. Willsen's office at 11:00 the next morning.

"Mr. Gordon, it's nice to meet you. Jess, it's good to see you again."

I got right to the point, "Dr. Willsen, what's going on with Megan?"

Dr. Willsen turned to Jack and said, "Mr. Gordon, I think you said you wanted to open this conversation."

"What's going on, Jack? What's wrong with Megan?"

"Jess, this meeting is not really about Megan. I'm sorry. I've never lied to you before. Forgive me."

"Jack, what's going on here? I want to know, and I want to know now!"

"Dr. Willsen, did you get the lab reports from the hospital?"

"Yes. So far, there is no major indication of heart problems. There was, however, a significant problem with Jess' potassium levels."

"Which means what?" I asked.

"Which means," Jack started, "that you've been keeping secrets from me."

"What?"

"Jess, we're here because I love you and I don't want to lose you. I finally understand where you were after all those meals we ate together. I finally understand that history is repeating itself. I finally understand how you lost so much weight in the last six months. I finally understand the meaning of bulimia."

"Congratulations. What does that have to do with me?"

Dr. Willsen started saying something to me. "Jess . . ."

I wouldn't let Dr. Willsen continue. I knew what he wanted to say and I didn't want to hear it. "Listen, Dr. Willsen, this scheme Jack thought of . . ." was all I could blurt out before Dr. Willsen interrupted me.

"Jess, eating disorders are not my specialty. Dr. James Fuller is a close friend of mine. He's a psychiatrist. His specialty is eating disorders. He can help you."

"I don't need help."

Jack rested his elbows on his knees and put his face in his hands. I never saw him look so helpless. It took several moments before he spoke. "Jess, you're often catatonic. You're passing out. What if you passed out while driving the kids to school?"

The thought of that possibility scared the hell out of me.

"Jess, I love you, but you went right back to that whole thing. Didn't you?"

I loved Jack too much to lie. "Jack, I can control this."

"Jess, it's already controlling everything you do. What's your weight down to?"

"About 95 pounds."

"That's what you weighed when you went into the hospital."

"Yeah, Jack, but . . ."

"Jess, I can't let you die."

"I'm not going back to the hospital. Got it?"

"Jess . . ."

"Jack, understand me. I'm not going back."

"At least give Dr. Fuller a chance to help you."

"I don't need his help. I'm not going back!"

* * *

Chapter Six

The Choice Point

Months had passed since Jack hoodwinked me into seeing Dr. Willsen. I never called or saw Dr. Fuller because I believed there was no need to. I knew I was often feeling depressed, but I was positive I could handle it on my own. When Jack tried to talk with me about my condition, I told him there was nothing wrong and that I did not intend to change my lifestyle. Those conversations were usually very abrupt.

"Jess, you're delusional."

"Jack, you're getting to be a pain in the neck. Knock it off."

Those few sentences between us usually resulted in us not talking for a few hours. It didn't bother me, but I could see it upset Jack. Unfortunately, I did not intend to appease him. "Why should I change?" I asked myself. Then I would always answer myself in the same way, "I won't. There's nothing wrong." I was bent on living my life my way, no matter the consequences.

Physically I felt OK, although I couldn't look at the fat cow that faced me in my mirror. No matter how hard I tried to lose additional weight, I hovered between 93 and 96 pounds.

For a while, I was forced to live in a world of status quo. Status quo was defined as working my ass off at my job, dealing with the kids and their problems, dealing with Jack's nagging, and often crying myself to sleep alone in the bedroom because Jack chose to sleep elsewhere rather than get into another argument.

By the second week of September, the kids were back in school and the country was mourning the first anniversary of 9/11. The news clips of the towers falling and the memorial services on television increased my depressed state. If I had the ability to think rationally, I would have understood that I was jumping head first into hell, but the eating disorder poisoned all possible rational thinking. Consciously, I told myself that my troubles of the past were gone. I swore to myself that I was still in recovery. Nothing and no one could convince me otherwise, although the increased frequency of evidence was slapping me in the face each time I passed out and found myself regaining consciousness on the floor. Most of the time, I passed out when I was alone. A few times it happened when the kids were around. Whenever it happened when Jack was around, we followed the all-too-regular pattern of him taking me to the emergency room to get checked out. Each time they told me my potassium levels were low and that I had to start on a more healthy diet plan. Each time I told them I would, then went home and ignored everything they said.

Jack, bless his heart, refused to give up trying to help me, no matter how much I verbally abused him about his saintly intentions and actions. Dinnertime, and the time after dinner, became somewhat of a game between the two of us. He and the kids would eat a normal meal that I had prepared, and I would eat only a few small forkfuls of "safe" food in the same amount of time. Then, after the kids left the table and Jack helped me with the dishes, it became a situation where he followed me around the house to prevent me from getting to a bathroom to purge the little I ate. Sometimes I thought back to the times when Jack didn't know I purged. I recalled how difficult it was for me to throw up after eating, and I remembered how I had the luxury of limitless time to empty my stomach. Now, however, Jack became the "food police." He shadowed my whereabouts, and I could sense he had his ear on the bathroom door whenever I went to the bathroom just after eating. But I was sly, and purging had become as simple for me as breathing. I quietly filled a glass with water and poured it loudly into the toilet to mimic the sound of me peeing as I silently purged. I made sure he could hear me roll off some toilet paper to fool him into thinking I was wiping myself.

I flushed the toilet to get rid of the evidence and then I ran the water to make him think I was washing my hands, although I only used the water to remove the mouthwash smell from my breath.

Jack was becoming increasingly alarmed at my condition, yet I fought his every attempt to help me. Countless times he nagged me with his "Jess, you have to take care of yourself" speech. Either that or he was a constant and annoying roadblock to the toilet. As far as I was concerned, it was like having one of the hospital matrons living in my own house. I was losing the image of Jack as my husband. I thought of him as "one of those against me." He kept trying to keep me away from my purging high, and he was pissing me off.

With no reluctance or remorse at all, I had become a perfect cheat. I knew how to hide my laxatives in my tampon box, knowing that Jack would never think of looking for them there. By this time I was also heavily into diet pills. A nurse friend of mine from the hospital got me a never-ending supply, which I kept hidden in a bottle that used to contain my antidepressant medication.

Once again, I had become withdrawn from the rest of the world, including my co-workers and friends, my husband, and my kids. All wifely and motherly urges were set aside without compunction. Yes, I was physically there for my kids, but that was it. I picked them up from school, made their dinner, and helped them with their homework. However, as soon as Jack got home, I separated myself from all of them. I was no longer the supermom I used to be. I became a self-centered, selfish, and worthless individual who lived in her own little world, and I didn't care. All I cared about was losing weight and getting rid of that disgusting fat cow image in the mirror.

Early in December, I felt increasingly depressed. I excused it as part of the oncoming holiday season and the pressure the gift list and shopping always had on me. My way of combating it was to increase my food restriction, increase my laxative dosage, increase my use of diet pills, and purge as often as I put anything in my mouth. In addition, I secretly started to smoke. Ordinarily, smoking is just considered a filthy habit which, if continued, can lead to serious health conditions over a long period. However, since I had always suffered from upper respiratory tract infections due to chronic and severe asthma, smoking can only be considered a self-destructive behavior.

On Monday the ninth, things went from bad to worse. I had already picked the kids up from school. They were upstairs working on their homework and I was in the kitchen to prepare dinner. I remember turning on one of the gas stovetop burners, getting a large frying pan from the cabinet, feeling light-headed, and feeling my heart race unusually fast. The next thing I remember was hearing Megan's voice as I woke up on the floor with the frying pan still in my hand.

"Mom, what's wrong with you?"

"Nothing, Megan."

"Then why do you pass out like that?"

"Megan, forget about it."

"But, Mom . . ."

"Honey, I love you. Don't worry."

"Mom, it scares me."

"Megan, let it go."

"I can't."

"Megan . . ."

"Mom, you need help. You're sick."

Suddenly, every emotional nerve in my body erupted in rage.

"Between you . . ." I screamed as I slammed the frying pan on the counter, ". . . and your father . . ." twice more I slammed the frying pan on the counter. "You don't tell me what to do, little girl. Got it?" Again, I slammed the frying pan on the counter. Megan's body shook with fear as she stared with disbelief into my angry and terror-filled eyes.

I raised my hand with the frying pan to slam it again, but stopped when I saw Jason at the kitchen door and noticed Megan's body quiver as though an electric current just shocked her. I softly placed the pan on the counter and left the kitchen to go outside to have a cigarette. My hands shook as I lit it up. I wasn't wearing a coat and the temperature must have been close to thirty-two, but it wasn't the weather that made my hands shake. I realized the terrible thing I just did to my daughter.

For the first time in months, I finally felt emotion, and it was all negative. I hated myself for my actions. I hated myself for how I hurt my innocent little girl. I hated my life and I wished it would end.

Although I shivered ceaselessly from the cold, I couldn't go inside. All I could do was chain smoke and, by my fourth cigarette, I saw the sun set against a fiery red sky. That's when I heard the phone ring and went inside to answer it.

"Hey, Jess," Jack said calmly to me from the other end of the phone, "how are you?"

"Could be better."

"I know. Megan called me here at work. She was crying."

"Jack, I'm so sorry."

"Jess . . ."

I started crying hysterically and had difficulty talking through my sobs. "Jack, I lost control and took it out on my baby. I'm so sorry. I'm so sorry. My poor baby."

"Jess, we need to talk. I promise. No lectures. No demands."

"Jack . . ."

"Please."

"Jack . . ."

"Jess, please talk with me. Not now. Tonight."

I could hear in Jack's voice that he started to cry. It got to me. "OK."

"Jess, I love you."

"I know you do. I know you do."

"I'll try to leave early. Don't cook. I'll bring some pizza home for the kids."

"OK," I said as I hung up the phone. I stood there holding the phone on the cradle. My knees felt weak, so I slowly lowered myself to the floor, where I cried for several minutes until Jason came in.

"Mommy, why are you crying?"

"Come here, sweetheart. I did something very wrong today and it makes me feel very sad."

"You mean because you yelled like that?"

"Yes, sweetheart."

"It scared me, Mommy."

"It scared me too, sweetheart. Can you forgive me?"

"Sure, Mommy."

"Jason, I love you. I need one of your special hugs."

"Sure, Mommy," he said as he wrapped his arms around me. I cried into his shoulder. "It'll be OK, Mommy. You'll be OK."

Just then I saw Megan at the door. "Precious, please come to me." Megan approached me hesitantly. With one arm I held Jason and, with the other arm, I hugged Megan with as much strength as I could muster.

"Precious, I beg you to forgive me. Please find it in your heart to forgive me."

Megan's face was against mine. I could feel her tears run down my face. "Oh, God, what have I done? Children, please forgive me. Please forgive me."

* * *

I was in the kitchen when Jack got home early with the pizza. He put it on the table and we just looked into each other's eyes without saying a word. After several moments Jack slowly walked toward me and hugged me. Again, I started to cry.

"Jess, things will work out," Jack told me as he caressed my back in a massaging motion. His touch comforted me. I thought about how the two of us had not been intimate for the past several weeks, and all those nights Jack didn't sleep in the bedroom to avoid me harassing him whenever he tried to help me. I thought about how lucky I was to have him as a husband and friend, then I started falling into a deep depression because I was killing the wonderful relationship we shared for decades. At that moment, I felt like a pitiful and worthless human being.

"Jess, I'll take care of the kids. Why don't you go upstairs, put on some music, and relax."

All I did was nod my head. Jack gave me another strong hug and then let me go. My back was to him as I walked out of the kitchen, but I could feel Jack watch me as I left the kitchen and went upstairs to the bedroom.

I wasn't in the mood for music. There was no kind of music for my depressed state. For the next three hours, as though in a trance, I laid on the bed with the lights off and stared at the evening shadows of leafless tree limbs swaying on the ceiling.

When Jack opened the bedroom door, the single 100-watt bulb in the hall seemed to flood the bedroom with light. Jack must have seen me squint so he quickly turned the hall light out and closed the door when he entered the room. I didn't move. I couldn't. Jack sat besides me, took my hand and caressed it lovingly.

"Jason is asleep. Megan is in her room watching TV."

"Jack, I'm so sorry."

"Jess, Megan and I had a long talk. She's OK now."

"I'm glad she's better. I must have scared her. But that's not what I'm talking about."

"What do you mean?"

"I want to apologize to you and the way I've been treating you."

Jack slowly bent down and softly kissed my lips.

"Jess, from the moment I saw you when we first met, you've lit up my life. Lately, I'm scared that light could go out. It scares me because I can't fathom living without you."

Again, I started to cry. Jack used one hand to reach for a tissue on the night table, but his other hand never let go of mine. "My beautiful Jess, I need your help," Jack said as he dabbed away my tears.

I didn't say a word. I thought to myself, "How can this worthless woman help you if she can't help herself?"

"Jess, this afternoon I promised you no lectures and no demands. I'm going to keep that promise. But I want you to promise me something."

Again, I didn't say a word. All that ran through my head was that Jack was about to say what I didn't want to hear and that I didn't want to listen to him.

"I want you to promise that you'll think about what I'm about to say. You don't have to decide anything, just think about it. OK?"

After several moments of self-debate, all I could do was nod my head in agreement.

"Thanks." Jack paused as though he had to gather up the courage for what he was about to say to me. Finally, he started. "Jess, I had a meeting with one of the doctors at the hospital today. I don't think you know him. His name is Dr. Robert Thatcher. His specialty is eating disorders, and he's got a national reputation for success with this stuff. He and another doctor wrote a big-selling book on the subject."

"Jack . . ."

"Yeah, Jess."

There was nothing I wanted to say to Jack that we hadn't said to each other many times before. For several moments Jack just held my hands in his as he looked into my eyes. His company soothed me. His touch comforted me. His support, even after all I put him through, made me weepy again.

"Jess . . ."

"Yeah, Jack." I looked into Jack's eyes expecting the "Jess, you have to take care of yourself" speech.

Calmly, Jack said, "We'll get through this."

I squeezed Jack's hand with one hand and caressed his face with the other. It was the first time in months that I saw him smile. Then I thought carefully before I took one of Jack's hands and placed it on the closed top button of my shirt. I had to think about it first because I knew it would lead to him desiring me, but I didn't care. At least, I didn't care at that moment. Jack opened the top button, then the rest of the buttons. Next, he opened the front clasp of my bra and kissed my breasts.

That night, as we climaxed together, it felt as though it was the first time we made love. I wanted to scream out with pleasure, but I was afraid of waking, no, scaring the kids. They had heard enough of my screaming for that day.

We fell asleep in each other's arms. I woke the next morning knowing my situation hadn't changed, but I also had a sense of positive resolve as I made breakfast for Jack and the kids. All I had was coffee. Jack was quiet. I think he was afraid of asking me my decision about seeing the doctor. Just as he put on his coat and got his car keys, I went to hug him and said, "Jack, make the appointment."

His smile beamed from one side of his face to the other as he kissed me goodbye and left without saying a word. The kids left a few moments later. That's when I took my second cup of coffee outside and had two cigarettes before I drove to work.

Jack called me later that morning. He told me I had an appointment with Dr. Thatcher in two weeks.

"Great," I said. What I really wanted to say was, "I don't want to do it."

* * *

Waiting two weeks for something I didn't want to do made the time pass slowly and intolerably. During the first week, I felt myself falling deeper into depression. I spent more time avoiding Jack and the kids. Usually, after Jack got home, I left their dinner on the stove, laid on the bed, and stared aimlessly around the silent and pitch-black bedroom. Millions of thoughts ran through my head. I kept asking myself these questions: "How far can I push and abuse my body with nothing extravagantly serious breaking down? How far do I have to go to put myself out of my fat cow misery? What do I have to do to die?"

I wanted to kill myself or die. Actually, I was hoping I would simply pass out again and fall into an eternal sleep. Death would be my savior, but it wouldn't take me.

During the second week of waiting, my depression became mixed with terror. I was horrified at the thought of being hospitalized again. I was adamant about not going back to an inpatient situation. I was terrorized at the thought of Jack sitting next to me as I divulged all of my secrets to the doctor.

The day before my appointment with Dr. Thatcher, it seemed like nothing made time progress, so I turned to music as a distraction. None of the contemporary artists in my CD or cassette collection captivated me. All of that music was too bland, and I was not in a bland mood. Instead, I went to my "ancient music," which is what my kids called my old vinyl records. All of my albums sat next to my record player, which, miraculously, still worked. Somewhere in those hundred and fifty dust-covered albums, I believed I would find the proper song or songs for my current mental state. After several minutes of searching, I found it. She had just the right voice and just the right lyrics.

The name of the 1973 album was *Laura Nyro—The First Songs*. The song I must have listened to at least fifty times that day was called "And When I Die." I turned on the record player and cued the needle to the top of the song.

I'm not scared of dyin' and I don't really care
If it's peace you find in dyin', well then let the time be here

Jack and my kids meant more to me than anything else in the world. The only thing that would separate me from them would be death. There was no way in hell that I'd let them hospitalize me again and put distance between me and them. No way.

* * *

Jack drove me to Dr. Thatcher's office so we would arrive a half an hour before the appointment. We were veterans and knew I'd have to fill out one of those five-page questionnaires about my medical history and current condition. I listed all of my medications, including the diet pills and laxatives. I wrote that I was previously hospitalized with an eating disorder. I even divulged that I was frequently admitted to the emergency room because of fainting. I wrote that I restricted and purged constantly, and I closed by admitting that my biggest problem was depression.

Finally, the decisive moment arrived when the receptionist said the doctor was ready to see me. At first, Jack remained in his chair. I looked at him like he was out of his mind.

"Jack, I'm not doing this alone."

"Jess, are you sure?"

"The only thing I'm sure of is that I don't want to be here. But, as long as I am, the two of you are going to hear it all at the same time. From here on in, no more secrets."

Jack opened the door for me to enter the doctor's office. Dr. Thatcher, with his thin build and salt-and-pepper hair and full beard, looked like the person I was supposed to see. I was glad he was in his fifties and not a young man. I didn't want to spill my guts to a kid just starting out in practice.

Dr. Thatcher looked at us, shook our hands, and said, "Hello," before we all sat down. At first, he said nothing as he reviewed the questionnaire. It amused me to watch him nod his head several times as he flipped through the pages.

"Well, Mrs. Gordon . . ."

"Jess."

"Well, Jess, how do you feel?"

"I feel like a worthless piece of garbage today, and today's a good day."

"I see," he said without showing any emotion. "Are you still on your antidepressant?"

"Yes."

"Are you still restricting?"

"Yes."

"And purging?"

"Yes."

"How often?"

"As many times as I eat."

"What about the laxatives and diet pills? Are you still abusing them?"

Jack looked into my eyes with shocked wonder, but he said nothing. I looked at him, and then I turned back to Dr. Thatcher. "Yes to both."

"What about the fainting spells?"

"My last one was about two weeks ago."

"And your suicidal thoughts?"

I didn't dare take my eyes off Dr. Thatcher at that point because I was too much of a coward to see Jack's expression. I paused to take a breath before answering, "Yes. I still have them."

"Have you made any attempts?"

"No."

"So these are just thoughts."

"Right. I won't take my own life."

"I see."

Dr. Thatcher paused to jot down several notes. Again, I never took my eyes off him to look at Jack. After what seemed like an eternity, he turned his attention back to me. "Jess, do you consider eating disorders a form of suicide?"

"Yes."

"I see."

For the next thirty minutes, Dr. Thatcher seemed to drill me with questions about my current and past eating disorder problems. All the time he stopped to jot down notes. Each time he paused felt like a rest between rounds of a pugilistic sparring match. I knew the session was about to end and that Dr. Thatcher would go for the knockout punch. I steadied my mind.

"Jess, why are you here?"

"Good question."

"And your answer is . . ."

"Not as good as your question."

"Avoiding it, huh?"

"As best I can."

"But I can't help you if . . ."

"Doctor, don't placate me."

"I didn't think I was."

"You and my husband both think I should go inpatient. Right?"

"Jess, you have all the classic symptoms, and then some."

"I'll tell you the same thing I told my last doctor: I'm not going back!"

"Even if . . ."

"I'll drop dead before I go back."

"That's a possibility."

Those words hit home. "OK, give me a reasonable alternative."

"Fair enough." Dr. Thatcher opened his desk drawer and took out a business card. "Her name is Dr. Marcia Hayes," he said as he handed me her card.

"And what does she do?" I asked without looking at the card.

"She's a nutritionist. She can put you on a plan that would increase your potassium and stabilize your weight."

"So you're saying my choices are inpatient or Dr. Hayes."

"Jess, let's talk about this expression: 'choice point.'"

"What does it mean?"

"There are three points to a choice point triangle. First, your symptoms increase and your health quickly decreases, possibly leading to death. Second, you maintain your status quo, which might also lead to death, only in a slower fashion. Third, you do something to save your life."

"I see."

"I hope you do. The choice is yours."

"Yes, it is."

"Our time is up for today. Would you like to schedule another appointment?"

I looked at Jack. He was looking down at the floor and rubbing both temples on his forehead with one hand.

"OK. Can you see me again this week?"

"Good. Let me see . . ." he said as he checked his calendar. "I can see you on Thursday at this same time. Does that work for you?"

"That's fine."

"Good. Think about the choice points. And please, give Dr. Hayes a call. Tell her I referred you."

"Thanks for today, doc." We all shook hands, and then Jack opened the door to let me out of the office. Not a word passed between the two of us as we headed to the car and then drove home. Even after we got home, neither of us said a word.

I ordered in some pizza for Jack and the kids, then I went upstairs and lay down on the bed. The room quickly darkened after sunset. I never went to sleep. The echoes of my confessions haunted me. Around 10:30, Jack came into the bedroom. He didn't say a word as he washed up and got into bed next to me. After a few moments, he rolled over and kissed me on the cheek.

"Jess."

"Yeah."

"You did OK today."

"Did I?"

"Yeah. I didn't like what I heard, but you were honest with him, and with me. Thanks for that."

"Yeah."

"Jess, no one is going to tell you what to do. All the cards are face up on the table in this win-or-lose situation. All I can say is I'll back whatever decision you make."

"Jack . . ." Suddenly, out of nowhere, I started to cry. I guess the pressure of the day finally took its toll. Jack reached over and held my hand.

"Jess, you showed a great deal of courage today."

I still couldn't say anything. All I managed to do was turn my head to face Jack. "Jess, you'll do what you want to do and have to do. I know that. But there is one thing in this world I never want to do."

I lifted my eyebrows as though to ask, "What?"

"Forgive me for what I'm about to say." Jack paused. "I pray you get through this so I don't have to stand next to the kids as we bury you. Fight it, Jess. Fight it. We'll fight it together." Jack leaned over and kissed my cheek.

"I love you, Jess." Jack never let go of my hand as he fell asleep. He was lucky he had the pleasure of unconsciousness to soothe his distraught mind. I didn't. I was still awake, in my clothes, and reliving my torment when the alarm sounded for me to get up for work.

I prepared breakfast for the kids and left it on the kitchen table before I went upstairs, showered, and dressed for work. Jack came up just before he was about to leave. We didn't say a word. He just hugged me, stared into my eyes, kissed me, and left. The kids were already gone by the time I got downstairs. I got my coat, cigarettes, and coffee, and went outside. The winter sun was unusually strong that morning, so it wasn't too cold. After I finished two cigarettes and my coffee, I went back inside. Dr. Hayes' card was next to the telephone where I left it yesterday. I called and left a message for her to call me at work. She did. We set up an appointment for Thursday before my appointment with Dr. Thatcher.

On Thursday, I went to Dr. Hayes' office without any expectations. Again, I had to fill out one of those long questionnaires. Again, I divulged everything. It didn't matter anymore.

Dr. Hayes was a tall, thin, pretty woman who wore her auburn hair in a French knot. She wore little or no makeup, and she didn't need it. She was quite professional and pleasant with me. She started by asking me about my current dietary plan and raised her eyebrows several times when I told her about my restriction, purging, and my abuse of laxatives and diet pills.

"Mrs. Gordon . . ."

"Jess."

"Jess, Dr. Thatcher has referred many of his eating disorder patients to me. Many of them have been in the same condition you are in now." She took out a piece of paper from her drawer. "Here is a dietary plan that has worked several times."

Dr. Hayes handed me the plan. I looked at the amount of meals per day and the size of the meals. I didn't want to insult her. In my mind, I said, "This lady's crazy if she thinks I'll eat like this, and I'm a fool for paying for this nonsense out of my own pocket without insurance reimbursement. I guess that makes me crazier than her!"

I looked Dr. Hayes straight in the eyes as she said, "Jess, what we have to do is to help you to break this cycle."

"Doctor, if I could break this cycle, I wouldn't be here."

"Are you not willing to?"

"Doctor, with all due respect, it's not that I'm unwilling. I'm incapable. I'm addicted to this lifestyle and I'm incapable of changing it."

"Jess, don't you understand that the alternative is inpatient care?"

"That's one option, but I'll be damned if I'm going to take it. I will not take myself away from my kids and husband. If the eating disorder doesn't kill me, that will."

Those were my last words to Dr. Hayes that day before we said our farewells. Moments later I buckled myself up in the car to prepare to drive to Dr. Thatcher's office. I wondered if all of Dr. Hayes' eating disorder patients were like me, or was I unique.

My second visit with Dr. Thatcher went much like the first, except that Jack wasn't scheduled to be there. It was something that Jack and I had agreed to. Jack felt that as long as I didn't need him there, he didn't have to take off from work. My thinking was that Jack knew everything there was to know. I didn't want to inconvenience him again with the same details. Dr. Thatcher made no headway with me because I gave up no ground toward doing what he wanted. Our only resolution was to agree to see each other again the next week.

My third visit started exactly like the first two sessions. "Jess, how do you feel?"

"I feel like a worthless piece of garbage today, and today's a good day."

"I see," he said again without emotion. "Are you still on your antidepressant?"

"Yes." The rest of the session was just a rehash of the earlier sessions.

I left Dr. Thatcher's office that day knowing it would be almost two weeks before I would see him again. The first thing that got in the way was New Year's. After New Year's he was scheduled to travel to a few cities to promote the book he co-authored, *Never Thin Enough*, which he had given to me as a gift in hopes it might help me. It didn't. I never read past the front cover.

That evening, Jack asked me how the appointment went. I told him that it was the same as the other appointments. Jack tried not to show his disappointment, but I knew him too well for him to hide it. I told him Dr. Thatcher was still suggesting I start inpatient treatment.

"What do you think about that, Jess?"

I answered Jack emphatically, "I'm not going back."

Over the subsequent few weeks before my next appointment, Dr. Thatcher's gentle and persuasive manner generated new thoughts and feelings in my consciousness. I began to admit to realizations that I had previously denied. First, I stopped lying to myself that nothing was wrong and that I was still in recovery when the scale read 90 pounds. Second, I admitted to myself that my eating disorder was nothing more than a slow form of suicide and, unless I did something, I was going to die at any given moment. In fact, I almost did.

Two days before Dr. Thatcher returned from his publicity tour, I passed out again. During each of the previous fainting spells, I never knew exactly how long I was unconscious. I couldn't explain it, but this time felt different. It felt like it took me much longer than usual to open my eyes. Actually, while I was unconscious, part of me hoped I would never open my eyes again. It scared the hell out of me.

Jack found me on the floor and, as usual, took me to the emergency room. That's when the second event happened. I was laying in bed waiting for the routine blood tests and examination to learn that my potassium levels were low. All of a sudden, a nurse two feet away shouted, "Code blue! Code blue!" Being no stranger to a hospital, I understood that the patient next to me had gone into cardiac arrest. Death was no longer a desirable abstract concept. Death was wafting about the unconscious patient next to me behind the cloth curtain. The thought of death coming for me through that cloth curtain and never seeing my kids again made my body shake uncontrollably. Someone shouted, "Clear!" I knew that huge volts of electricity passed through that patient's body to bring it back to life. I reacted as though the paddles were against my breasts and my body writhed as though I was just shocked into consciousness. Moments later I passed out from the emotional trauma. No one knew.

Jack, who had never looked worse in his life, was at my bedside the next morning as I awoke. My release papers were in his hand. He kissed my forehead for several seconds without saying a word. I took his hand and started to cry.

* * *

Chapter Seven

Desperate Times

The drive home from the emergency room was silent, except for the words "Code blue!" and "Clear!" reverberating in my mind. Each time I remembered those words, my body quivered. I thought about dying and never seeing my kids again. I imagined Jack, Megan, and Jason in a cemetery, consoling each other as they stood over my coffin. My depression and desire to die were so emphatic that I wasn't sure if I cared how much misery I would cause the ones I loved the most. It scared the hell out of me to think I had forced my life's journey to this pathetic juncture. I had reached my choice point, and I had to make a decision.

I never did learn if that patient in the emergency room lived or died, but I knew something changed as far as my life was concerned.

Two days later I saw Dr. Thatcher. The session started with the usual question. "Jess, how do you feel?"

"I feel like . . . I feel like . . . something's changed."

"How so?"

"I still feel like a worthless piece of garbage, but I think I'm ready to go inpatient. I don't want to, but I think I better."

"Why?"

"Because I want to die too much. If I had the nerve, I would kill myself."

"Jess, aren't eating disorders a slow form of suicide?"

"No."

I stopped myself from saying another word. For the past several months, I had consciously hoped I would die from my eating disorder. I remembered asking myself, "How far do I have to push my body until I finally die? How far do I have to go to put myself out of my fat cow misery? What do I have to do to die?"

I could see Dr. Thatcher's eyes focused squarely on my eyes as though he could read the thoughts going through my mind. After several moments of silence, I looked directly into Dr. Thatcher's eyes and whispered, "You're right."

"Jess, what else has changed?"

"I want . . ." It was difficult to say the words. I took a few deep breaths to exhale some of the depression, humiliation, anxiety, and worthlessness I felt about myself. I stared at the floor so as not to see any judgmental expression on Dr. Thatcher's face. "I want to see my kids grow up. Going inpatient is the only way that will happen."

The rest of the session was different from any of the other sessions because Dr. Thatcher immediately gave me the names and telephone numbers of two hospitals to contact. The first was Springdale Hospital in New Jersey. The second was Queensland Hospital in Pennsylvania. I asked him about the New York hospital I was in almost fifteen years ago, and he informed me that it no longer existed. I also asked if there were any qualified centers in New York, and he told me there weren't any.

Just before the session ended, Dr. Thatcher repeated his question, "Jess, what else has changed?"

I had no answer. "What do you mean?"

"Jess, what else has changed?"

I took several moments for reflection. Then it dawned on me. He must have known what I was about to say because I saw a small smile on his face as I once again stared him straight in the eyes and finally responded, "I want to save my life. I've made a decision not to kill myself."

"Exactly," he said with a look of satisfaction and success on his face.

* * *

When Jack got home, he was elated when I told him what had happened at my therapy session. He couldn't stop hugging me, kissing me, and telling me how proud of me he was for my decision to go inpatient. That night we didn't make love, but he held me in his arms as we fell asleep together.

The next morning I decided to stay home from work in order to get on the phone with the two hospitals. I wanted to act quickly before I changed my mind. I called Springdale Hospital first. A receptionist answered. "Springdale Hospital. How can I help you?"

I took a deep breath to summon up some courage and said, "Hello, my name is Mrs. Jessica Gordon. I'd like some information about your eating disorder program."

"Certainly. One moment please."

The receptionist put me on hold. Within seconds, I heard a man's voice. "Hello, Mrs. Gordon. My name is Dr. Barrow. I'm the director of the Eating Disorder Unit."

"Oh, hello." I was a little startled and almost intimidated that the director took my call. I was expecting the receptionist to get back to me. "Dr. Barrow, I'm looking for some information about your program."

"Certainly. Who is the patient?"

"Me."

"I see. Well, this unit has been in operation under my direction for the past twelve years. We have found that when the patient wants to be helped, we have an extremely high success rate."

"Very good. How does Springdale Hospital differ from Queensland Hospital?"

"Both are very fine programs. Our biggest difference is how we handle our daily therapy sessions."

"How so?"

"Most hospital group-therapy sessions deal with a patient talking for a few seconds, or a few minutes. We found that patients listening to other patients in an in-depth therapy session provides greater help to the person talking, and the people listening."

"I see."

"Otherwise, our programs are very similar, except we pride ourselves on having exceptional chefs. You know, the better the food tastes . . ."

Dr. Barrow chuckled, paused, and asked, "Mrs. Gordon, how long have you had an eating disorder problem?"

"Between one and two years, this time."

"This time?"

"Yes. I was inpatient with an eating disorder problem fifteen years ago. I was in recovery for over thirteen years. During that time, I gave birth to two children, worked, and led what most people would consider a normal life with normal eating patterns. Now I'm watching my life spiral out of control."

"I see. What is your current status?"

"In regard to . . .?"

"Your eating disorder."

"I'm anorexic, bulimic, I abuse laxatives and diet pills, I'm extremely depressed, and I suffer from suicidal thoughts. However, I've never taken any actions toward those thoughts, and I'm under a doctor's care."

"What's the doctor's name?"

"Dr. Thatcher. His office is here on Long Island."

"Is that the same Dr. Thatcher who is the co-author of *Never Thin Enough*?"

"Yes. In fact, he recommended your program."

"Splendid. Mrs. Gordon, we can help you. When would you like to come in?"

I wasn't prepared for that question. "Come in? You mean check myself into your hospital?"

"Exactly."

"Dr. Barrow, thank you. But I need to make a few calls and think about this."

"Mrs. Gordon, you need help. We can help you."

"Thank you, Dr. Barrow. I'll get back to you."

"Very good. I hope to hear from you soon. Good luck, and have a good day, Mrs. Gordon."

"Thank you." I hung up the phone and started to shake because I was losing my nerve. The realization of leaving Jack, Megan, and Jason for an extended period drove me crazy. I poured myself a cup of coffee and lit a cigarette at the kitchen table. That in itself was unusual because I always smoked outside the house for fear that Jack would smell the smoke and give me a hard time. Since Jack and the kids were not going to be home for hours, I didn't care. Within a few minutes, I lit my second cigarette and called Queensland Hospital. A receptionist picked up and I started with the same request for information about their program. This time, instead of the director of the unit getting on the phone, the receptionist fielded my questions. She answered all of my questions politely and professionally, but it didn't have the impact that Dr. Barrow's conversation had. I was impressed that he had taken the time to try to help me.

That night when Jack got home, I talked about my impression of the two hospitals. I told him I wanted to enter the Springdale program and that I didn't want to put it off. It was Thursday night. Jack wanted to stay home from work on Friday so he could drive me out to New Jersey while Megan and Jason were in school. I made a counteroffer of Saturday. Jack hugged me, told me he loved me at least ten times, and agreed. We didn't make love that night, but once again Jack hugged me as we went to sleep together. It felt wonderful to be in his arms. I felt at peace. I felt scared.

* * *

The next morning I called Springdale. Again, the receptionist picked up. I had a hard time saying, "Hi, this is Mrs. Gordon."

"One moment, please."

"Sure."

Within seconds, Dr. Barrow said, "Mrs. Gordon, I'm glad you called."

"Dr. Barrow, how nice of you to take my call."

"Mrs. Gordon . . ."

"Jess."

"Jess, I'm here to help you."

"Thank you. I appreciate that. I've decided to enter your program. Can I check in tomorrow?"

"I'll be here. You made a wise decision."

"I hope so."

"Pack a suitcase with your necessities."

"I can't believe I'm doing this again."

"Jess, you are doing the right thing."

"Thank you, Dr. Barrow. I'll see you tomorrow."

"Excellent."

We hung up. I lit another cigarette, poured another cup of coffee, and started to shake at the realization of what I had just committed myself to do. I knew I had to take this step. It was either this step, or death.

* * *

Friday was an excruciating day for me. As soon as Jack, Megan, and Jason were out of the house, I went to the kitchen, poured my first cup of coffee, and lit my first in a series of chain-smoked cigarettes. "Out of control" would have been a kind way of describing my condition. I tried testing myself to see if I could actually eat something and hold it in. I prepared a slice of toast, put a hint of butter on it, cut it in half, threw one half in the garbage, and ate the other half. Thirty seconds later, I felt nauseatingly full. I ran upstairs to the bathroom, shoved one finger down my throat, and purged the toast and coffee. My emotions were negatively rampant. In about twenty-four hours, I would be in a hospital dining room with a full meal in front of me, and I would be expected to finish it without the ability to purge it if I felt too full. Within minutes I was upstairs rummaging through my various hiding places and chugging down a handful of laxatives and diet pills. I wasn't appeased. I made another pot of coffee and chain-smoked another half a pack of cigarettes over the next two hours. By 11:00 I was upstairs and popping pills again. When I got back to the kitchen, it smelled like an ashtray, so I opened the windows and turned on the ceiling fan.

My feelings of anxiety, self-doubt, self-hate, and worthlessness were higher than any other time in my life. Suddenly I started shaking and I felt my heart racing. I remembered the old cliché of someone's life passing before their eyes just as they are about to die, because that is what was happening to me. All of the memories were negative except for meeting Jack and giving birth to my kids. God, how I love those three. Instinctively, I laid down on the kitchen floor. I thought: "I finally did enough damage to myself to die by my own actions, and I don't care. At least I won't have to face the inpatient program." I lost consciousness just as my face touched the cold, tiled floor.

It must have been at least two or three minutes before I opened my eyes. I was depressed that I was still alive. Slowly I dragged myself into the chair to regain some strength. For thirty minutes, I just sat there. Finally, I had the strength to stand. I called Jack and told him I was having a hard time, but I didn't say a word about passing out because I knew he would run out of work and drag me off to the emergency room.

Jack was his usual self. He reassured me that I was taking the proper actions by going inpatient, and that today's anxiety was probably normal for my situation. He hung up after telling me he loved me.

I lit a cigarette and went for the phone book. There was only one person who could talk with me with any real understanding of my condition. I found the number and called it as I prayed the number was still in service. I heard one ring, then the second, and then I heard her voice. With great trepidation and fear of embarrassment, I managed to whisper, "Kylie?"

"Yes."

"This is your long-lost rotten friend who is being hunted by the food police."

"Jess. Is that you?"

"Kylie, please don't hate me. I hate myself enough for the two of us."

"Oh, Jess. I missed you."

"Thanks for not hanging up on me. I would have deserved it."

"OK, sister. What's going on? You sound like shit."

"I'm going inpatient again tomorrow. I feel so worthless."

"Jess, has the depression led to suicidal thoughts?"

"Yes."

"Besides restricting, have you started purging?"

"Yes."

"Laxatives and diet pills?"

"Yes."

"Passing out and seeing the floor when you open your eyes."

"Yes."

"Welcome to my hell. Jess, that's where I was when you met me. That was how long ago?"

"About fifteen years."

"Damn. It seems much longer than that."

"Kylie, where are you now with this stuff?"

"I fell apart about five years ago and did a third stint. I didn't want to go. All I wanted to do was die. I guess I felt like you do now. But I went, I broke the cycle, and I've been OK for the past five years."

"Where did you go?"

"Springdale, in New Jersey."

"That's where I'm going tomorrow."

"Dr. Barrow, huh?"

"Yeah."

"He's a good guy. He cares. They'll help you. Then it's up to your therapy sessions outside the hospital. That's a crucial element for recovery."

"Kylie, I passed out this afternoon. I didn't want to wake up."

"Yeah, kid, I know. Been there and done that. But listen, you can get through this. You can put yourself back together."

"I don't think so."

"Jess, I know you. You can do it. Break the cycle."

"I couldn't even eat a half a piece of toast today without purging it."

"That's today. Tomorrow, you'll have food police patrolling your every bite. Hey, you don't want to lose your privileges, do you?"

"Actually, this time I'm more concerned about losing my life."

"It's a package deal, Jess. Keep your privileges and you'll save your life. Jess, I'm so happy you called me."

"Desperate times called for desperate measures. Kylie, you're terrific."

We must have talked for two to three hours. It was the best therapy imaginable for me. By the end of our conversation, Kylie had almost convinced me that my life had value and meaning. I kissed the phone before placing it back on the cradle, then I just stood there for a few minutes until I finally let go of the phone and went outside for a cigarette before packing my suitcase for tomorrow's journey to an undesirable territory.

A few hours later, I had dinner with Jack and the kids. Two minutes after the table was cleared, I snuck up to the bathroom, put my face in the toilet, stuck my finger down my throat, and heaved my guts up. The taste of the vomit was repulsive. As I rinsed my mouth, I prayed it was the last time I would taste my vomit for that reason, but I didn't feel confident.

When Jack and I got into bed, he said he wanted to make love to me. I kissed him and started to cry. I wanted him to hold me, to give me his strength, but there was no way I could feel sexual pleasure with him on the eve of my inpatient agony. I explained that to him. As usual, he was his loving self. We cuddled into each other's arms and fell asleep silently.

I woke at 4:30, went downstairs to make a pot of coffee, and went outside for my first cup of coffee and a cigarette as Jack and the kids slept. Mixed emotions tortured me. I wanted help, but not at the price of losing my husband and kids for an extended period. The thought of being away from them for any amount of time was excruciatingly painful. Jack came downstairs just before sunrise. He came outside with his cup of coffee and was kind enough not to chastise me for smoking. Little did he know it was the tenth cigarette of the morning. He took my hand, kissed my cheek, and we watched the sunrise together. As the sunrise started to climax, I squeezed Jack's hand and said, "I pray this is the sunrise of a new and better life for all of us. Jack, you're the best in the world."

* * *

Jack and I drove Megan and Jason to each of their friends' homes. Each time, I hugged each kid as though I were never going to see Megan or Jason again. I remember Megan saying, "Mom, I hope you feel better soon." When I hugged Jason I lost control and started to cry. My little man said, "Don't worry, Mommy, the doctors will make you all better."

"Sure, honey. I love you."

"I love you too, Mommy."

I got into the car and closed the door. Jack pushed the button to lock the doors. The sound reminded me of jailers locking prisoners into their cells. My whole body shook from panic. Thankfully, Jack didn't notice. Suddenly, each of those sixty days and 180 meals replayed themselves vividly in my mind as Jack drove us closer and closer to my next imprisonment in New Jersey. Tears streamed down my face. Jack reached over and held my hand. Except for a few moments, he tried to hold my hand the entire time during the nearly two-hour ride from Long Island to New Jersey.

We were about twenty minutes away from the hospital when Jack got off to fill up with gas. The attendant saw me crying, so I quickly turned my head away. I was embarrassed and ashamed of myself. One thought ran through my head: "How long will I be away from my kids and my husband?" I didn't know. I never asked Dr. Barrow how long the program took. I felt stupid for not asking such a basic question.

Fifteen minutes later Jack turned into a side road. We could see a modern-looking medical facility. Although the building consisted of mostly glass walls, I imagined it to be a prison. Jack parked. When we got out of the car Jack started for my suitcase on the back seat. "Jack, leave it there."

"But, Jess . . ."

"Please. If I decide to stay, you can always come out for it."

"What do you mean, 'decide to stay?' I thought . . ."

"Honey, please. Let me do this my way."

"OK, Jess," he said as he came around the car, took my hand, and started to walk toward the entrance several yards away.

My knees felt like they were going to buckle and I'd fall to the ground from the anxiety. We walked slowly into the entrance. Jack spoke with an obviously overweight male security guard. "We're to here to see Dr. Barrow." He looked immediately at me and gave me a polite little smile. I stared into his eyes. It's as though they said, "Here's another woman starving herself to death." I said nothing.

"Dr. Barrow's office is on the second floor," he said with a customer-service type of smile. "It's down the main corridor and on the right. You can't miss it."

"Thanks," Jack responded, then he led me to the elevator.

I felt like a condemned prisoner being led to an execution chamber. We got into the elevator, got off at the second floor, very slowly walked down the corridor, and arrived at a glass door with Dr. Barrow's name printed in painted black letters. Jack opened the door without letting go of my hand. My knees buckled slightly. Jack noticed. "Jess, you're doing the right thing."

"Then why do I feel like crap?"

Jack closed the door and let go of my hand only to put his arms around me and hug me. He kissed my cheek.

"Jess, I know this is tough for you. It's tough for me, too. I don't want to be away from you, and I wish to God we didn't have to be here. But being here means you'll get better and get over this stuff. I don't want to lose you."

The image of Jack, Megan, and Jason standing over my grave flashed into my memory. "OK, Jack. Let's do this. Let's start it and get it over with."

Jack opened the door again and we entered Dr. Barrow's waiting room.

Dr. Barrow's receptionist smiled when she saw us. It made me nauseated how everyone smiled at us as though this was a wedding reception or some other happy occasion. "Hello. And you are . . . ?"

"This is my wife, Jessica Gordon. She's here to see Dr. Barrow."

"Oh, yes. We spoke on the phone. How nice to see you."

"Nice," I said to myself. Is she oblivious as to why I'm here? "Nice to meet you. Is Dr. Barrow available?"

"Yes," she responded. "But first, I'll need you to fill out these forms and answer this questionnaire."

"Sure."

"Have a seat and take as much time as you need. Oh, and I'll need to copy your insurance card."

Jack handed her our insurance card. I took the clipboard, sat down, and started the irksome task of answering absurd and privacy-invading questions. Twenty minutes later I handed the still-smiling receptionist the completed paperwork. She looked it over as though grading me on a test, shook her head with approval, made a few notations, asked us to have a seat again, and picked up the phone. "Dr. Barrow, Mrs. Gordon is ready to see you now." There was a short pause before she said, "Very good."

It impressed me that Dr. Barrow opened his office door so quickly to meet us. "Mrs. Gordon, how nice to meet you."

Dr. Barrow looked like a doctor. Even if he wasn't wearing his white coat and you saw him on the street, you would guess that he was a physician. He wore a dark suit, white shirt, solid blue tie, and wingtip shoes. His mostly grayish hair was impeccably cut, as was his beard.

"Nice to meet you, Dr. Barrow. This is my husband, Jack."

Dr. Barrow shook my hand, then he shook Jack's hand. "Please, come in. Let's talk."

He led us into his office and toward two plush leather chairs. After closing the door, he proceeded to his desk and sat down. At first he reviewed my paperwork, then he looked at me directly and said, "Mrs. Gordon, I notice you don't have a suitcase."

"Well, Dr. Barrow, I planned on meeting with the doctors at Queensland Hospital later on today. I still haven't made up my mind as to which facility to enter."

"I see. Well, let's see if we can persuade you to stay here."

"Do your best, Dr. Barrow. At this moment, I don't want to go inpatient here or there. I'm scared. I'm horrified. I have no idea how long I'll be away from my husband and kids, and I hate that feeling."

"Your feelings and concerns are appropriate. First, let's start with the amount of time. The most you can be here is twenty days, but this is January, so I doubt you'll use your full insurance time during this stay. And let's hope this is the only stay you'll need."

"I don't understand. The last program I attended lasted thirty days."

"Yes, but insurance policies have changed since then. Now, medical coverage for this procedure lasts a maximum of twenty days in a calendar year."

"And you think that's enough time to get me into recovery?"

"Well, it won't just be your time here. When you are discharged from here, you'll go into an outpatient therapy program. Simply put, we break the cycle; they work to keep it broken."

"And you find this works?"

"Yes."

"What is your success rate?"

"At least 80 percent."

"Twenty percent failure. That's a large number."

"It's up to the individual."

"Do you think I'll be part of the eighty or twenty percent?"

"Mrs. Gordon . . ."

"Jess."

"Jess, you're in a serious condition. We are here to help you if you are ready to be helped. Do you think you're ready?"

"I think so. I think I have to do something."

"You're right. You have two kids who need their mother."

"Perhaps that's why I shouldn't stay here, or anywhere."

"You misunderstood my meaning. Jess, we want you to stay here."

"Thank you. But, like I said . . ."

"Jess, let me rephrase that. Based on our conversation and your paper-work, you need to come in here. Now."

I turned my eyes away from Dr. Barrow and stared out his window at the trees surrounding the hospital. He didn't have to say the words, but I was sure of his intended meaning. He was thinking that if I left his office without committing to the program, I'd get back in the car, not go to Queensland, and continue my self-destructive pattern. I didn't look at Jack, but I felt his eyes were watching me and waiting for my decision. The journey to my choice point was over. Slowly, and reluctantly, I turned back to Dr. Barrow. "OK."

"Thank you, Jess. We'll do everything possible to help you."

"I hope you're successful."

"I hope we're both successful." I turned to Jack, "Well, here we go again. Honey, would you mind getting the suitcase?"

Jack leaned over and kissed me. "It would be my pleasure. Thank you. You did the right thing."

"I hope so."

"Jess, I'll leave you two alone for a moment so you can say goodbye. Mr. Gordon, you can hand off the suitcase with reception. They'll get it up to Jess' room." Dr. Barrow got up from behind his desk and approached Jack. Jack stood and extended his hand to Dr. Barrow. "It was nice to meet you," Jack said.

"Nice meeting you, too."

"Take good care of my girl."

"That's what we're here for." Dr. Barrow closed the door behind him when he left his office. I was still seated. I didn't have the energy to stand. Jack knelt down on his knees in front of me. "Jess, you can do this."

"You have more faith in me than I do."

"The time will pass quickly, and you'll be better."

"I wish I had your confidence."

Jack stood, leaned toward me, kissed my lips a few seconds, took my hands into his hands, and said, "Call me when you can. Jess, I love you."

"Take good care of Megan and Jason."

"No problem. Ready?"

"No, but yes."

Jack held my hand as we left the office. Dr. Barrow was waiting for us in his reception room. "Jess, I'll show you to your room."

"Wonderful."

Jack hugged me and said, "I'll get your suitcase. See you soon."

"Yeah."

Millions of thoughts ran through my head as we waited for the elevator. I still couldn't believe I was back in this situation. I wondered what my room-mate would be like. I dreaded that first meal. I longed for all of my pills, and I was dying for a cigarette.

My room had southern exposure, so the late-afternoon sun poured into the room as Dr. Barrow opened the vertical shades. "I always love the view of the forest this time of day." My eyes quickly inspected the room. There were two beds; one had clothes on it. There were also two dressers, two plain wooden chairs, and a sink with a fine strainer over the drain. There was, of course, no bathroom or shower.

My suitcase arrived within a few minutes. Without asking my permission, the attendant who brought my suitcase just opened it and searched it for any prohibited items. Of course, he found nothing. I was no novice to this routine, so I left my paraphernalia home in their secret hiding places. When he came to my carton of cigarettes, Dr. Barrow interjected, "Smoking is only outdoors."

"No problem."

The attendant's eyes turned toward me and focused on my purse.

While handing it to him, I said, "Of course." He checked it, cleared it, and handed it back to me. The ritual was over.

Dr. Barrow extended his hand and said, "Good luck, Jess."

I shook his hand and said, "I'm here to give it my best shot."

"Good. Dinner is served at six. Therapy follows dinner."

"Wonderful. I can't wait." Dr. Barrow and I shook hands, and then he turned and started toward the door. I called out, "Dr. Barrow . . ." I paused a few seconds.

"Yes."

"Thanks for convincing me to stay here. I don't want to be here, but I know it's the right thing to do."

"And you're right. Let us help you help yourself."

"That's a deal."

"Excellent. See you at therapy after dinner."

"OK."

For several minutes, I stared into the leafless forest. My dominant thought was to get the hell out of there. "Screw this," I said to myself. "I want to be with my family and in an environment where I'm comfortable. Chuck it all. I'll just go off the deep end." At that point I had to sit down. All sights and sounds were blocked from my consciousness. I don't know how long it took until someone knocking on my open door broke into my active thoughts. "Yes."

"Mrs. Gordon . . ."

"Yes. Call me Jess."

"Mrs. Teac will see you in ten minutes."

"And she is . . . ?"

"Oh, sorry. She's our nutritionist. She's in room two nineteen."

"Thank you."

Ten minutes later I was seated in front of Mrs. Teac's desk. She was on the heavy side with huge breasts that surged through her white coat. She wore thick makeup to cover her age-related wrinkles. I sat patiently before her as she reviewed my file, then said, "Mrs. Gordon . . ."

"Jess."

"Jess, how much have you been eating recently?"

"Almost nothing."

"I see. Well, we'll start you off on a 1,200-calorie plan and work you up from there. You'll have a choice for each meal. Just fill out the next meal's menu at each meal. Do you have any questions?"

"No. I know the routine."

"Very good. The best of luck to you."

I smirked as I said, "Thank you." I thought to myself as I returned to my room, "Yesterday I couldn't keep down a half a slice of toast. How the hell am I going to keep down a full meal?"

Except for one or two staff members, the corridor was empty, as was my room when I returned and sat in the chair. The solitude and silence didn't last long before voices of many women broke in. One of those voices said, "Hello," as my new roommate entered our room. "I'm Claire Johnson."

"Jess Gordon."

"Welcome."

"Thanks."

Claire was extremely unkempt. It looked like her shoulder-length hair hadn't seen a brush for days. Of course, she was thin, and she was obviously several years older than I was. I was glad about that. I was concerned they would put me with a teenage girl and that we would have nothing in common.

It was an hour before dinner. Claire and I started introducing ourselves. I hoped I could form a friendship with her similar to my friendship with Kylie. However, when Claire started explaining that she had no idea of why she was there, all expectations of a future friendship waned.

"All I did was lose a bunch of weight," Claire said. "Now, they have me away from my daughter and husband for no good reason."

Claire was in complete denial of her eating disorder. I remembered how I was the same way when I entered my first inpatient situation. Then again, I was first learning what eating disorders were all about back then. I remembered when Kylie first defined bulimia for me. Now, I was an advanced practitioner. That made me think, "I'm back with my sisters. I wonder what new techniques I'll discover in these therapy sessions."

The more Claire spoke, the more I considered her not all there mentally. The expression "space cadet" came to mind, but I didn't mention it to her. My final thought before the dinner chimes sounded was, "Lady, you're an amateur compared to where I am at this point."

"Well, time to face the food," I said.

The dining room was just down the hall. When I walked through the door an attendant told me my seating position. Each person was assigned a permanent seat so they would know who you are and the meal you would be served. After only a few seconds of waiting, the moment of truth had arrived. It was time to face my enemy, battle it, and conquer it. Placed before me was a dish filled with chicken and a baked potato. A second plate with salad and a third plate with bread and butter surrounded my main course. It took at least a minute or two before I picked up my knife and fork. I could feel the eyes of the attendants watching until I put the first piece of food into my mouth. By the second bite I was feeling full. I put my knife and fork down onto my plate. Again I felt all eyes on me. One attendant, like a prison guard, started to approach me. Then the woman next to me noticed what I did and said, "Keep going. They'll let you get away with not finishing your first meal, but they're pretty strict. You'll have to finish the rest of your meals."

"Yeah, I know the routine. This is not my first time in one of these places. Thanks."

The attendant backed off. I guess she thought to herself, "She got filled in. No sense in pushing the point further."

By the time coffee and tea were served, I had finished half of my meal. Considering where I was before that night, I actually felt quite successful. I knew what was expected of me and, no matter how difficult it would be to accomplish that goal, I wanted to do the right thing.

As usual, all the bathroom doors were locked when we exited the dining room. I followed the crowd of women into the evening therapy room and took a seat in the rear. It slipped my mind that I didn't have to be concerned about volunteering any conversation or thoughts. The session began the moment the last woman took her seat.

"Good evening. We have some new faces here tonight, so I'll say a few words about our evening therapy program. All of our participants are involved on a voluntary basis. We believe in detailed group therapy sessions. Our volunteers submit written answers to our background questionnaire. Each night we try to delve into one person's background and behavior. We try to help them to see something new within their character with the hope they can modify, or eliminate, negative actions or behavior patterns. Either you are the voluntary patient in an in-depth therapy session, or you are the proverbial 'flies on the wall.' Our objective is for you to learn about yourselves through other patients' lifestyles, experiences, and current situations. Anyone interested in becoming a volunteer can pick up a blank questionnaire at the end of this session. I'll ask you all to hold your comments and questions to our Q&A time. Let's begin. Tonight we'll be talking with Sara."

Sara looked like she was about five foot three. She didn't look emaciated, which surprised me. I learned later that she exercised frequently and religiously and that she bulked up with muscle. For someone so young, she had an extremely sad face.

"Good evening, Sara."

"Good evening, Dr. Barrow."

"Sara, when was the first time you were involved with restriction or bulimia?"

"I don't know. I don't remember."

"How old are you now?"

"Twenty-one."

"Were you ever at a heavy weight?"

"Yes. At ten I was heavy. I was chubby, but I didn't look like what I weighed. I never did that. If you looked at me, you wouldn't say she's 202 pounds. Like, I was tall, I carried . . . I'm big boned, so it's not like I was fat. I was fat. But it's not like I was a roly-poly. You know?"

"How tall are you?"

"Five seven and a half."

"When did you start dropping down from the 202?"

"When I was like twelve years old. I did it in a healthy way. I didn't restrict. I just ate the right way. If I wanted something, I would have it. If I gained a pound, it would come off. But nothing to the extreme. The extreme, oh yeah, the extreme came when I was sixteen."

"Define 'the extreme.'"

"Oh, I went on this crazed diet. Three eggs a day and three grapefruits and water and coffee. That's how it started, and that's how I lost all the weight. I lost, like, a lot of weight. 100 pounds. Maybe 125 pounds. And just from there, it was always diets, diets, diets, diets, got to lose weight, got to lose weight. And that's it."

"What do you think prompted going into that extreme situation?"

"I just couldn't deal with myself no more. The fact that I couldn't deal with this fat on my body no more. It's disgusting."

"When was the first time you saw a therapist?"

"When I was . . . I don't know. When I was nineteen, maybe. Yeah, I was nineteen."

"So you saw a therapist three years after you hit that first extreme."

"Yeah. Well, like the bulimia and the real restriction and the obsessive thoughts and all that shit didn't come until I was nineteen. That's when it came into play."

"What happened when you were nineteen?"

"I don't know. I have no clue. I don't know at all. Just the fact that I wanted to lose weight. I got thin, and I wanted to get thinner and thinner and thinner and thinner and thinner."

"In your mind, was there a person you wanted to be like?"

"No. Just bones. That's it. Just thin. I wanted to see bones. I wanted to look emaciated. I still want to look like that."

"Have you ever gone through bouts of depression?"

"Yeah. When I first started losing, losing, losing. That was three years ago. That's when the depression kicked in. It was a horrible feeling. I just didn't want to do nothing. You just feel like there's a cloud over your head. You don't want to go nowhere. You just don't give a shit about anything. It's as if you have no hopes or nothing. I just think, 'Let death just come already. Let me just die already. Let me just get really, really anorexic and just die.'"

"Where do you think the depression came from?"

"The doctors say it was because of the lack of nutrition and obsessing over the weight loss and all that. 'Til this day, I'm in depression. I'm in and out of it."

"What kind of medication do you take?"

"They put me on Prozac, and then I stopped taking medication because it makes you get fat. It makes you get happy. And happiness equals fat. So, I don't go near medication."

"Why do you think, 'Happiness equals fat?'"

"Because everyone who is happy is fat, and when you're happy, you're eating food. And when people eat food, they get fat."

"Do you have thoughts of suicide?"

"Yeah. Always. I, ah, there are points in my day when I can't get through it no more. I'll never . . . I don't have the nerve to actually commit suicide, but . . . I'm too afraid to do it myself. I can't cut myself or anything but . . . sometimes I just pray to God that I won't wake up in the morning. Just take me because I can't go through another battle. Every day is a battle."

"What are you fighting?"

"My eating disorder. Not even fighting with it. Just dealing with it because I can't escape it."

"When you look in the mirror, what do you see?"

"A fat person. I'm fat. I'm huge. I look in the mirror . . . I can't even look at myself in the mirror no more. I see a chipmunk face. I see a big jelly stomach. Ooh, I can't. I don't see anything that's thin."

"What got you into therapy for your eating disorder?"

"My brain may have got me there. When I started throwing up . . . when I felt like I ate a little bit too much and I would throw up, it got to the point where I knew there was something wrong, and I told my mother I needed help. And that's when I started seeing a therapist."

"How did that go?"

"With that dumb thing? She was horrible. She just stared at me. I spoke to her and she just looked at me. That lasted for two months. Then I found another therapist for almost a year and a half, and then she told me she couldn't treat me no more. She told me, 'You're crazy.' Then I went to another place in New Jersey. They told me . . . they told me they couldn't help me no more because I was too crazy for them. So, I told them to go fuck themselves and I left. I was there for like a month."

"It got you angry. Didn't it?"

"Yeah."

"What's interesting is that you kept going. You kept seeking help instead of just quitting the idea of therapy. You kept going."

"Yeah."

"Do you think it might mean you were seeking survival?"

"But I'm not seeking survival."

"Do you attend therapy because you want to? Are you here because you want to be here?"

"I honestly don't know why I'm here or go to therapy. I'm never going to give up my eating disorder. It's my life. If I give up my eating disorder I'll get fat, and I can't do that."

"Are you anorexic or bulimic?"

"I hear that I'm anorexic bulimic because I restrict a lot and I don't binge. If I eat something I feel I'll gain weight from, I throw it up, and then I have to exercise. Hypergymnasia . . . I have that."

"How much do you exercise a week?"

"A lot. I work out six days a week, sometimes seven, two hours in the morning, and then an hour at night."

"What type of exercise do you do?"

"I do cardio and weight training at a gym."

"What is your favorite exercise?"

"Running."

"How do you feel after exercising?"

"Good. I mean, my mind feels good, but the pain in my body . . . I have to run ten miles a day. It's ten miles a day 'cause I have OCD, too. So if it's not, like, planned out properly, it won't come out right. So I have to run ten miles a day. My mind feels better that I did it, but my body is wrecked."

"How does the OCD show itself?"

"I have to go to the gym in the morning and at night. If I don't, I feel like I'm going to gain weight. I have to run ten miles. I have to keep on asking people if I've gained weight, or if I've lost weight. I have to always check my bones in the mirror. My hip bones, my spinal cord, my shoulder bones, my collarbone, I have to always check them out."

"When do they look right to you?"

"If they're coming out, if they're sticking out, that's the way I want them to look."

"The more you see your bones, the more success you feel?"

"Yeah. They'll make me feel good for like a couple of minutes of my day."

"What happens on those days when they are not as sharp?"

"I feel like shit. I don't want to know nobody. I don't want to know nothing. I just want to sit in my bed. I sit home. I don't go out. That's it. I'm fat. I won't go out."

"Are you in a relationship now?"

"No. I can't give my time or my energy to anyone else. It has to be for me. I have to go to bed early. I have to wake up early. I have to get my workout in. I can't have someone else take up my time."

"What kind of work do you do?"

"I do reception work. It's convenient because I can go in at 1:00 or at 3:00. It's two days a week from 3:00 to 7:00 and three days a week from 1:00 to

7:00. So I still get my morning workouts in and I get my night workouts in. So it works for my schedule."

"Do you have any ideas for future work?"

"No. I don't think I'm going to be around in the future."

"What do you think will take your life?"

"My eating disorder."

"How?"

"Because I already feel it. I feel like I'm losing."

"What symptoms do you suffer from?"

"My teeth are a mess. I have caps. I have root canals. My teeth are all eroded. My hair falls out. I have osteopenia in my spine. It's a bone thing. I usually don't get my period. The last time I had it was like two months ago. The time I got it before that was like a year ago. So I don't get a period. My body aches. I get dizzy. I get light-headed. My ankles hurt. My feet hurt. I can't walk sometimes. I just keep on pushing myself and pushing myself."

"With those body pains, especially in the ankles, how do you get through ten miles of running?"

"I take Advil and put patches on my ankles."

"Do you have any triggers?"

"Yeah."

"Tell me about them."

"When people eat, I can't take the noises when they eat. It makes me, like, I want to throw up. That may trigger me to throw up–if they're making noises while they're eating. If they're sitting down, if I see something, like they're fat, it makes me feel crazy. It may make me want to throw up, or I'll have to restrict. I snap very easily. I'll be fine one second, and if someone makes a noise and, like, I don't know, it makes me just want to stick my fingers down my throat and get stuff up. I don't even have to stick my fingers down my throat. All I have to do is like exhale a little bit and it brings stuff up. Yeah. Sometimes all I have to do is cough and it brings things up. Yeah. Once, I was in my car and I was driving to the gym. I just got out of work. I coughed and this asparagus just came shooting out of my mouth."

"What types of foods do you eat? How often?"

"I eat vegetables–a normal serving. A serving of fruit. A protein. A tablespoon of fat oil. And, that's it."

"How often?"

"Every day."

"Once a day? Twice a day?"

"Oh! All divided up. Like, for breakfast, I'll eat an egg. After gym I'll have a cup of fruit. Then, for lunch, I'll have some asparagus. At 3:00 I'll have a cup of carrots. And then by 5:00, I'll have–if I didn't have my fat in the morning with my egg white, I'll have it with one of my vegetable servings. On the other hand, maybe I'll have a fat-free yogurt, or a no-sugar, fat-free frozen yogurt."

"How often do you purge?"

"It depends. Normally it happens when I'm feeling anxiety, or when I feel like I want to eat something and throw it up. It could be three times a week or four times a week. Or, it could be that two weeks go by and I didn't throw up."

"Do you ever binge?"

"A binge to me is like eating a candy bar. Two candy bars. That's like a binge. That's like, holy shit, I'm going to gain pounds. That's a binge for me."

"How often do you do that?"

"It happens, like, sporadically, like maybe once a month."

"What do you think brings that feeling on?"

"I don't know, but I don't like it, and after that . . . That's why I try to stay away from that, because the next day I don't feel like myself. I feel like shit. I feel like I let the fat person come out of me. And I won't . . . That's why I try to stay away from the binge. Like the binge is something that I don't like. Like, it's OK if I take a bite of a cookie because I know I won't gain weight from that. And I can throw it up."

"How long after you eat do you purge?"

"Oh, like, right after. Maybe fifteen minutes. If someone's there and I can't throw it up, I'll throw it up in my room in buckets, in bags, and then I'll go to the dumpster and throw it out."

"What is your relationship with your scale?"

"My scale? My mother threw it out on me because I was obsessed with it. I know I have more muscle on me now than I ever did, and my body fat is lower, so I know that the scale isn't anything because you can hold onto water. You can gain 5 pounds with water and it's not fat. So that's why I just go by my clothes and the mirror. I don't go by the fucking scale. It doesn't do nothing. It'll just make my mind worse. I'll use a tape measure."

"How often?"

"It depends. Like once a week."

"What parts do you measure?"

"My hip bones. My inner thighs. Above my knee. My calves. My arms. And my butt."

"What happens if you see a number that you don't like?"

"Then I take charge."

"How do you take charge?"

"Further restrict. And work out more and harder."

"Fifteen miles instead of ten."

"No. I know I can't do fifteen miles because then I'll be dead on the floor. I know that."

"When you see your bones very sharp, do you feel successful?"

"Yeah. That's when I feel happy."

"How long does that feeling last?"

"It depends. Either like a few seconds or a couple of minutes."

"If you could throw a magic switch right now and have something tomorrow morning, what do you think you would want?"

"I would have the body that I want—to be extremely, extremely thin. I would be happy. And I would never get fat again."

"Thank you, Sara. You did a splendid job tonight. Does anyone have a question for Sara?"

Another young woman stood and asked, "Do you ever want to have a baby?"

Sara rolled her eyes with disgust and answered, "Hell no. I'm killing myself to be thin. Pregnant women are nothing but fat cows."

There was silence in the room.

Dr. Barrow asked, "Any other questions?" He waited a few moments. There was no reply. "Well, I have one comment. All of you here have heard me say, 'We can help you if you want to help yourself.' Think about that as you reflect on Sara's session here tonight. Any other thoughts? No. Very well, we will meet again tomorrow. Remember, ladies, if you wish to volunteer for the evening session, please fill out one of these forms. Thank you all. Have a pleasant evening. Oh, Sara, let's chat a few minutes in my office."

I went back to my room. Claire was there. Without even looking at me, Claire commented, "That little girl is out of her mind."

"Is that what you think?"

"You can't think anything else."

"At least she's not in denial," I said to jab at Claire's consciousness, but the remark flew right over the space cadet's head. "Unfortunately, Sara wants to lose more weight, so this disorder will kill her. She's taken the wrong choice point as her objective."

"Choice point?"

"We can talk about it tomorrow."

"Yeah. Goodnight, Jess."

"Goodnight, Claire." I prepared myself for my first night away from Jack, Megan, and Jason, got into bed, and stared at the ceiling, thinking about what Sara had said. Parts of my mind empathized with her thoughts and problems. We both restricted. We're both bulimic. But that's where the similarities ended. I thought to myself, "That girl won't see age thirty. She doesn't see her suicidal lifestyle. Instead, she seeks death as her salvation. That poor girl. I hope one of these doctors is smart enough to turn her around before it's too late."

Another thought came to me. Actually, it was the image of being the last person on a very long line. It's a terrible feeling to think that everyone before you on that line is better off than you are. Then I felt a little guilty because the image of Sara came along and got on the line behind me. Suddenly there were still many people better off than I was, but Sara now represented someone worse off than me. Actually, it was the truth. I've begun to fight my depression and I'm in this hospital to try to save my life. Sara, on the other hand, prays for death as salvation. It made me wonder if I'd meet more women in this hospital who would take up possible positions between Sara and me, or, worse yet, get to the end of this long line of eating-disorder sufferers. Heaven help those unfortunates at the rear of the line who are worse off than Sara. I'm not religious, but I thanked God I'm not at the end of the line anymore. I actually prayed that one day I might actually reach the middle or even the front of the line and look back at all the people behind me who are less fortunate than me.

Tears started streaming down my face, but not because of my thoughts about Sara. I was still dealing with my own depression. I didn't want to be there. I wanted to be with my kids. I wanted to be with my husband. I wanted to be in the comfort of my home, but I wasn't. I remember falling asleep as a tear ran down my face and onto my pillow.

* * *

At breakfast the next morning I paused and stared at my food before I picked up my fork. All I could think was, "Eat this food. It will get you home." I was the last one to leave the dining room. I didn't care. I finished the meal. I felt a sense of accomplishment, but I also felt nauseatingly full. It was a disgusting feeling, but one that I had to get used to until my body got used to eating normal portions.

Lunch was the same chore as breakfast. Once again, I had to build up courage to pick up my fork to start eating, especially since I still felt full from the breakfast meal.

Once again, I was the last one out of the dining room. I didn't care. I felt pleased with myself that I finished the food on my plate, and I felt even more nauseatingly full from the lunch meal. I felt so uncomfortable that I went to see the attending physician to find out if this was a normal reaction, or if something was wrong with me. The doctor explained that it was a reaction from my extended period of restriction and bulimia, and that I should continue eating the full meals, even though I felt so full. He also told me to see him again if the feeling persisted after several meals so he could prescribe an antinausea medication to help me through this adjustment period.

After seeing the doctor, I got dressed to go outside to walk around the grounds. Aides or spying video cameras lined the path all along the way. I thought that some exercise would help to burn off some of the meal. It did. The cool, fresh air and a couple of cigarettes helped me to think about my situation and what I had to do to improve it. It allowed me to reflect about how much I loved my kids and husband, and how I hated to be away from them. Before the evening meal, I called Jack and must have spent an hour and a half on the phone with him. It was great to hear his voice, and it gave me a chance to express my uncomfortable feelings to him. Jack was great with me, as usual. He only spoke words of encouragement. He told me, "Jess, I believe it is difficult. You went through a rough time, and you're going through a rough time now. Keep doing what you have to do to get out of there, and to stay out of there."

I went straight to dinner after talking with Jack. I took less time to pick up my fork, but the strain of eating didn't diminish. I ate the full meal, felt terrible, and headed to the evening therapy session. We never knew who was going to speak that night. Little did I know how much the next patient was going to affect me.

* * *

"Good evening, everyone. Tonight we're going to talk with Denise."

Denise was tall, about five foot eleven, thin, and the most immaculately manicured woman I had ever seen. Most of the women at the hospital didn't care about their looks. Most of the women at the hospital didn't even care if they took their next breath, which made Denise's grooming that much more unusual.

"Denise, thank you for volunteering."

"My pleasure, Dr. Barrow."

"Let's talk about your life prior to the start of your eating disorder. Were there any special negative situations?"

"Yes. Infertility. It was devastating. Absolutely devastating. At first, I was so close to having children. I got married at age twenty-seven. I was working. I was doing a graduate degree at that point, and many of the women around me at church were having children. Everyone was having three, five, seven, nine children. Those women stayed home. I said, 'How pathetic. Get a life.' You know? But three or four years into my marriage, while I was working on my second graduate degree, I suddenly felt unfulfilled. I wanted to have children."

"Do you have any children now?"

"No. No. I pursued every avenue. I did . . . this was before insurance covered this, but I did three in vitro fertilizations, six intrauterine inseminations, and I had two operations. I had hysterosalpingograms, laparoscopies, and an operation on my fallopian tubes. I did everything. I created a lot of embryos.

I'm pro-life, so to me, that's life. I had embryos planted in my uterus, waited three-and-a-half weeks to find out if they took hold or if I repeated my menstrual cycle. Each time my period returned because the embryos failed to take hold. It was devastating. I started to fall apart from the stress, the disappointment, and the humiliation."

"At what age did your eating disorder start?"

"I was close to thirty-nine years old. I never experienced any form of an eating disorder before that age."

"Have you gone through states of depression?"

"Yes. At age twenty-two, I experienced a state of mania that was out of control, and I didn't know what it was. I hadn't slept for months. Finally, my general practitioner picked up on it. Isn't that amazing? I went to him for sleeping pills. You know, this was about twenty years ago. He saw me and said, 'How long has this been going on?' I was on top of the world. Everything was great. I just wanted to sleep. He only gave me a two-week supply of Halcion. He told me I needed to see a psychiatrist. He said, 'You are completely manic. I think there is something wrong.' So I experienced more mania. I had depression before the infertility, but never as bad. I would crash and I would take the popular antidepressant of that time. It worked. I didn't need hospitalization. You know, it was not paralyzing. It was just there. It's the infertility. It was a matter of taking all those hormones, all those drugs, all those procedures, and being in and out of anesthesia. Plus, I was going on and off my medication, because every time I would go for my cycle, I would tell my doctor that I was stopping my medication because there was a possibility I would conceive. So I was going on and I was going off. Then each attempt to conceive resulted in failure, and that really brought me down. I just crashed. I had to take a leave from work."

"You said you were married at twenty-seven."

"Yes."

"He's your ex-husband at this point. Right?"

"No. I wish he were my ex-husband at this point. He's a very angry person, and we're stuck at settlement, you know, with property and money, and it's going through the court system and unfortunately it's litigated. The judge is going to end up making all the decisions because he won't move in the negotiations."

"You wrote that he was abusive."

"Yes."

"How?"

"He was always emotionally abusive. I wasn't aware of that. But at age twenty-eight, through my mid-thirties, I thought he was my best friend. I just got used to him being critical of things. I learned from my therapist that my husband shouldn't do or say the kinds of things he was saying to me. He would insult me. He was always doing things to provoke, to trigger, to get a reaction, but I wasn't fully aware that this is cruelty. This is just plain-out mean. This is abusive. I come from an upper-middle-class family, and I traveled to Europe many times. My parents have homes on different islands, and he was able to take advantage of that and have a good life being married to me. Then he would insult it all. So I just didn't realize. I think, in my own way, I was just tolerating and accepting it."

"Why? You're an intelligent woman. You saw things that were bothering you."

"I wasn't as aware then as I am now. I saw things that bothered me, but I would just give him the benefit of the doubt or extend kindness. He came from a family background not similar to mine at all. We had some good moments, and I think it's kind of what got me stuck."

"Were there money problems?"

"Money was never an issue. If I wanted to buy a piece of jewelry, I just did it. There was money. We didn't live off credit. There was always, between our salaries, enough to do what we wanted. When we purchased our home, we were a good team. When I tore out the house and took the carpeting off and took paneling off, there was never a question in his mind about my actions. When I furnished it with Ethan Allen furniture and a piano, he didn't question it. I went through this subject in great detail with my therapist, and he said, 'Your marriage is not a marriage. It's more like a business operation.' Looking back now, perhaps that was true."

"Who controlled the finances? In other words, who handled the bank accounts and who did the bill paying?"

"He did all the bill paying. He did the taxes. He managed every account, and all of the accounts were in both our names."

"Did you see that as a control issue?"

"No. It was just convenient for me. However, he did things with the money that bothered me. They bothered me mostly because those actions expressed his personality, and I didn't do something soon enough to stop it."

"Like what?"

"About five years ago, behind my back, he started to invest a lot of money. He would loan it to people at high interest rates. An example would be to loan $100,000 at an interest rate of 21 percent. He went up to the legal limit, and I caught him doing it. He promised in front of the psychiatrist he would never do it again, and then he did it three more times."

"So he stayed just below the border line of illegality."

"Yes."

"Do you think he had affairs?"

"Yes. Well, no. He was online a lot with women. I'm aware now that a year and a half ago, he was partying. He was seeing people."

"How did you feel when that happened?"

"At that point, thank goodness, I was becoming stronger. I was beginning to see my current therapist. He gave me a lot of support and insight. It was less difficult because I was seeing more and more of my future ex-husband's true nature. I was beginning to look back over my years of marriage and coming to the realization that it wasn't so great. It caused me grief. My therapist said, 'He's not your husband anymore. You just have to detach yourself and realize that it's over.' You see, I was postponing and delaying the inevitable because a part of me thought there was no way to manage a home by myself, work full time, and pay all the bills. You know, my husband always fixed things, repaired things, put things together, bought things . . . I just got so comfortable with things of that nature. I thought, financially, I wouldn't be able to manage it, so I held on to him for a longer period of time. Finally, I did a pro and con list of whether or not to leave him. That list proved one thing– my life would be better without him. I filed for divorce immediately."

"It sounds like you were able to make a quick mental separation once you made a decision."

"Absolutely. But understand, three years before that moment, I communicated to him very clearly that I was unhappy and that I was considering a divorce. He never thought I would have the strength to do it and follow through with it. He was dead wrong."

"In your questionnaire, regarding your eating disorder, you wrote, 'It all started Christmas 2001.'"

"Yes. I can remember the day my eating disorder started the same way a person might remember the day they had their first cigarette."

"Denise, you thought you were overweight at that time. You were about to attend a family function, and you were willing to wear clothes that you felt were 'inappropriate' for that occasion."

"Yes."

"Why did you do this and then, later, feel embarrassed from it?"

"I had to do it because those were the only clothes that fit. I was never heavy in my life. I gained weight after all that infertility, the depression, and the drugs. I don't know how much weight I gained, but it was enough to bother me and to say, 'That's it. You're heavy. You're fat. Pull yourself together and get back to your normal self.'"

"Had you tried dieting prior to that?"

"No. I don't diet. I don't think I ever dieted. I think while I was in high school in the 1970s, people would talk about the starvation diet. I think that's where I got the idea from. The girls would say, 'I'm going on a starvation diet.' We would lose a couple of pounds and, you know, it was like a fad. We wanted to lose weight."

"So you turned off food, at least most of it."

"It started December 25, but it wasn't until April, three or four months later, that it became an extreme situation. I was put on a medication, Lithium, that causes weight gain. I was losing weight in January and February and March and feeling good about myself. I was exercising and said, 'There's no way that this is going to be taken away from me just because of the medication.' And so, the day I started Lithium, I recall, I said I'm absolutely not going to gain weight on this. I just stopped eating. I think I probably went down to about six hundred calories. I had no idea. I was clueless. I didn't even know how many calories were in a given food. I just remember being determined that I wasn't going to let this interfere with my weight loss plan."

"Did your husband say anything to you about your restricted eating program?"

"When I became very thin he became more insulting and cruel. When I was starving myself and almost dying, he encouraged it."

"Which? The death or the lack of eating?"

"After I got extremely thin, he encouraged me to lose even more weight. I didn't know if his intent was to harm or just to make comments. I had become so accustomed to him teasing me that I would just say to myself, 'That's his style. This is how he speaks to people, and this is how he speaks about people.'"

"You wrote about April and the onset of depression. What do you think brought that on?"

"I was unhappy at work at that time. There was just a lot of stress and there was an awful amount of tension and arguing at home. One way of dealing with unhappiness in the past would be to get depressed. I don't know how deliberate this depression was. But, when I fell into it, it was so strong that I had to take a leave and go on Lithium."

"What symptoms were you seeing? Was it constant sleeping? Constant crying?"

"No. I wish I could cry. I still can't. The depression altered my mind chemically, and I just didn't have the energy to fight it. I was completely aggravated. I couldn't function. I couldn't drive, turn on the TV, or open a book. I certainly could not teach 132 teenagers a day, even though that's where my career was for twenty years. I just shut down. In the past, when that happened, my husband used to support me and help me. This time around, his goal was to keep me in that state."

"What comments were you getting from other people about your weight loss?"

"In the beginning, everyone said, 'This is great. You made the decision to lose the weight and you're doing it. Wow!' Everyone was saying they wished they had my discipline. I didn't know I was anorexic. I had no idea what I was doing. I was clueless. I just looked great. Then my mom noticed I wasn't eating. She made a comment here or there, but it was my psychiatrist who noticed and came down very hard on me."

"How long had you been seeing him at that time?"

"I was seeing him once a week for four years."

"Were you confident with his treatment?"

"Oh, yes. Yes. Very comfortable and happy. Yes. I had a very strong relationship with him. I trusted him."

"When you saw him, did you express your feelings and emotions, or did he just prescribe medication and say, 'See you at the next appointment?' In other words, was he a psychopharmacologist?"

"No. He refused to be that way. He said it is unethical to prescribe medication to someone and see them a month later. I did overcome a couple of major issues in my life through those sessions. One was my brother's death. He died when he was sixteen, which was a serious issue for me."

"He was very young. What was the cause of death?"

"I'd rather not talk about it."

"Was it illness? Self-inflicted?"

"Does it matter? One day we laughed together and the next day he was dead. I loved him. He was gone and . . . It took twenty-one years for me to start to grieve and move on. My psychiatrist never gave up. It was very serious. I was very close to my brother. The other issue that we worked on was my desire to commit suicide. I just couldn't get beyond it. I always wanted to die. Whenever I'd think of my brother, I just always wanted to be with him. When my brother died, I wasn't suicidal at all. It all started with my infertility. Then there was tension in my home, but I wasn't aware of how bad it was. Then I missed my brother. When you put it all together, I wanted to die. I couldn't see beyond that. I was hospitalized, and then hospitalized again, and again, but my psychiatrist refused to give up. He was there twenty-four hours a day. If I had a thought, I would call him at 11:00 p.m. to tell him, 'I want to die.' He said, 'Any other doctor would have put you into the hospital twenty times.' But he's against hospitalization unless it is really necessary. Finally, he took me to a psychotherapy workshop in Manhattan. He said, 'I'm going to be with you during this workshop, and then we're going to be able to resolve this.' They asked me to briefly describe my issue. I said, 'I always want to die. I want to be with my dead brother.' That's all I said. Nobody knew the details. The workshop therapist told me to lie down on the ground. He had someone else lie next to me on the ground that represented my dead brother. All of a sudden, I felt very uncomfortable. I wanted to get up. He said, 'No, you can't get up yet.' I said, 'But I don't want to be down here.' He said, 'You can't get up yet.' I just felt uncomfortable. I said, 'No, I just changed my mind. I don't want to be lying next to my dead brother.' I got up. He said, 'It's easier to die than to live. Right?' I said, 'Yes.' He said, 'Denise, imagine I'm your father and this woman is your mother. As your father, I'm telling you, 'No more. End the cycle. End the cycle.' The woman next to him said, 'End the cycle. No more. No more.' It was the first time I ever felt that my parents wanted me alive, and they wanted the cycle of suicide and people killing themselves to be over with. For the first time I felt I could end it. I could end the cycle. I felt empowered. From that day on, I realized I didn't want to be six feet under the ground with my brother. I missed my brother terribly. For twenty years, all I wanted to do was to be with him, but when I was lying down on that floor next to him, I became very uncomfortable. The workshop worked. I finally had my wish through this scenario, and I didn't like it."

"But you weren't truly finished with suicidal thoughts. Were you?"

"I was finished with the thoughts of killing myself to be with my brother."

"OK, Denise. Let's take this in another direction. Were you a popular woman in high school and college?"

"Oh, especially college. Charismatic. Involved in every extracurricular activity."

"Did you date much?"

"Dating wasn't a priority for me. I did date in high school. I dated someone for two years. I was very close to my Christian faith. I maintained my virginity. When I went to college, I was very serious about studying. It was a very academic experience for me. I hung out with people who were very bright. No one would ever get below a 3.7 GPA for a given semester. I didn't go out and drink on those Thursday nights or Friday nights. I did here and there. I experienced what a shot was, but I didn't engage in it often. I don't feel like I missed out on too much. I did have a couple of relationships in college. In my senior year, I started to go out on those Thursday nights, and I had so much fun that I said, 'Oh, my goodness. I can't believe this. This is fun.' So I was kind of like a late bloomer."

"As a child, did you feel nurtured?"

"There were some real difficult, tough times. My father has bipolar disorder, and I remember him cycling and how it affected the family, but he worked hard, and there were five kids. So my mom did the best she could raising five of us."

"How did his bipolar disorder affect you?"

"It affected my siblings more in a negative way. As a group of five kids, I hate to say it, but I was my father's special or prized child. I never experienced physical abuse, but my siblings did. My father never laid a hand on me. If I was affected in any way, it happened when he was manic. He got involved in a million projects. That's how I lived my life in high school and college. Playing one instrument was not enough. I had to play every instrument. I was in every honor society. I had to go all out in everything. That's my father's personality."

"Let's discuss the sight of your bones and what they represented. You wrote that you didn't like seeing your bones. And yet, you enjoyed looking thin and the comments your thin appearance generated. Later, you wrote, 'Being very thin was my biggest accomplishment, and bones became my trophy.'"

"I learned from my therapist that my bones became my trophies. He was the one who came up with 'trophies.' I told him that being thin was my biggest accomplishment at that time, not in life. People would say, 'Oh, wow, look at her!' They said it with a sense of jealousy. I was able to lose the weight, and lose more and more. I could abstain and walk away. I saw everybody eating cheesecake, desserts, and pasta. Day in and day out, I heard people say, 'Oh, if I could just lose 5 pounds.' While they just talked about the desire, I took action. Look, I'll tell you about the bones. Things bothered me. When I stepped out of the shower and walked on the tiled floor, it hurt my feet. When I went into the car and put the seatbelt on, just the pressure of the seatbelt against the skin, I felt the bones. When I sat down on a very comfortable couch and felt my bones instead of insulation, that troubled me."

"So your bones became a trophy, and a source of physical pain."

"Yes."

"Your bones made you feel a sense of accomplishment."

"Yes."

"You felt like you reached your 'perfect' self."

"Yes."

"Prior to that day, you felt everything in your life was successful and accomplished through your perfectionism."

"Yes."

"Who was the first one to point out your problem?"

"My psychiatrist. He became alarmed and began to weigh me every week."

"Did he ever use the expression eating disorder?"

"He said, 'Anorexia.'"

"How did you respond to that?"

"I denied it. I didn't even know, really, what it meant. I said, 'I'm fine.' He urged me to eat. I tried to explain to him that it wasn't a big thing for me. He's a good guy, and a great psychiatrist. He didn't know that if I saw 118 pounds one week, I'd want to see 117 the next. I always hoped for lower numbers at each visit. Each time I dropped another dress size, I felt more accomplished."

"More perfect in your own eyes."

"Yes."

"As you lost more and more weight, you felt more in control and more successful."

"Yes. I remember feeling elated and successful when I went to a party and there were all of these great appetizers, foods, and the desserts. I could control myself and just ate two carrot sticks for the entire night. I would say, 'Oh, how great. How wonderful. Isn't it great that I can do this and nobody else can? Look at the people at this party who are overweight and who are overeating and overindulging, and yet they say they want to lose weight. I'm the strongest one and the most disciplined one in the room.' That's how I felt. I recall always being able to walk away from food."

"You wrote about Thanksgiving of 2002 and how you felt like you looked like a model in a new Hilfiger outfit."

"Yes."

"And yet this model almost passed out from malnutrition and had to be taken to the hospital."

"Yes. I went to the emergency room."

"In your eyes, you still looked beautiful."

"Yes."

"Do you think other people felt the same way?"

"Other people probably thought I looked like a Holocaust survivor."

"What did you see when you looked in the mirror?"

"I was suffering from malnutrition, and the mirror showed me a gorgeous woman."

"Is it what you saw, or how you denied what the mirror showed?"

"You sound like my psychiatrist."

"Thank you."

"I didn't think I was starving myself at that time."

"What do you think now?"

"My doctor said, 'You're starving yourself.' I said, 'No, I'm not. I'm not hungry after church.' He repeated, 'You're starving yourself.' At church after that visit, I deliberately ate two forkfuls of coffee cake. Then I told him about it. But then I realized that he didn't mean starving yourself just in the terms of things physical. I was starving myself of socialization and enjoyment. You see, when you walk away from food, it's a very powerful thing. I mean, it's sad, but it's powerful."

"Let's talk about your physical symptoms around Thanksgiving of 2002. You wrote, 'My hair was falling out. I lost my period. I was catatonic.'"

"At times."

"And yet you also thought you were looking beautiful and doing great."

"Yes."

"Let's talk about that contradiction. You still weren't sure you were anorexic. You still weren't sure there was anything wrong. You were just having those fainting spells."

"Yes. I did get very sick that November. But I didn't make the connection with that and the weight loss. On occasion, when I was driving to work, or teaching, I would feel faint. My heart, at times, would pitter-patter."

"When did your psychiatrist first use the word anorexia?"

"I don't remember."

"Let's use Thanksgiving of 2002 as a time frame."

"Oh, before that. At least three months before that."

"So, here you had your psychiatrist telling you what the problem is, and you denied it."

"No. He said, 'Are you still losing weight?' And I said, 'Yes.' And he said, 'There's a word for that.' I said, 'What?' He said, 'Anorexia.'"

"So he put the diagnosis on the table."

"It wasn't like it was a diagnosis. He said, 'There's a word for that.'"

"That's right."

"Yeah. But I just thought, 'I went on a diet and lost the weight.'"

"Exactly. You denied the diagnosis. In the same way you denied there was anything wrong. You thought you looked gorgeous. You were pleased with yourself. You were successful. You're the kind of person who demands success. Once again, you had reached a point that you were in control of something."

"Right."

"Where you hadn't been before."

"Right."

"And yet, the diagnosis was on the table and you walked right past it and continued to decline."

"Well, I really didn't discuss it with my doctor. He insisted on weighing me every week."

"Why do you think he did that?"

"He told me that he had to because he is a medical doctor. It would be unethical if he didn't. But I complained a lot about it. He just said, 'I'm a medical doctor, and I need to know.' We had a really good rapport and relationship for four and a half years before that. I thought it would be ruined because he insisted I be weighed at the beginning of every session. I just got very angry and went on the scale. And I just said, 'Well, next week I'm going to be 2 pounds less, and I don't care.'"

"What did he say about that?"

"He really didn't address it too much. He urged me to eat. He tried to explore why I didn't eat. He tried to see if I was still suicidal and doing it this way. No. It's not like he ignored it. I was resistant to talk about it."

"In your mind you were thinking, 'I have no problem. I'm OK. I feel OK. I look OK. I don't want to be bothered with the scale because I'm OK.'"

"Yes, and that scale was ruining our relationship."

"Soon after, you had your first meeting with your therapist."

"Yes."

"Your therapist came right out and, from your description, was very blunt about your eating disorder. Would you agree that both of your doctors were concerned that you were in a pattern that was detrimental to your health?"

"Well, yes."

"You wrote that you felt intimidated by your new therapist."

"Yes. He was too blunt. He pulled no punches."

"Did you think to yourself, 'I don't want to be bothered with this new guy?'"

"Absolutely. With my psychiatrist, I just denied it because I didn't know too much about anorexia. He just wanted me to eat more. He didn't understand that it was deeper than that."

"What was it about your new therapist that made an impact on you?"

"First, he scared me with his nonsubtle approach. He told me I could be hospitalized and that women die from this. He explained the symptoms. I had a lot of them, like the urinary tract infections and sore throats, the loss of menstruation, and loss of hair. I kind of got scared during that first session because I had too many of those symptoms."

"You were finally introduced to the physical effects of malnutrition. You didn't want to see him again, did you?"

"No."

"But you did. Why?"

"I was surprised that I made another appointment. I thought he said things that I didn't think he had the right to say. He said I was vain. He called me a perfectionist. He said my standards were too high. I think he probably went a little too far. I thought that this was like a reality show. I was surprised. I said to myself, 'Why go back for more punishment?'"

"Why did you?"

"I needed to get my psychiatrist off my back. The promise was that I would see an eating disorder specialist and he promised he would stop weighing me if I would. Out of all the therapists I interviewed, that doctor seemed to be the most competent."

"So, your decision was simply based upon the lesser of two evils."

"Yes."

"It wasn't based upon the multitude of detrimental physical symptoms you were suffering from."

"No."

"You simply wanted your psychiatrist to stop weighing you."

"Yes. That had to come to an end. Our sessions could not start like that anymore. Then, one session, I just refused to be weighed. He refused to do any therapy with me, and he refused to write any medication for me. It took thirty minutes for me to finally get on the scale. I said, 'This can't happen anymore. I swear to God. I'm going to find someone else.' I said, 'Please, please, please. Don't weigh me anymore. Please don't.' It was interfering with our rapport."

"Do you think that the scale symbolized acceptance of a possible problem and that by not getting on the scale . . .'"

"I just . . . look, I just didn't want to see the numbers. I didn't want him to see the numbers. I would see a number and it made me more determined to be at a lower weight the next week. I told him, 'This is detrimental. This is not good. This is not working for me because I just want to get thinner and thinner. If I see the same number the next week, then I'm just going to starve myself more.' He didn't get it, but my new therapist got it right away. He knew that weighing me was not going to work. I still don't like to be weighed. I still refuse to be weighed. I saw my gynecologist a couple of months ago. I said, 'I'll weigh myself, thank you.' Or, I told him how much I weighed. It's very . . . I don't like it."

"It's very what, Denise?"

"It's . . . I just don't like to see a number that, perhaps . . . what if it's unexpected? What if it's a pound or two higher? Right? I just prefer to tell people, on average, this is my weight. Let's move on. Take my blood pressure."

"At that time, did you ever equate your eating disorder with suicide?"

"No. Nobody wants to starve themselves to death. It takes too long. It's just not quick enough. If someone wants to commit suicide, they can just kill themselves. They could suffocate themselves. It's so much easier. I don't think anyone wants a slow death."

"You wrote about being in a hospital and making a suicide attempt."

"Yes. My second hospitalization was because of an attempt at suicide. I used a plastic bag and detergent. I was put on suicide watch when I was admitted because my doctor thought I was too much at risk. It wasn't just ideation. I had intent. I had a plan. He seemed very concerned. We had only known each other for seven or eight months at that point. He had reason to admit me."

"What did you do?"

"Suffocation. I was almost successful the second time. I used a plastic bag. I was almost dead. I was dizzy. I was losing consciousness. I thought, 'Great!

You did it this time.' Then I threw up. I hated the feeling of vomit on my face and ripped the bag off my head. Then I said, 'Oh, well. This didn't work.'"

"Was there another attempt after that?"

"No. But there were two more hospitalizations after that."

"You were still dealing with depression?"

"Yeah. Big time."

"In other words, you still had the desire, but you weren't going through with it like you did twice before."

"Right. Well, I had . . . I was getting a gun. I applied for a gun and did all the paperwork. Then one day my husband opened the mail before I got home, and he saw the paperwork for the gun. He called my doctor. I was just a week away from getting a gun permit. The suffocation didn't work, so I tried to get a gun. And then my psychiatrist wrote a letter to the government and said that I was not allowed to purchase a gun. Now I'm on the government computer records. I was really angry then. I felt like my rights had been violated under the Constitution."

"Were you more angry at the fact that your husband and doctor prevented you from getting that gun, or that you failed at your attempt to use that gun to kill yourself?"

"I was angry for both reasons."

"I see. You never failed at anything you tried. Did you?"

"Not even close."

"You wrote, 'I achieved excellent grades in school. I was in all the honor societies. People of equal intelligence constantly surrounded me.'"

"Yes."

"You are an intelligent woman who always applied that intelligence."

"Absolutely. I enjoyed it. I love challenges and conquering them."

"And you never felt failure."

"Never."

"Throughout your entire life, you were a role model of success. You faced challenges and achieved what you desired."

"Right."

"Except with giving birth."

"Couldn't. That sucks. I had no control over that."

"And yet, you could see a woman with a 16 IQ giving birth."

"Right."

"That bothered you. Didn't it?"

"Absolutely."

"You had all this intelligence. You were mentally and financially able to reach out to all the best infertility doctors. But you didn't reach success."

"I could not make those embryos attach to my uterine lining and, darn it, stay there, and divide, divide. Please divide. It's like I didn't have that control. It was very . . . it was very disturbing. Very depressing. It takes life completely out of you. It was devastating. Devastating."

"Was there anything special about the day you put the plastic bag over your head? Was there any connection to your depression?"

"I was in the hospital for probably a week prior to that. It was Mother's Day. I was thin. I was . . . there was this closet. I'm not talking about a walk-in closet. It was extremely narrow, and I could actually fit into it. I closed the door. I tied the plastic bag over my head because I just needed to escape. I did. I was in pain. Great emotional pain. There was fierce self-hatred. I realized at that point that I didn't like myself. I thought I understood what it was about. I was wrong. If I understood it, I wouldn't have engaged in anorexia to the degree that I did. All I felt was an uncontrollable hatred toward myself."

"Why?"

"Because of my infertility. Because I made bad decisions. I began to see the negatives in my marriage. I couldn't believe I had allowed myself to reach that position. My marriage was supposed to last forever. The anger I felt for having failed my marriage was overpowering, but I decided not to disclose the intensity of my fears, the continuous loss of appetite, the fierceness of my self-hatred, and the dreadful mistakes I made."

"Denise, did you knowingly do anything to ruin the marriage?"

"Absolutely not."

"Yet you blamed yourself for your future ex-husband's actions."

"Yes."

"It was the second major failure in your life, with infertility as the first."

"Yes."

"And you had never experienced any sort of failure prior to those two situations."

"No. Never. Not even close."

"Denise, you chose Mother's Day to take action. It was not just an ordinary day for you. It symbolized an unresolved failure in your mind. Now tell me why you took that plastic bag off of your head when you were so close to the death you sought?"

"Because I threw up."

"Denise, why did you take that bag off of your head when you were so close to the death you sought? Think about it."

"Because my vanity hated the vomit on my face."

"Try again, Denise. Look inside. You know the answer."

"Dr. Barrow, I . . . I wanted to live. It's like when they laid me on the floor next to that person who was supposed to be my brother, and I got up. I wanted to live."

"Good, Denise. Very good. Now why did you enter this program?"

"I don't want to die from anorexia."

"Once again, you made a decision to save your life."

"Yes. Yes."

"What was it like eating your first meal?"

"It was hard."

"Did you feel incapable of eating?"

"Yes. I had no idea how starting to eat again would be so mentally and physically uncomfortable when I was losing all that weight. My body just didn't know what food was. It didn't know what to do with the food. I didn't know that my digestive system was not working properly. It affected the small intestine and the large. Even the enzymes in the saliva that help break down the food didn't function properly. Chewing was a chore. The smell of the food nauseated me. I started to cry. I had a tremendous amount of gas. I was bloated as if I looked nine months pregnant. If I didn't have the gas, I had the constipation. I said, 'Oh, my God! What did you do to your body?'"

"You have been here ten days. What is it like now?"

"It's still difficult, but I set a goal of recovery for myself. I won't let myself fail. I can only go into recovery by eating."

"I like that statement, Denise. 'I can go into recovery by eating.' It sounds like a slogan we should hang on the wall. And with that excellent statement, it's time to say thank you for your most excellent session. Congratulations on your first steps toward recovery."

The other ladies in the room gave Denise a spontaneous round of applause, and many approached Denise to shake her hand and offer words of encouragement. I was one of them.

For a few moments I stood and stared in Dr. Barrow's direction. I saw the volunteer session questionnaire forms on the table. My staring at the forms caught Dr. Barrow's attention. "What do you think, Jess?" he asked as he approached me.

"I think I'd like to fill out one of those forms this evening."

"Excellent."

Dr. Barrow handed me a form and one of the hospital pens.

"You'll have it in the morning, Dr. Barrow."

"I'll look forward to it."

"That day we met in your office, you were right, Dr. Barrow."

"About what?"

"I'm glad you convinced me to stay."

"Me, too. Have a pleasant evening, Jess."

"You, too."

* * *

That night I spilled my guts into that form. I kept drawing parallels with Denise's life. That overwhelming desire to die was no stranger to me. We both had lived with someone else's bipolar disorder. We both had brother issues. Her brother was dead. My brother tried to kill me. We both lived through the negative physical effects of anorexia and wound up in a hospital as a result. Denise had been abused by someone she trusted, her husband. I was abused and raped by someone I trusted, my guidance counselor, Lucy.

Denise and I were sisters of sickness. We were depressed and taunted by outside pressures we couldn't control, and we were both willing to die rather than learn how to cope and survive. What she said made sense. "It's easier to die." But the one other thing we had in common was a decision to try to save our lives. Denise and I took separate roads to get to this one miserable destination.

But there were also things significantly different between Denise and me. While her husband became a negative factor in her life, Jack was just the opposite for me. I can't remember one time when Jack represented or provoked a negative thought, even when he tried to keep me from purging. Although I didn't like it, I understood he was trying to help me and showing his love by his actions. I have to be one of the luckiest women in the world to have such a great guy. Even though I wound up in that hospital because of all the crap I subjected myself to, I'm convinced I've been lucky. First, I'm lucky to be alive. Next, whereas Denise was desperate yet unsuccessful in her attempts to have children, I have two wonderful children. I appreciate and I'm grateful to have two children I love so much. "Lucky": I find it a very strange word to apply to my existence. I can't remember ever calling myself lucky before. Labeling myself lucky refreshed my soul, made me feel good, and temporarily empowered and rejuvenated me.

That night I fell asleep without crying. The next morning I woke feeling energized. I looked forward to breakfast, a long walk, lunch, another long walk, dinner, and the evening therapy session. I wondered what new thoughts and attitudes would be born by listening to tonight's patient.

* * *

The therapy room quieted down as soon as Dr. Barrow entered and took his seat at the front table. He paused for a few moments to review the questionnaire of the therapy patient for the night. Dr. Barrow looked at her, seated a few feet away, without his usually optimistic facial gestures. After a deep sigh, he opened the session. "Tonight we'll be working with Carol."

Perhaps because of her short, cropped hair and extremely small, almost nonexistent breasts, I thought Carol was the first male to join the group. I was wrong. My immediate impression of Carol was that she looked like the type of person who would jump headfirst into the deep end of an empty swimming pool. She was shorter than most women at the hospital and stood only about four foot eleven. She wasn't thin; she was emaciated. Unlike most, she wore long sleeves, which surprised me because the crowded therapy room often got quite warm.

"Good evening, Carol."

"Hi, Dr. Barrow."

"Carol, what are your thoughts about listening to the other women who have volunteered for these sessions?"

"Listening to stories of people with eating disorders triggers me. I know that when I hear about someone with an eating disorder that has a heart attack or other health problems, it doesn't scare me out of it. It doesn't make me say, 'Oh, my God, I'm not going to do that.' It makes me think, 'Ooh, I'm jealous. They're sicker than me.' Some people are scared off by it. However, it puts me in a competitive-nature kind of mood. The greatest trigger for me is someone going into detail about their problem. For instance, in one book I read, the author went into descriptions about what bones were showing. I enjoyed the author's descriptions of her face and her body. I would say to myself, 'Oh, I don't see those bones on me.' Or, the book would describe a lot of numbers when she was losing weight really quickly. There was a part that said, 'She was 57 pounds, then 53 pounds.' I said, 'Hey, she's walking around at 53 pounds and my doctors are yelling at me for being . . . whatever . . .'"

"I see. Let's talk about your childhood. Tell me a little bit about your relationships with your mother, father, siblings, and friends. Did you get along well with your parents?"

"Probably. As a little kid, I remember things going pretty well. Nothing really sticks out in my mind. But then, around age ten, I felt my mother was being overbearing and manipulative."

"You're how old now?"

"Twenty."

"At ten, how did you react to your mother's imposing her will on you?"

"By starting my eating disorder. From there, it was a power struggle with eating. My dad sat on the sidelines. Sometimes my mom whispered to him to tell me what to do because she thought I would listen to him."

"The power struggle, could it also be defined as a control situation?"

"Yeah. I could control what went into me, and she couldn't. It was all about her manipulative ways. I mean, I was young. There were just ways of hiding food. Looking back, I could see that my mom was on Weight Watchers, and my sister started Weight Watchers. I was in the fourth grade and said, 'Hey, I want to be on Weight Watchers.' Looking at my mom and sister, I started being afraid that I would start looking like them."

"Was it only your mom's behavior, or did something else happen that caused your eating disorder?"

"It was a combination. I won't forget what my sister did."

"Older sister? Younger sister?"

"Older sister. She's six years older. We were at a restaurant for my birthday. I ordered my favorite dish. I ordered seconds afterwards. I was always a skinny kid. I could eat whatever I wanted to. My sister said, 'Ah, you're such a pig.' As I was chewing whatever I was eating, I just felt, 'Yuck.' After she said that, I spit it out. Then things just kind of added to it. I was in overnight camp, and kids were making fun of me because I was nerdy. But people were always complimenting me on being thin. 'Oh, you're so lucky you're so thin.' I was so afraid of losing that. So, it's kind of a combination of my mom controlling 'Where are you going?' 'Who are your friends?'—a combination of that control aspect and what happened in camp. And just generally, I remember in school, they handed us packets on puberty and they showed us a diagram of a woman changing. I looked at that picture and said, 'Oh, my God. I don't want to look like that! I'll look fat!'"

"Did you know anyone else with anorexia at that point?"

"No. I had no idea what it was."

"You were uncomfortable with being nerdy, but you were happy when people said how lucky you were to be so thin."

"I've always been nerdy. I was the type who would get a ninety-five on a test and not be satisfied. A ninety-five was good, but when I got a ninety-five, I wanted a ninety-six or ninety-nine. I had an obsession with numbers. And then, especially with the camp, people would call me thin, but then I would look at third graders. At the time, I was in the fourth grade. I would say, 'Oh, look at how thin they are.' It was always as though I was comparing myself to people who were thinner. Sometimes I'd think to myself, 'Well, I'm thin according to their standards, but not according to my standards.' I always wanted to be not just thin, but thin by my standards, not compared to all other people."

"Have you ever been overweight in your life?"

"What? Never!"

"OK. So at ten years old, at that meal, you decided to change your eating habits."

"It wasn't exactly like it was a complete turnaround. That was kind of the straw that broke the camel's back. It wasn't like I was eating normally up until then. Gradually, after that meal, there were a lot of rituals. In the morning, I would have to cut my Nutri-Grain bar into four pieces, and I could only eat one piece. There was a certain way to measure out the cereal. There was a certain time that I had to eat. There were just a lot of rules. That's when my OCD started. I had rules for food and other things."

"Your mother set up rules for you. You could do this, you couldn't do that. Was this just rebellion? Were you just saying, 'Mom, I'm going to take control here, and you have no choice.'"

"Maybe. I mean, she was a lot more protective than other parents. My eating rules started to become an overbearing response. Yeah, maybe I can see it, I guess, as me wanting to have control–especially over my own body."

"The OCD. When was it first diagnosed?"

"It wasn't diagnosed until age eighteen. My sister has it, my mom has it, and my grandpa has it, so I wasn't diagnosed when I was home because obsessive behavior was just normal. You know, checking things and tapping things. It was like, 'Oh, I thought everyone did that.' When I went to college, my roommate noticed that I was checking my alarm clock for thirty minutes. She stared at me in a weird way. I tried to make up an excuse. It was then I realized, 'Oh, maybe people don't do that.' So, I had symptoms. I'm not sure about earlier than age ten. But after age ten, I remember."

"Do you think the eating problems fell right into the OCD?"

"Well, it's kind of weird, the relationship between OCD and my eating disorder. With the eating disorder, I have control. I chose the rules. I say to myself, 'You can only have this amount or that amount.' Whereas, with the OCD, it makes the rules that I have to follow unwillingly. It chose me. I didn't choose to have it or want it. It just tells me to say a certain ritual in my head, like count. It was like something outside of me made me do it. The OCD came from outside of me, and the eating disorder was within me."

"Did you always have excellent grades in school?"

"No. I switched schools about the same time the eating disorder developed. Before that, I was a slacker. I was bored and I would get into trouble. I would talk in class and things like that. When I changed schools, I decided I would be a completely new person. I mean perfect. That was fifth grade.

I decided no more laziness and no more being a pig. So, being a better student and being more disciplined in my life went along with the eating disorder. But being that way caused new problems. All of a sudden, I heard them saying, 'Oh, who is this new kid coming in and getting good grades?' They had their social order, and I was kind of disturbing it. They also thought I was spoiled. I didn't have to do my own laundry. I went to camp over the summer. They kind of looked at me like, 'Oooh.' It was basically . . . I don't know if it was directly this, but there weren't a lot of Jewish kids there. And there's something about a Jewish mother. A lot of them are overbearing. Well, at the time, I thought they didn't like me because I'm a loser."

"Why did they consider you a loser?"

"There was something wrong with me. Something wrong that made people not like me. I got into things that annoyed people, but I really didn't care. I was kind of very . . . I was quirky and silly. I thought of myself as this kind of fat kid who was rebellious–someone who did not fit in."

"Have you ever felt invisible, like you didn't exist in 'their' world?"

"Sometimes . . . well, probably around the time the eating disorder started, I watched people in the playground and just kind of . . . I was sort of separate, like there was kind of a wall or something. They would do their own little thing, and somehow they interacted with each other. I was kind of like separate and they didn't notice me. But, mostly, just kind of . . . kind of like I'm just watching a movie of everyone around me and I'm not part of it. I'm just watching it."

"Have you ever gone through extreme depression?"

"Yeah."

"When?"

"Well, there were different episodes. Probably, I think the first case of . . . I guess I would say regular depression . . . I'm not sure what level. This was my junior year and senior year in high school. I had lung surgery. It made me . . . I was just very depressed after that. I guess it was an anxiety-provoking situation, and it just made me feel lousy. I guess I was in a lot of physical pain. Then again, in college I was dealing with depression the entire time. It wasn't until recently, like the past year, that it became more severe and I needed hospitalization to resolve it."

"The lung problem. What brought that on?"

"It was spontaneous. Just generally collapsing. I needed surgery for that."

"Were you ever hospitalized before that?"

"When I was ten, I was hospitalized because of medical problems from the eating disorder. I lost a lot of weight then. I was fainting. I was in the hospital for a week. They were giving me IVs and they tried to figure out what's wrong with me, and I lied to them. So they had an eating disorder person come, like a specialist, and I lied to every single one of his questions."

"What were the questions? What were the lies?"

"Like, I knew that they were looking to see if I had an eating disorder and I didn't want to end up . . . my mom, when I wasn't eating, my mom used to say, 'You're going to end up in an eating disorder unit.' So when they asked me things like, 'Do you think you're fat?' I said, 'No.' 'Do you like to eat food?' 'Yes.' I kind of feel, at that time period, they were focusing on the gymnastics and the ice skating. They kept asking questions like, 'Do you do that? Or that?' 'No, I just sit around.' They kind of had this idea that, like, 'Well, she's pretty young. She's not a gymnast.' So they ended up not diagnosing me with an eating disorder. I was basically able to pull it off. I convinced them that I was just a picky eater, and they bought it. They said, 'Oh, OK, your constant weight loss may be a virus.' Looking back, it was ridiculous. I lost 20 percent of my body mass, ended up in a hospital, and they said, 'Just a virus.' So, I pulled it off. I never . . . I went to the eating disorder specialist once, and he didn't diagnose me. But then the treatment from then on was identical to someone with an eating disorder, just minus the therapy. I still had to drink supplements. I still had to go to the doctor every week, but they didn't know I had an eating disorder. They thought I wanted to gain weight. So, when I went to the doctor, he said, 'OK. Let's see if I can fatten you up.' Normally, they wouldn't say that, at least I hope they wouldn't say that, if I had an eating disorder."

"Were you seeing a therapist?"

"Just the doctor. They didn't think there was anything wrong. They just thought I was a picky eater."

"So you were actually eating when you had to, and getting away with not eating when you could."

"Yeah. And then, what ended up happening was just . . . Because of the lunch, really, I would end up going to the doctor and not gain any weight. So he would just add more Ensure. So I had this gigantic afternoon snack and dinner, and a gigantic snack before going to sleep. So, eventually, I mean, I just couldn't stop the weight gain."

"Were you angry?"

"Yeah. Of course, it seemed . . . it was different. Even though it felt terrible, most of the weight I gained went vertical, so it wasn't as noticeable."

"That second bout of depression, were you hospitalized for it?"

"Yeah. I was trying to think. The first hospitalization was after the freshman year. That was a residential program for OCD. That was because the OCD was getting out of control. And so it's kind of different from like a 'hospital' hospital. It wasn't a locked unit. You could go in and out."

"Were you happy with the treatment you were getting?"

"Yeah. I mean, it's actually hard to get into the program because there are only three such programs in the entire country. You had to be very self-motivated to get in there. So I really wanted to go in there. It helped a lot. It was hard, though. But even then, I was almost thrown out of that program because they basically had a contract with me saying that I had to be healthy physically to be there. They couldn't accommodate an eating disorder. So I would sneak into the bathroom and throw up and things like that. So, even then, it was always about hiding it and trying, almost like, the eating disorder was kind of like this . . . It's like adapting and trying to hide and not be caught."

"Tell me about the second time you were hospitalized."

"The second time was for the eating disorder. That was inpatient and a terrible program. This was around my sophomore year. They had some therapy. I saw a psychiatrist. They start you off on an all-liquid diet. All Ensure. It originally got up to 4,000 calories. I thought I was going to explode. So it was basically, we spent our time eating, and then sitting on the couch was kind of like, oh, God, your stomach hurt. I felt like a beached whale sitting there. But it was also a very triggering environment to see all these really, really emaciated patients and wanting to be like them. Whenever I looked at an extremely thin person, like, I would say to myself, 'I want to look like you.'

And they thought the same thing about me. Everyone there thought they were the fattest patient there."

"What percent were you below your 'normal' body weight?"

"I'm not sure exactly. They had this program . . . if you were more than 15 percent below your expected body weight, then you were on this all-liquid Ensure diet. So I was on that program a little bit. I think I was about 20 pounds underweight. Something like that. I felt like I looked totally normal. And now, when I look at pictures of myself from that time, it's like, 'whoa!' I didn't see it then. But now, when I look at pictures of myself, I think I looked terrible. I thought to myself back then, 'Why do I need to go into the hospital? I'm just a tiny bit underweight.' Looking at those pictures makes me feel confused. It's like, why didn't I see it then?"

"Are you comfortable looking at pictures of yourself today?"

"Sure. I think I look OK now."

"I see. Carol, when you feel hunger, do you feel more successful and more in control? Did you enjoy your hunger?"

"Yes. I enjoyed it. I had, like, different periods of . . . because I don't . . . when I was younger, when I was about ten, whenever my stomach growled, when I felt it, when I heard it, that was like success. That was good. In college, when I felt really hungry, eventually, after a while, you don't feel hunger because, like, you go so long you just get used to it, so you don't notice it. When I would walk around feeling light-headed or dizzy or something, I felt better about myself. Like, look how disciplined I am. I felt like I was more studious. When I was in control of my body and food, I was more in control of the studying, 'cause I kind of linked the two together."

"By age ten, you thought your mother was overbearing. This must have put more stress on that situation."

"Yeah. My mom would also get on my dad's case. She would tell him that he's too thin and that he's not eating enough. So it was like she was trying to force both of us to eat."

"We talked about anorexia. Tell me about your bulimia."

"That was more in college. It might technically be considered purging anorexia. It wasn't so much bingeing as it was, like . . . I'd have a meal with my parents, or if I went out for dinner with a group of people, I purged that meal. But my bingeing, more this past year . . . I don't meet the full criteria to call my purging anorexia bulimia. Things that I purged were things that I enjoyed too much while I ate them. 'Cause that was like a sin. I couldn't do that. That was, like, really indulgent. And I had an image of myself of lying down and watching TV and spilling out all over the place. It's too out of control to enjoy food."

"When you purge, what's going through your mind?"

"You mean, right when I'm finished?"

"Before, during, and after."

"Before, it's like I feel I'm dead. I would just fill myself up. Sometimes in my apartment, I would have a lot to eat. I would binge on some things. It didn't matter. It was just filling me up. I would have a huge amount of pickles or pretzels, something like that. It was just all about eating more and eating more and I'm not allowed to taste them. I just kind of shovel it in and kind of really eat fast. And then I kind of like have that feeling that I never really felt full, and then finally this, like, panic sets in, 'Oh, my God. Look how much I ate. I have to get it out now. Get it out now.' I can't wait two seconds. I would just run to wherever to get it out. And then, as soon as it gets out, it's like, 'Ahhh.' So it's kind of like I'm out of control, I let myself go out of control for a period of time, and then I gain back control by throwing it up. I don't know, the whole thing was . . . it was basically a good distraction from any emotions I felt. If I'm feeling depressed, if I'm feeling anxious, I just focus on the food coming in and going out. The bingeing and purging was something to be ashamed of. But the restriction was something to be proud of."

"How do you react to the taste of vomit in your mouth?"

"The more I did it, the more I was disgusted with the bitter taste in my mouth. But I had to. I had to get it all out of my system."

"When you binge, how much do you consume?"

"I would frequently binge on junk food. A binge for me would be like two single-serving bags of chips. And, if I enjoyed that enough, that was enough for my binge. And then there are other times. Sometimes I would eat two bags of chips and two candy bars. It was never like . . . for me, that was an enormous amount and it had to be thrown. It was too much. It was basically more than a normal person would eat at one time. I can look back now and see that it wasn't a huge amount."

"Is bingeing, purging, and restriction the only way you dealt with emotions?"

"No. Around the same time I started purging, I started cutting myself. I guess the advantage with the cutting is that you can hide it. It's easy to hide it. No one knows. I'd bet most of the people sitting in my class had no idea that I was cutting, purging, or restricting. All those things were for the same reason, an emotional release. The cutting just kind of went along with it. I used it for . . . one psychiatrist said I used it for emotional regulation. Either if I feel too many emotions, if I feel too sad, too anxious, too overwhelmed, then I had to release those emotions and just get them out. It's kind of like the idea that I can't control my emotions, but I could control the pain I would feel by cutting. And then I would also cut if I felt too normal, too little emotions, and I would do it if I needed to feel something. If I kind of wanted to feel pain."

"How did you react to the sight of your own blood?"

"When I first started, the cutting and the blood felt really good. It was like this high. This release. Kind of similar to, like, the vomit. Then, after a while, it didn't do enough. I just kept doing it more and more and more and more and more until I was doing it hundreds of times and it just wasn't doing it for me."

"Did you ever get the same high as the first time you cut yourself?"

"No. It's the same thing with restriction. You lose more weight, but it's never enough. And that's when I . . . I kind of, well . . . I decided to stop cutting, well, not stop, but not do it as much. One time, I cut too deep. I had to go to the emergency room. I was almost ready to die. After that, I decided that it just wasn't good. It just wasn't good enough anymore. It wasn't painful enough anymore. It would just take more and more each time. The instrument had to get sharper. I had to cause more damage. It had to be deeper. It had to be more and more and more. I just kept trying to get back that same high, but I couldn't. That's when I moved to burning and stuff with a straightening iron and a curling iron. That was also a lot of just pain. But I definitely noticed periods of just, the cutting and burning and purging went together. The purging usually didn't have to do with when I was feeling fat. It was more like an emotional thing."

"Are you still cutting?"

"No. It's been like a month now. I'm making progress."

"Since you started, is that the longest you've ever gone without cutting?"

"I don't think so. I think I went longer before. But I always . . . the reason I stopped was because I realized it just wasn't doing it. Like, I was just starting to realize it's not going to make the emotions go away. It's just going to make the emotions get worse, 'cause afterwards I got so mad at myself. 'Look what you did. You went a month without doing it and now you're cutting yourself.' I'd beat myself up afterwards. I kind of used other motivators. It was too expensive to buy all that stuff."

"What do you use to cut yourself?"

"A range of things, like razor blades, X-Acto knives, and box cutters. One time I tried hard to give it up. I threw out all the sharp utensils in my apartment. Then, one night, I got so depressed I felt I had to cut. I looked around. There was nothing sharp in the house. Then, after rummaging around, I remembered a gift from my mother that was on the shelf in my closet. It was never opened and still in its original wrapping paper. It was a blender. I took the blades out. It didn't do too much for me, but it sufficed for the moment. It's funny. My mom happened to call two days later and asked, 'Did you ever use that blender?'"

"I said, "Sort of . . .'"

"Does your mom know about the cutting?"

"Yeah. I eventually had to tell her because it was kind of noticeable when I was at the beach and wearing pants because I couldn't wear a bathing suit. She asked me why. And also, there would be the bills from CVS for Band-Aids and everything. They got expensive. And then, when I went into the emergency room, she kind of got the bill. She was very, very upset. She just flipped out because, to her, that was like a sign of craziness. I was going to lose it and get locked up. That was kind of like one of those things like you only heard on TV."

"Do you think her concern was reasonable?"

"Well, like, I guess so."

"Do you love your mother?"

"Yeah, but sometimes I hate her. I feel like she wants to help, but sometimes she just doesn't know the right way to do it. Or, she'll always be very controlling and yelling . . ."

"When she yells, how do you feel?"

"I usually just feel enraged, and I yell back. It just goes back and forth. Back and forth. Lately, I mean lately, it's yelling because of being in the hospital a month ago. And then, almost going to the hospital a few weeks ago. And the school; they are worried about me being in school."

"Why were you hospitalized in the last few months?"

"This past one was just for being suicidal. But the one before that was for a mixture of eating disorder stuff, but mostly depression."

"What medication are you on?"

"I'm on Lithium, Luvox, Ceraquill, and some other stuff."

"Some people think Lithium makes you gain weight. What effect did it have on you?"

"I was very afraid of Lithium. I said to my doctor, 'I heard about Lithium and blah, blah, blah, blah, blah.' I didn't gain anything on it. And mostly, from what I've heard, a lot of the weight gain from the medications is that you become less depressed. All of a sudden, your appetite increases. But my appetite stayed the same. I'm still trying to work out the medications. The problem is that I mess it up. When you're underweight, the medications don't work at all, pretty much. And when you're purging, the medications don't stay in your system. So the eating disorder really screws up the medications."

"Let's switch topics. Are you currently in a relationship with anyone?"

"Yeah."

"How long has this relationship been going on?"

"Over two years."

"How did you meet him?"

"We met in class. He's a grad student. Our relationship has been pretty rocky, with my stuff, with going to the hospital, or things, just things like not being able to have a normal dinner with him. For a while, I couldn't eat in front of him."

"Why not?"

"I felt like a pig. You know, I didn't want him to see me eating. Or, eating and purging. So there was a lot of, just, things like, if he put his arms around me, I didn't want him to do that. I didn't want to sit on his lap. You know, because I thought I would crush him. So it was kind of, it was a lot of, there's still a problem with the affection part of it. And just being ashamed of my body and all those things really interferes with the affection."

"Have you ever made love with him?"

"No."

"Has he ever seen you with your clothes off?"

"No."

"Does he know about your depression and eating disorder history? Have you ever discussed it?"

"Yeah. I mean, he's very supportive because he himself struggles with depression. He's on medication. I've had two boyfriends before him. They just said, 'Suck it up and get over it.' But he's understanding that way, and I have a problem with affection."

"A problem giving it, or getting it?"

"I guess it's both. I didn't want to receive it."

"Why is that?"

"I don't know. I think it's a combination of just, like, I don't really allow myself to experience emotions. It just seems out of control, or, I'm kind of always detached and observant. So you can't really, like, observe yourself being affectionate. You know what I mean? You have to be in the present."

"Does he love you?"

"I think . . . well . . . Yeah. I assume so."

"You've known him now for two years. Has he ever said so?"

"He has. I don't say it a lot because I don't want to say it just to say it."

"But you feel you love him?"

"Yeah. And I guess sometimes that causes a lot of confusion for me. I mean, how can he possibly love me? I'm not deserving of it."

"Why not?"

"I guess I think of myself as kind of like, I don't know, some flawed, evil, fat, ugly, deformed, bad person."

"If I could hand you a magic pill, what would you want that pill to fix?"

"My depression and pain. I almost feel like my pain is invisible and that you can't see it. And so, I'm kind of afraid that my doctors won't believe me, or everyone's going to believe I'm all better and won't help me. But at least like . . . here at the hospital, I see sickly looking patients. I'd think to myself, 'Look at how much discipline they have.' I'd think, 'Wow, they're in a lot of pain, and other people see it.' Now, my pain is like my scars. My pain is all covered up. I just seem like, kind of like, I'm not going to get better because there is something fundamentally messed up about me—something that's always going to be wrong, and there's nothing to change it. As long as I'm me, there's just something wrong about it. That's kind of like, environment, the suicidal thoughts, and punishment. It's like the only way, really, to get rid of my pain is to get rid of myself. So it's kind of like this hopeless feeling that no matter how many people I see, no matter how many medications I take, no matter how hard I try, it's never going to get better. What I say always is that when other people, like, get better from it, I say to myself, 'Wow, they can do it because they're working harder, and I'm just this evil person.' I go around convincing myself that I'm OK. That's how I always feel. Like, oh yeah, I'm still going to class, and basically, in my eyes, it's like, oh well, I'm still alive, so I'm OK. I'm validating myself. Oh, there's worse people out there."

"When you look at yourself in a mirror, what do you see?"

"When I look in the mirror, I don't see a face, I don't see a body. I just see like different parts. I stand there and spend hours picking at my skin. I pick at my pores. So it's kind of like I look at my face and the only thing that exists are pores, and everything else around doesn't exist. I look in the mirror and it's kind of a good distraction. I look at all the marks on my body, instead of seeing my body as a whole."

"Are you proud of those marks?"

"Oh, no. I'm extremely ashamed of them. I hide them. A large portion of my wardrobe has to be put aside because I can't wear that stuff."

"Let's say there are two magic switches on the wall. The first switch puts you at a healthy weight and makes you a relatively happy, secure, and loved person. The second switch makes you dead. Which switch would you flip?"

"Without a doubt or moment's hesitation, the second switch. I would welcome death instantly."

"Carol, why are you here? Was it your choice?"

"No. My mother forced me into this program. So did my school. They said they would throw me out if I didn't go into an eating disorder recovery program."

"So, it's not so much that you're looking for recovery. For you, it seems like the more important issues are staying in school and dealing with your mother."

"You got that right. I love school. My grade point is 4.0."

"That doesn't surprise me, Carol. I hope what we do here will get you back into school."

"Me, too."

"Well, everyone, it looks like we've reached the end of another session. Carol, I'd like to thank you for sharing your thoughts with us in such an open fashion. Wonderful job. Wonderful job. And, with your permission, I'd like to continue talking with you for a few minutes in my office."

"Sure."

* * *

The more I sat in on the evening therapy sessions, the more I believed that Dr. Barrow was right. By listening to the stories of the other women, I was learning more about myself and finding things I had to address with my own personality.

I found it ironic and sad that the other women and I had something in common. At some points in our lives, we all tried to be "perfect." In fact, we all tried so hard to be perfect that we wound up sick and, frequently, mentally disabled as a result of that unattainable perfection we sought for ourselves. Carol took that "perfect little girl" syndrome to an extreme, as did Denise. Denise was so perfect she attempted suicide multiple times, and Carol has hundreds of scars over her body from self-mutilation.

When I got back to my room, Claire tried to talk with me about Carol, but I was in no mood to converse with my space cadet. I just nodded my head a few times when her voice sounded like she addressed a question to me. Within ten minutes, I excused myself from the conversation by feigning a headache. I got into bed and felt unable to fall asleep because of various introspective concepts running haphazardly through my thoughts. I didn't fight them. I let them flow.

I recalled Denise's tales about her abusive husband. I labeled myself lucky because I have the greatest husband in the world. He would do anything for me. I have a husband who loves me more than I'll ever realize. I have a husband who would never come close to abusing me. Then I thought about Carol and how she felt she doesn't deserve to be loved by her boyfriend. How sad that must be. Sometimes people can't find love to share with someone else, but everyone should feel deserving of love.

Then Carol's descriptions of cutting herself and how she used it for emotional control brought my thoughts back to Megan. I could never understand why Megan cut herself. Perhaps Carol finally opened my eyes as to why Megan cut herself. Was Megan also using it as an emotional control to get over her fears and anxieties? Perhaps she was. After all, it started when she was in an extremely frightened and depressed state. Perhaps it gave her the same "high" as it did for Carol.

The final thing I remember contemplating before falling asleep was whether I would be chosen for a therapy session. It was great to be a fly on the wall. It already had benefited me. But, being in the hot seat had to be different. Dr. Barrow seemed like a great therapist. He got his patients to open up and divulge their most private and innermost thoughts, fears, and conflicts. He seemed to help put those negative feelings and fears into a different light for his patients. What would happen with me? How would I react? I wasn't sure, but I was anxious and curious to find out. I had already begun to break the cycle and had started eating, albeit with difficulty. Now I wanted to break the emotional cycle of my debilitating depression. As I'd come to learn, an eating disorder is a mind and body sickness. I was starting to heal my body, but my mind had recovered only a miniscule fraction of what it needed to get to. As long as I was there, away from the ones I loved so much and trying to heal myself, I might as well go for the gold and come out a woman on the road to a physical and mental recovery. God knows how much I wanted it and needed it.

* * *

The next morning at breakfast one of the attendants handed me a sealed envelope. I had no idea what it contained, but something made me control my curiosity. I refrained from opening it in public. When I finished my meal, I got dressed to go outside for a long walk. Finally, I sat down in the sun under a tree. I lit a cigarette and opened the envelope. It was from Dr. Barrow. It said I had been chosen as the patient for that evening. He asked me to answer a few questions so he could have more details about some of the things I had written about in my questionnaire.

I sat there for several hours under the scrutinizing eyes of a matron and mused over each question before writing a concise answer. It was obvious that the better information I supplied, the more tools he would have to try to help me. Before I knew it, it was time for lunch.

I kept to myself during the entire meal. I didn't want anyone else's thoughts or petty problems interfering with my task at hand. It wasn't until just before dinner that I completed the assignment and handed it to Dr. Barrow's still smiling assistant. The interesting thing for me was that her smile didn't bother me as much as the day when I first met her.

* * *

The buzzing therapy room went silent as soon as Dr. Barrow entered and took his seat at the front table. He smiled at me and checked his papers. I took a deep breath to compose myself. I had been through many therapy sessions before, but none with so many people who were about to hang on every syllable I uttered, or none with so many eyes staring at me as though I was the center ring of a three-ring circus. It was intimidating, but I remembered that I was the one who asked for it.

"Good evening, everyone. Tonight we'll be working with Jess. Good evening, Jess."

"Nice to be here, Dr. Barrow."

"You've been here for six days now. How is it going for you?"

"Better than I expected."

"What did you expect?"

"When I first arrived, I expected to walk out of your office and go home."

"Why didn't you?"

"If I left, it would only have been a matter of time before I died from my eating disorder. As recently as two days before checking in, I passed out from low potassium levels, and I wanted to die. Fortunately, that experience scared me back into wanting to live."

"Well, obviously, you're not in denial."

"Been there, done that, don't want to do it again."

"Thank you for that beautiful transition. Jess, you were chosen for tonight's session because of something you said during our first telephone conversation. Do you remember your expression, 'This time?'"

"All too well."

"So this is not the first time you went inpatient for your eating disorder."

"No."

"What would you say is the biggest difference between the cause of your first inpatient stay and this one?"

"The first time I fell into my eating disorder was by accident. The second time, it was because my life was out of control."

"What do you mean by 'accident?'"

"Well, the first time it started was because I wanted to lose 10 pounds to look better in my wedding dress."

"That was over twenty years ago. Wasn't it?"

"Yes. What I learned is that an eating disorder can be caused by a personality type that seeks approval. Well, when I lost my weight, I heard the expressions I've heard other women say here. 'Oh, you look great. I wish I could have the discipline you have.' I looked so much better after I lost a reasonable amount of weight, and I loved the approval. I never got approval from my parents. They weren't the nurturing type. So getting approval and having that 'I want to be perfect' type of personality pushed me right into a downward spiraling pattern. I thought that the more weight I lost, the more approval I would get. I didn't. Little did I know that the approval would eventually turn into criticism once the weight loss went out of control. But by that time, the ritual was too well ingrained. At that time, I denied that I was out of control and threatening my own life by my personality type and malnutrition."

"Can you elaborate on that point?"

"I'll put it this way: losing weight became akin to a drug habit. It's like when people take a prescription drug to help themselves with a medical problem and then they wind up addicted to that drug and nearly dying from the medication that was supposed to help them. My habit, my addiction, became an obsession. Fifteen years ago, I went inpatient weighing 90 pounds. That was 40 pounds below my safe weight. I got out believing I was in full recovery and would never revert to that habit. I was like a cigarette smoker who gave up smoking for good, and I was glad I had given up the habit. I gave birth to two children without ever caring about how much weight I gained because the health of my children was the only thing important to me. I stayed in recovery for over thirteen years."

"That was a long time."

"Yeah, I thought I had this thing beat. Then my life went out of control."

"How so?"

"Let's start with my job. I work part-time, but I'm considered a manager at the hospital I work at. We were installing a new computer system, and I'm not very good with computers. I had to rely on others to get the job done, and I'm usually a very self-sufficient person. I don't like relying on others. Plus, I knew that if I didn't do the job perfectly, the hospital and medical records and the health of thousands of people could be jeopardized. That scared the hell out of me. Then I started having problems with my daughter when she entered junior high school. At first, I thought it was just a high-anxiety adjustment period for her. She had been a good student, but in junior high her grades dropped considerably, and her behavior, which had been good, went to hell. I got notes from her teachers on a daily basis. Then I learned she started cutting herself. I had no idea what prompted that. Listening to these sessions has actually given me a better understanding about why people do that. I felt my daughter's life could be lost. I pictured coming home one day and finding her in a pool of her own blood. My fears and my life were out of control. I started suffering from anxiety and depression. I needed to have control over something, and the only thing left to control was what and how much went into my mouth. What I'm learning is that I never controlled what went into my mouth. It controlled me. A heroin addict doesn't control the heroin, the heroin controls, and tries to destroy, the addict."

"Your first inpatient stay was a result of laxative abuse and anorexia."

"Yes."

"What has changed?"

"Now I'm back to laxative abuse and anorexia. I abuse diet pills. I'm bulimic. I suffer from depression, for which I'm on medication, and I've been fighting suicidal thoughts. I have an obsessive and addictive-type personality. I started smoking. I still desire that 'perfect person' personality, but I'm living anything but a perfect life."

"Jess, let's go back to your childhood. What negative factors might have influenced your behavior or personality type?"

"I had the kind of childhood that kids shouldn't have. First, let me say that my parents aren't bad people. In their own way, they're lovely people. But, with that said, I'll start by saying my father was a fool for taking me and my brother with him when he went on a date and cheated on my mother, who found out about it that same day. That night, my mother took my brother and me out of the house to live with relatives. I hated that. I thought I'd never see my home again. My parents weren't nurturing at all. As a result, and as an attempt to receive any type of nurturing, I formed the 'I must be perfect' or 'good little girl' personality. It was the only way I received any nurturing or positive feedback from teachers, friends, or relatives. I lived my life and judged myself by what others thought of me, not by what I thought of myself. I never knew what my parents thought of me. Unless they said something negative, I never heard from them. Unlike most parents, neither of them ever attended an open school night, nor did they ever speak to one of my teachers about how or what I was doing in school. They had nothing whatsoever to do with my schooling. My mother let me down. She could have helped me enter womanhood. Instead, she made my first period one of the most embarrassing moments of my life. One of the other women this week spoke of living with someone with a bipolar disorder. I love my brother, but he suffers from bipolar disorder. He constantly blew up in my face. I'll never forget the day I had a friend over and he ran around the house naked with a large kitchen knife, trying to kill us. He should have been sent to jail or an institution. Instead, the police dismissed it as though nothing happened. There was the time my father's mistake set the house on fire. We had to move out while the house was renovated. My parents and brother went to live with relatives. I thought I was so lucky that I got away from my brother and went to live with my guidance counselor. I had sessions with her for a year prior to that. I thought I was safe. I thought her taking me into her home put me into a safe and nurturing environment. That's what I thought until I was fifteen and she raped me, then she kept me in an unwanted lesbian relationship for over a year. Oh, yeah, I had a 'wonderful' childhood. I was the poster girl for the most-messed-up child of the year. Then I met my phenomenal husband. I thought all of my life's tragedies were over. I thought I was finally going to live happily ever after."

"You thought you found your knight in shining armor who would protect you from the rest of the world."

"He did. He would do anything for me. He would protect me from every negative thing and person in this world. He just couldn't protect me from myself. I became my own worst enemy. I got myself into my first round of eating disorders. He tried to get me out of it. With his help, I got myself into recovery. But recently, I got myself into my depressed state. I have thoughts of suicide and a constant desire to die. He tried to get me out of it. Part of the reason why I'm here now is because of his help and my doctor convincing me to be here."

"Jess, what are you looking forward to?"

"I'm looking forward to getting out, staying out, and never returning to an inpatient situation."

"Good. And what do you think you've learned so far from your stay here?"

"I've come to understand that wanting to kill yourself is wrong and a sick way to live."

"Are you just saying that, or do you understand that now?"

"I understand it, but it still consumes me. I still hate who I am. To begin with, I'm a terrible mother."

"What makes you think that?"

"Because I'm here as a result of my self-destructive and suicidal behavior. For a long time, I didn't care if I saw my kids grow up. That makes me a worthless and terrible mother."

"We'll get back to that thought in a moment. First, I'd like to know why you are here."

"I'm here because I don't want to die. This is a new and very recent change in my attitude. Like I said, until a little over a week ago, I lived with constant suicidal thoughts. I was just too much of a punk chicken to take my own life. Then I was in the emergency room two days before I checked in here. The patient in the next bed went Code Blue. Death was no longer a virtual concept. Death was physically close. Death could have reached out its hand to my bed and taken me forever. That incident changed me. Death was suddenly as real as that person dying in the bed next to me. I still don't know if that person ever took another breath. But the best reason I can tell you why I'm here is to break the cycle."

"Are you doing that?"

"I think so. For over a year, I restricted as much as possible. Or, if I put anything into my mouth, I purged it. Plus, I popped laxatives and diet pills like they were candy. It got so that passing out from low potassium levels became a normal routine. I've lost count of how many times I woke up with the cold kitchen tile floor against my face. What if I passed out while driving my kids somewhere? I didn't care about losing my life, but I sure as hell didn't want to murder my kids. They would have been innocent victims of my self-destructive behavior. That's not right. I have to be the worst mother in the world."

"What makes you say that?"

"Because I'm here instead of being with them."

"Jess, try this. You're a good mother."

"Why?"

"Because you're here."

"I don't understand."

"OK. Let me put it this way. Your eating disorder puts you in your secret and private place, and it separates you from your family. Doesn't it?"

"Yes."

"You often live in your own world in order to hide your eating disorder."

"Yes."

"Jess, by going into recovery, you'll go back to spending quality time with your kids and husband instead of sneaking away to practice the self-destructive habits created and controlled by your disorder."

"I hope so."

"Jess, what do you want the most?"

"I want to get rid of my depression. I want to change my choice point. I want to see my kids grow up. I want my husband to continue loving me, and I want to finally love myself. I want to break the cycle. I want to get into recovery, and stay there. I don't want to ever be in this kind of place again. I hate being here, but I'm here to save my life."

"That sounds like a perfect thought to end tonight's session."

* * *

Chapter Eight
Little Or No Effect

I t was difficult falling asleep that night. I kept replaying what I said at my therapy session earlier that evening in my mind. "What did you expect?" Dr. Barrow had asked. I remember giving him somewhat of a glib answer because I was nervous. Now, however, it was one o'clock in the morning, I was still awake, and I was asking myself that same question and looking for an honest and realistic answer. For the past six days I had been eating, I had stopped the laxatives, and there was no way for me to restrict or purge. That was fine, for now. I had broken the cycle here in the "bubble." They call an eating disorder unit a bubble because it's a protected and safe environment. I had no choice but to follow the rules and live a healthy lifestyle. What would happen when I was out of the bubble? What would happen when I saw fresh wounds on Megan's arms from cutting or, worse yet, found her in a pool of her own blood? What would happen when I was alone with my secret stash of laxatives, and there was no one to stop me from restricting, or to inspect the toilet before I flush?

I distinctly remember Dr. Barrow asking, "What are you looking forward to?" and "Jess, what do you want the most?"

I remember my exact answer to both questions. "I'm looking forward to getting out, staying out, and never returning to an inpatient situation. I want to get rid of my depression. I want to change my choice point. I want to see my kids grow up. I want my husband to continue loving me, and I want to finally love myself. I want to break the cycle. I want to get into recovery, and stay there. I don't want to ever be in this kind of place again. I hate being here, but I'm here to save my life."

The truth is that I still hate myself. The truth is, I am still my own worst enemy. The truth is, this disorder controls me, I don't control it. My habit, my addiction, is an obsession, and I'm afraid of giving it up because, if I do, I'll become nothing more than a worthless, fat cow.

The next morning Dr. Barrow, as required by my insurance company, was going to call me into his office to review my status. He had done that with all the other girls and me every two days since we'd been there. My intention was to convince him I was ready to leave. I was ready not because I was sure I had beaten this disorder, but because I wanted to get back to my family. I wanted out, even if it was for the wrong reason.

* * *

I entered Dr. Barrow's waiting room and immediately captured the attention of his still-smiling receptionist. "Good morning, Jess."

"Good morning."

"Dr. Barrow has another patient in his office. He'll be with you shortly."

"Thanks."

The digital clock on the receptionist's desk read 10:19. There were no magazines and nothing to do. At first, I studied his receptionist. I couldn't tell how tall she was because I never saw her stand. Her face was pleasant looking. She was neither pretty nor ugly. Just common. From the crow's-feet and other wrinkles, I'd guess she was in her mid-fifties and at this job since the unit opened. She was neither fat nor thin. Her hair was blonde, probably from a bottle, and every strand was perfectly in place, unlike mine.

By 10:25 I started to get fidgety. That's when I took my attention off of the receptionist and stared at the doctor's door. At first I wondered how many women sat in this room wondering if they were going to be released; then I rehearsed my reasons why he should release me from this eating disorder prison.

At 10:29 Dr. Barrow's office door opened and an extremely young and extremely thin girl exited crying. "Caroline, your parents will be here in about an hour." The two hugged. "I'll miss you, Caroline," Dr. Barrow said in a fatherly tone. "I know you tried your best."

"I did, Dr. Barrow," she replied through her sobs.

Dr. Barrow took out a pack of tissues and handed one to her. She wiped her eyes and left the room still crying. Dr. Barrow's eyes remained on her until she was out of the room and turned into the corridor, then he turned toward me, gave me a very small grin, and said, "Good morning, Jess. I'll be right with you."

Dr. Barrow returned to his office and closed the door behind him. If I didn't know better, I'd say he needed a few moments to let out his frustration and release possible feelings of failure and other emotions pent up inside him. "Yeah," I said to myself, "even therapists and doctors have their down moments, only they know how to deal with them. I don't."

I turned to the receptionist and said impulsively, "Dr. Barrow better keep those tissues handy for me." There was no response. "What was that all about? She's so young."

"She's eleven. She's been suffering from anorexia for the past two years. This was not her first inpatient situation."

"How sad. Why is she leaving? She looks like she still needs help."

"Well, you know that any insurance company's inpatient/outpatient care covers a maximum of thirty days for the calendar year. Today is day thirty for her. Her parents cannot afford to pay for treatment out of pocket. They were here yesterday. Instead of getting the insurance extension they hoped for, they signed release forms and waivers."

"Wait a second. You mean the insurance company knows this kid is a hard-core eating disorder victim and all they did was say, 'Goodbye. Sorry. There's nothing we can do for you.'"

"That sums it up."

"That's incredible. No. It's disgusting. Will she have any form of outpatient care?"

"There's no insurance coverage left for this calendar year. The system isn't perfect."

"Perfect! The system stinks. That kid could die from starvation between now and the first of the year and some numb nut in an insurance company white tower will only say, 'Sorry, kid, your insurance ran out for the year. If you survive, see us again next year.' Shouldn't her doctor decide what's best for her, not the insurance idiot who has no clue what this is all about?"

The receptionist kept her eyes on mine without blinking, but she remained silent and didn't answer my question. For the first time, I took notice of the nameplate on her desk. Her name was Deborah. I had a feeling Deborah had experienced this type of scene before. For the first time, Deborah wasn't smiling. Something in her facial expression made me think Deborah agreed with me about the treatment of the little girl, but she wasn't allowed to express her feelings to a patient. We continued staring at each other for several seconds until I broke the tension of the silence, "Heaven help her, and all those in her position. This disorder is terrible enough. It's a shame some idiot doesn't care if that little girl lives or dies."

Just then, Dr. Barrow's door opened. "Come on in, Jess."

I guess I still hadn't calmed down. As I sat down, I blurted out, "Dr. Barrow, is it true about that little girl?"

"Let's talk about you, Jess," Dr. Barrow said as he sat down, reached for my folder, and buried his eyes in it. It was obvious he wanted to change the subject. "I see your weight has improved nicely since you joined us. You're up to 105. Good for you. How do you feel?"

"Just marvelous!"

Dr. Barrow's wry face indicated he understood the sarcasm and anger in my voice.

"Sorry, Dr. Barrow. I'm feeling pretty good."

"That's good."

"Yes. The medication you prescribed seems to be helping my depression."

"It's probably a combination of the medication and the fact that you are not suffering from malnutrition."

"Yeah."

"Jess, I'm thinking of releasing you. How do you feel about that?"

"I'd love to get home with my family."

"Do you think you are ready?"

"Honestly, I think so. You and the people here have helped me to break the cycle, which I couldn't do on my own. The laxatives, the purging, and the restricting are gone."

"Do you intend to continue treatment with Dr. Thatcher?"

"Absolutely."

"Jess, here is a list of recommended therapists for your outpatient treatment. It's vital that you continue therapy once you leave, or everything you've accomplished here might be for naught."

"I understand perfectly," I said as Dr. Barrow handed me a list of therapists in the tri-state area. "I'll get back to you this afternoon."

"Very good. Once you give us a name, we'll contact that doctor for you and forward a copy of your records." Dr. Barrow paused before continuing. "Jess, you understand that insurance coverage is an important factor."

"All too well."

"You've only used eight days for this calendar year. Should you need it, and I hope you don't, you still have twenty-two days of inpatient and intensive outpatient coverage left. Should you slip and need additional help, don't hesitate to contact me."

Something inside told me to get out of his office before he changed his mind. I stood, offered my hand, and said, "You can count on it, Dr. Barrow. I'll get back to you this afternoon with the name of the therapist. And just let me say, from the moment we first spoke on the phone, you've been a gentleman, a professional, and a nice guy."

"Well, you did all the work, Jess, we just gave you a helping hand. Here, you can use my phone to call your husband and make plans. I'll step outside so you can have some privacy."

I started dialing Jack's number at work before Dr. Barrow got out of the room. His phone rang twice before I heard his voice, "Jack Gordon here."

"Hi, hon."

"Jess, is everything OK?"

"Everything's fine. I get paroled tomorrow. Come and get me."

"Oh, Jess. That's great. I've missed you."

"Jack, you'll never know how much I've missed you and the kids. Get me the hell out of here."

* * *

Sunday, February 9, 2003, was a confusing day for me. Jack picked me up early from the hospital. The kids weren't with him. He arranged for them to get home a few minutes after we got into the house. It was confusing because I couldn't decide if I should congratulate myself or castigate myself. I was pleased with my weight because I got it up to a point where I was out of immediate danger, but I knew it would take a good therapist to keep me there and convince me to improve. I shouldn't have needed convincing, but I did. I didn't feel like I was on a secure road to continued recovery. In fact, from the moment we left the hospital, my thoughts obsessed on my secret laxative stash and the freedom to purge if I felt the desire. Obviously, those were not good signs for continued healthy behavior, neither was my decision not to attend the required intensive outpatient care program I was scheduled to start on Monday. I knew I didn't have the emotional strength to commute from Long Island to New Jersey for three days a week to eat two meals a day at the hospital and attend group therapy sessions. My rationalization was that I would start private therapy on Monday with my new therapist in Garden City, Dr. William Clark. I didn't look forward to the appointment.

The eight days in the hospital were somewhat pleasant, but I had my fill of doctors, therapy, and questions. My appointment with the therapist meant I would have to fill out another one of those annoying questionnaires and parade my disorder and transgressions to another stranger. I felt apprehensive. I felt anxious. I felt like I'd had enough of this garbage for a while and needed a break, but couldn't have one.

Jack was his usual and great self as we started the two-hour drive home from the hospital. Not once did he question me about what had happened in the hospital. His only comment about the situation was that I looked so much better. He told me several times that the kids looked forward to being with me again, and how happy he was to see me.

I turned on the radio when we approached the New Jersey Turnpike. A soft piano played slowly. It fit the kind of mood I was in. It was a song I didn't know and, at first, I enjoyed it. The lyrics asked a question: If you had a chance to get what you want, would you take that chance, or not? But then the song jumped into a heavy rap rhythm. Megan must have tuned to that station the last time she was in the car with Jack. My nerves were too shot to take that kind of music, so I turned the radio off. But the lyrics I heard got me thinking. In a way, that was the mental position I was in. Would I capture and hold onto the beginning of this recovery, or would I just let it slip? I wasn't sure of the answer or, at least, I wasn't ready to answer the question honestly, not even in the privacy of my own thoughts.

The ride home became an intermittent nightmare from the moment we hit the Jersey Turnpike. First there was stop-and-go traffic from Exit 7A past Exit 8A. The approach to the Outerbridge Crossing was a parking lot. The Staten Island Expressway was backed up the entire length to the Verrazano Bridge. The Belt Parkway crawled from the time we got on until my exit at Sunrise Highway. The expected two-hour trip turned into a three-and-a-half-hour calamity. I couldn't wait to get out of the car and be home again. Then, a few blocks from home, I started thinking about what it would be like getting into the house and returning to a "normal" life outside the bubble.

When I walked through the front door, I was emotionally out of control. Jack didn't notice that my hands were shaking as we walked into the silent and lifeless house. Part of me actually wanted to turn around and get back to the hospital, where there were no choices about eating, no purging, no restricting, no laxatives, and no apprehension about doing what I would normally do to abuse myself at home.

Jack called the parents where each of the kids was staying and asked to get them home. Both houses were on our block, so I knew it wouldn't take long to see them. I waited and watched by the front window so I could greet Megan and Jason as they arrived. Jason approached first, accompanied by his friend's mother. She waited by the sidewalk and watched as Jason safely entered the house. She was kind and courteous enough not to come in and cause me any more stress from her visit. I politely waved to her to thank her, then quickly closed the door, kneeled down, hugged Jason, and kissed his face a hundred times. Jason laughed at all the attention and kisses, and it made me laugh. I couldn't remember the last time I laughed, and the feeling lifted my spirits. I knew I missed my kids, but I didn't know how much until that moment.

"I'm happy to see you, Mommy. I missed you. Do you feel better now?"

"I'm so happy to see you, too, honey. You don't know how many times Mommy thought about you last week. I love you so much."

"I love you, too, Mommy. Is it OK if I finish up my homework now?"

"Sure, honey." I watched Jason walk up the steps as though I hadn't seen him in years. Just as he turned out of sight in the upstairs hallway, Megan opened the door. I hugged her and started kissing her the way I kissed Jason. Megan, however, didn't think it was cool for a mother to show such affection.

"Come on, Mom. It's not like you've been away for years."

"It felt like it, honey. I'm happy to see you."

"Glad to see you, too. I'll be in my room."

Jack was standing next to us. He noticed something on my face, but didn't say anything until Megan was upstairs and he heard her door close.

"It was an interesting week with her."

"How so?"

"I think she missed you more than she's willing to admit. Jason, on the other hand, took the situation in stride. He's a hell of a great little kid."

"Yeah, and they have one hellava great mother," I said with great sarcasm.

"Yes, they do," Jack said as he hugged me. I knew Jack didn't get what I meant. He kissed each of my cheeks before he kissed my lips. "Jess, I hope you're on your way to where you want to be."

"Me, too."

"It's almost five. I have a feeling you're in no mood to cook. What do you say I order in some Chinese?"

Jack's mention of food jolted me back to the realization that I was out of the bubble and back into the real world. Cooking and eating were the last things on my mind, but I knew that he and the kids had to eat, and I knew how much the kids enjoyed Chinese food. "Sure, hon. Great idea."

It was close to six before the food arrived and the four of us sat down to eat together. I paused before I ate my first forkful. I wondered whether this was my first meal toward recovery. The mealtime was basically pleasant. Jason was extremely talkative and told us all about his sports activities at school and a few big tests he had, and how proud he was for getting good grades. The mention of good grades almost annoyed Megan. Unlike Jason, she'd had a test or two and didn't fair as well. Throughout the meal, I noticed Jack trying to observe what and how much I ate. It bothered me. It felt like the food police were still watching me as they did in the hospital. I put on a good show for him and finished a normal-sized meal. When we finished eating, I suggested that Jack and the kids spend some time together. Megan said she had schoolwork to do and excused herself. Jason asked Jack if they could throw the football around in the backyard. I insisted they go out and have a good time together. Jack didn't realize it, but I had ulterior motives for my suggestion. Jack and Jason went upstairs to wash, then came down as I was loading the dishwasher. Although I had eaten as much at each meal in the hospital, I felt uncomfortable and full, and it bothered me. The moment I heard the backyard door close, I turned on the dishwasher and headed downstairs, knowing all too well what I was about to do. I opened the downstairs bathroom door, locked it after I got in, lifted the toilet seat, bent over to the sight I had seen hundreds of times, stuck my fingers down my throat, and heaved up every bite of food I had taken in. I welcomed the disgusting taste of vomit in my mouth. I didn't feel shame or remorse for my actions. Instead, I felt great satisfaction knowing that every ounce of food that had entered my system was purged. My wooziness felt much like a drug-induced high. I rinsed my mouth with mouthwash, rinsed with water, and exited the bathroom. I was still light-headed and needed to hold on to the banister firmly to prevent myself from falling as I ascended the stairs to return to the kitchen.

A few minutes later, I finished with the kitchen and took out the garbage. I went upstairs and noticed Megan's door was open. Her radio was on and there were schoolbooks all over the bed. I knocked on the open door. "Hey, sweetheart, how did it go while I was gone?"

"Well, Dad and I butted heads a few times, but otherwise it was OK."

"What was the problem?"

"No problem. I was just in a bad mood, I guess."

"Because I was away?"

"Glad you're back, Mom. I hope things work out for you and you won't have to go back again."

"Me, too, Megan," I said as I hugged her.

"Mom, I better get to my homework. Things aren't great for me in school lately."

"What can I do to help?"

"You can let me try to do my homework. I hate this crap."

"Megan . . ." I paused. I felt that if the conversation went any further, we would have another one of those stressful talks about how she has to improve in school. This was no night for one of those talks. I was already emotionally drained and knew nothing would be accomplished. "Megan, I'm here for you. Let me know how I can help you."

"Sure, Mom. No problem. Have a good night."

"You too, hon."

I went to my room, washed up, got undressed, got into bed, and stared mindlessly at the ceiling. Strangely, I felt out of place in my own home.

The room was almost pitch black except for the light entering from the hallway. It must have been a few hours before I heard Jack and Jason get back into the house and walk upstairs. Jason came over to me and we kissed each other goodnight.

"I'll be in to tuck you in, Jason. Get washed up," Jack said.

"OK, Dad."

Jack approached me and sat on the edge of my side of the bed. "How ya doin'?"

"Fine."

"Sure?"

"Peachy."

"I'm glad you're home."

"I know. You're a good guy, Jack."

Jack just stared into my eyes for a few moments. It looked as though he wanted to say or do something, but he didn't. "I'll get the kids ready for bed."

"Thanks." Jack left the bedroom. I could hear him kiss and say goodnight to Megan quietly. Then I heard his footsteps as he went into Jason's room. I could hear him say how proud he was of Jason for doing well in school, then I heard Jason and Jack each say goodnight.

Jack returned to our bedroom, got ready for bed, and slowly got under the covers. I turned away from him. He approached me and kissed the back of my neck. Any other normal couple probably would have made love that night after being away from each other for so many days. We didn't. It wasn't that Jack did anything wrong or wasn't deserving of my affection, I just couldn't give it. Besides, my eating disorder prevented me from thinking of us as a normal couple. Jack got closer to me and held me in his arms. At first, I wanted to back away, but I didn't. Jack may have been frustrated. I wasn't. I was satisfied just to be in his arms. Within moments, Jack fell asleep. I wasn't as lucky. For the next three hours, all I could think about was my appointment with the therapist tomorrow morning. I didn't want to go there.

* * *

It was 5:15 when I woke to the sound of Jack's alarm. Jack noticed I was awake and kissed me good morning. I tried to turn over to fall back to sleep but couldn't. Instead, I laid there and continued where I left off last night.

I should have gotten up when I heard Jack and Megan raise their voices about her getting up for school and getting ready, but I didn't. I had neither the physical nor the emotional energy to face that situation. By 8:30, all three had come in to kiss me goodbye and wish me a good day. I was glad they were gone and the house was quiet. It meant there was less possible stress for me to deal with.

I got up, poured myself a cup of coffee, lit my first cigarette, and tried to compose myself for the upcoming appointment. I also had some toast for breakfast to pretend I was continuing my healthy eating patterns. However, two minutes after the last bite was finished, I was in the downstairs bathroom with the door locked, my face in the toilet, and my fingers down my throat puking up the coffee and toast. So much for that idea. Again, I was extremely hazy as I walked up the stairs. I had to hold on to the banister firmly to keep from falling. I returned to the kitchen table, had my second cup of black coffee with my fourth cigarette, and stayed there until it was time to get dressed and start for the doctor's office.

The doctor's waiting room was small and looked like it hadn't been renovated for over twenty-five years. There was some ridiculous rock music playing, and it got on my nerves, which were already shot long before I arrived at the doctor's office. The receptionist behind the window looked like a big-busted, mindless twit with red and purple hair, 4 pounds of makeup on her face, and mashed potatoes for brains. I said "Good morning." She did not respond except to say, "May I have your insurance card." I handed the card to her as the phone rang. She said nothing else to me. I heard her say into the phone, "What do you mean we're not going out tonight?" At that point, she closed the window to prevent me from hearing what she talked about. From her body language, I could see she was angry with the person she was talking with. She paid absolutely no attention to me, nor did she do anything to work on my appointment or insurance situation. Finally, I decided to knock on the window. "How about giving me the questionnaire so I can get started with that nonsense?"

Without saying a word, she handed me the questionnaire on a clipboard that had a pen attached to it with a short string that made it difficult for me to write. Twenty-five minutes later, she was still on the phone as I approached her window to hand her back the completed questionnaire. Instead of opening the window to take the form, she turned away from me. I just left the form on the windowsill and returned to my seat.

The situation was starting to piss me off, and I felt my anger and frustration rising. Another fifteen minutes passed until she finally got off the phone. I could see her duplicate my insurance card and get on the phone. I assumed she was calling my insurance company for authorization. Two or three minutes later, she hung up, then she quickly picked up the phone again. She pushed one button, which was probably an intercom signal to the doctor. That call only took a few seconds, after which she opened the window and said, "Mrs. Gordon, we're sorry to inconvenience you, but the doctor doesn't work with your insurance company. Would you like to pay by check or cash?"

"You're not serious?"

"About what?"

"Check or cash."

My temper skyrocketed out of control, and I blurted out without hesitation or restraint, "Listen, little girl, you can't be as stupid as you look!"

"Lady, that's very rude!"

"Rude was you talking to your boyfriend for almost an hour instead of doing your job and taking care of a patient. Rude was you not checking my insurance before I started filling out this damn questionnaire. Rude was that idiot of a doctor not keeping his appointment on time. Don't you dare call *me* rude when you and that idiot treated me in the most unprofessional manner possible. And, as for this crappy questionnaire . . ." The form never left the windowsill. I removed it from the clipboard, gripped it firmly, ripped it into hundreds of pieces, threw them into the air like confetti, and shouted, "That's what you can do with this crap."

Seconds later I was out of there and out of my mind with rage.

I can't recall living through such fury as I felt when I left that office. Little did I realize how much of a danger I was to myself, and others. I got to the car, started the engine, screamed to a point where it hurt my throat, pounded on the steering wheel, hurled the car into drive, floored the gas, and screeched out of the parking spot. Five blocks later I drove through a stop sign without noticing it until a car traveling perpendicular to me blasted his horn and swerved onto an empty sidewalk to avoid hitting me by the mere margin of an inch or two. Thank goodness that other driver was alert. He probably saved both of our lives by his defensive driving. I pulled over to the side, turned off the car, lit a cigarette, started to shake, and started to cry. Thirty minutes and three cigarettes later, I felt calm enough to start the car and start home again.

As soon as I got into the house, I made a pot of coffee, lit another cigarette, and picked up the phone. I heard two rings after I dialed. "Dr. Thatcher, please," I said.

"I'm sorry," his receptionist said politely. "He's out of town and won't be back for two weeks. Do you need . . ."

I interrupted her and said rudely, "Well, if I'm still alive in two weeks, I'll try to give him a call."

"May I . . ." I didn't let her finish. I hung up the phone and said aloud to myself, "No one gives a shit, just like with eleven-year-old Caroline. Well, if no one else gives a damn, neither do I."

The kids were out of the house when Jack got home from work. He looked exhausted, but I didn't care. I immediately blurted out the various catastrophes of the day. He hugged me as he said, "Everything will work out."

"How the hell do you know everything will work out? I don't want your sympathy. I want action. You're my husband. You're supposed to do something about the garbage those other people put me through!"

"Jess, calm down."

"Don't tell me to calm down. I'm angry and that's the way I want to feel!"

"I'll take us out for dinner."

"I don't have an appetite and don't want any damn dinner," I yelled as I got my coat and car keys and stormed out of the house without telling Jack where I was going. I didn't tell him because I didn't know, and I didn't care. I got to the car, remembered what had happened this afternoon, and just started walking aimlessly away from the house.

* * *

It was after 11:30 when I got home from my multiple-mile sojourn from the house to the shopping mall and home again. Jack and the kids were sleeping. At first I was angry with Jack that he had the nerve go to sleep without knowing that I was home safely; then I felt remorse for the way I took my frustrations out on him earlier in the evening. He didn't deserve what I did to him. I sat on the bed and gently caressed Jack's face. He didn't budge or wake. I was glad. I really didn't feel like talking or apologizing for my actions.

Even though I hadn't eaten dinner, I went downstairs to the bathroom, locked the door, put my face in the toilet, shoved my finger down my throat, and puked what little there was in my stomach. I did my mouth-rinsing routine, started up the stairs, and felt extremely faint. My instincts saved me. I sat down and blacked out. I doubt I was out for more than a minute or two. It was 11:55 p.m. when I got up to the bedroom, checked to see if Jack was still soundly asleep, and snuck an extremely large handful of laxatives down to the kitchen. I made myself a cup of instant coffee, downed the pills, got my coat, and went outside to have the first of many cigarettes. It was dark. There was no moon, but I didn't bother to turn the outside light on. I wanted solitude, and I was afraid a light might attract conversation with a neighbor returning home late.

I kept thinking about what had happened that day at the doctor's office, and not being able to get to Dr. Thatcher. More than anger, I felt depression. Again, I wished I had the guts to take my own life and end the madness I was living through. I hated myself, and I hated how people, except for Jack and the kids, didn't care. I knew where behavior like this was headed, and I didn't like it. I was out of Springdale just a short time, and I was already back in the same mental condition I was in before I entered. The smart and rational thing to do would have been to go upstairs, pack my bag, and prepare to return to the hospital at sunrise, but I wasn't acting or thinking in a rational pattern. I sat there convincing myself that this situation would blow over with the proper willpower. I couldn't face separating myself from the kids again, so I denied anything was extremely wrong and just kept lighting one cigarette after another over the next few hours.

Before I knew it, I saw it was 4:30 a.m. I went upstairs, got into bed, and was still up when Jack's alarm went off. I should have gotten up and told him I was sorry for how I treated him the night before. Instead, I closed my eyes to pretend I was sleeping and actually fell asleep.

It was 11:30 by the time I opened my eyes again. I was alone in the silent house, and it was a good thing. Because of the laxative overdose, I felt like I was going to die from a litany of symptoms: nausea, vomiting, abdominal cramping, diarrhea, bloody stool, dizziness, muscle weakness, painful urination, and slow respiration. For the next several hours, all I could do was run from the bed to the bathroom and back again. At 2:05 I wasn't sure if I'd feel well enough to pick Jason up from school, so I called his friend's mother and asked her to do me a favor. I hardly ever spoke to the woman, but she was polite and immediately agreed to help. After I hung up, I managed to find the energy to get downstairs to write a note for Jason to help himself to a snack before going out to play. I tacked it on the front door and left it unlocked so he could get in. It took all the energy I had left to get back upstairs and into bed again. Two seconds after my head hit the pillow, I was out cold. The next thing I heard was Jack coming into the house. "Jess, where are you?"

"Up here."

"Jess, are you OK? What's wrong?"

I sat up and almost felt like a normal person again. "Jack, I'm fine."

"Are you sure?"

"Jack, I'm fine. I'll get dinner ready."

"You don't have to. I called for some Italian food to be delivered."

"Thanks. That was a good idea."

"Will you join us for dinner?"

"Sure."

"It'll be here in about thirty minutes."

"Good. I'll grab a shower in the meantime."

"Are you sure you're OK?"

"Let it go, Jack."

"But . . ."

"Jack . . ."

"OK."

I got downstairs in time to finish setting the table just as the doorbell rang. Jacked called for the kids to join us, and we ate as though nothing had happened that day, or the night before. As soon as we finished eating, Megan said her homework was done and that she was going to a neighbor's house. Jason asked if Jack would watch some television with him. It didn't take much to convince Jack to spend time with Jason. Again, I had ulterior motives. I left the dishes on the table, got downstairs, purged, rinsed my mouth, and got back into the kitchen without anyone knowing what I did. I finished with the kitchen, got the garbage out, and got back into bed after downing about twenty laxatives.

* * *

Wednesday, Thursday, and Friday went by like a blur. They were the kind of days you put yourself on automatic and just do the things you have to do without thinking. I had fallen into my own normal daily pattern: breakfast, purge, lunch, purge, dinner, purge, and then get ready for bed after taking a heavy dose of laxatives. Some people wouldn't consider that a "normal" living pattern but, for me, it was. As those three days passed, I actually thought I was getting away with that lifestyle.

Friday was the only day I did anything out of the ordinary. I had called Jason's teacher on Thursday and requested an appointment with her on Friday. She was polite and obliged. I was concerned about Jason's behavior at school and his reaction to me being away at the hospital. His teacher and I met at 11:30. The good news was that Jason showed no unusual behavior during that time. His teacher told me she loved him because he was always so studious, his homework was always on time, and it always showed hard work was put into it. For a few moments as I left school, I felt great. I was on top of the world because I have such a great son. He's my pride and joy, and the pure love of my heart. Yes, for those few moments on Friday, things were great.

Saturday, however, all hell broke lose. First, Jack and the kids were home, which created extra stress I didn't have when they were all out at school or at work. Second, I passed out in the kitchen in the morning, and Jack found me on the floor. We had a war. He insisted I go to the emergency room. I insisted there was nothing wrong. Third, I found fresh parallel cut marks on Megan's forearm. It was time to have that conversation I avoided the night I got home from the hospital. I waited until Megan was alone in her room. At that moment, Jack and Jason didn't have to know what was going on. "Hey, sweetheart. Have a minute?"

"What's up, Mom?"

"You tell me."

"What do you mean?"

"I saw your arm."

"No big thing."

"Sorry, I don't see it that way."

"Forget it."

"I can't do that."

"Try."

"I can't."

"Then try harder."

"Megan . . ."

"Mom . . ."

"Are you feeling depressed? And if you are, what's it about?"

"Sometimes life just sucks."

"Yes, it does."

"Well, it did for me this week. I hate school. Sometimes I just hate myself. Forget it, Mom. They're just scratches. No big deal."

"Are you serious?"

"Sure."

"Dr. Thatcher gets back in a week. I'd like you to start seeing him."

"Why? Everything is under control."

Hearing Megan use the expression "under control" stopped me in my tracks because that's what I kept telling myself about myself. "Honey, if things were under control, then you wouldn't cut yourself."

"It's the cutting that puts things right for me."

"How?"

"Mom, you know I never did drugs. Sometimes I just need a little lift. The cutting does it for me."

Megan's words reminded me of what Dr. Willsen once told me. It also reminded me of what Carol said in the therapy session at Springdale. I found myself afraid and speechless. Megan took my momentary silence as consent for her actions. She kissed my cheek. "Luv ya, Mom. I'll be home for dinner. I'm meeting some of my friends," she said before she left the room and the house.

It took me several minutes before I finally got the energy to get up. I went downstairs to the bathroom, locked the door, and purged my empty stomach. Suddenly, there was a knock on the door. "Jess, are you OK?"

"Yeah, Jack. I'm fine. I guess something didn't agree with me."

"Anything I can do for you?"

"No, I'm fine."

"Sure?"

"Yes, Jack. I'm positive."

Jack was upstairs in the kitchen having a soda when I got there. "Jess, between this morning and this, I really think you should see a doctor."

"Thanks for your concern, hon. I'm fine."

Jack wanted to say something. Instead, he just looked at me with bewilderment and kept silent.

* * *

Dinner was exceptionally quiet that night. It seemed like Megan, Jack, and I were immersed in our own little worlds. Jason was the only one to speak. I guess he was the only one free of any cares or problems. Megan was the first to finish eating.

"I'll be with my friends at the mall, Mom. I'll be home by 11:00."

"Megan," Jack said as he reached for his wallet, "here's something for a snack."

Megan kissed Jack, then me.

"Later. Thanks, Dad."

Jason got up from the table. "Is it OK if I go down the block to play for a little while?"

"I'll take you over there," Jack replied. "Call me when you're ready to come home. Let me hear from you by 9:30."

"OK, Dad."

"Be right back, Jess."

"Sure."

I waited a minute or two after hearing the front door close. It was my opportunity to get downstairs to the bathroom without Jack's interference. After locking the door, it was fingers in and food out. Once more, I felt like I was going to pass out. I sat on the toilet a few moments before I felt I had enough energy to stand up. Once I stood, I needed to hold on to the sink with one hand as I rinsed my mouth and washed my face with ice cold water. It seemed to revive me a little, but I still needed the aid of the banister to get upstairs and back into the kitchen. I was surprised to see Jack was back already and doing the dishes. He said nothing, but his expression made up for that. It was as though he knew what I had been doing, but kept silent.

"Hon," I said very weakly, "I'll get the dishes."

"OK. I'll get the garbage out."

Something made me think that Jack took the garbage out to get away from me. Maybe it was paranoia. Maybe I was right. I didn't ask. He didn't tell. I was finished loading the dishwasher when Jack got back inside. It seemed like he was out there several minutes.

"Hey, Jess, how about some television?"

"Sure. Anything on?"

"With two hundred stations we've got to find something."

"You got a date."

I joined Jack in the den. "Do you remember the movie *Frankie and Johnny*? It starts in five minutes."

"Hey, big guy, I thought you don't like chick flicks."

"I like Pacino."

"You sure it's not Pfeiffer you want to watch?"

"You're kidding."

I kissed Jack's face. "Yes, I am."

Frankie and Johnny reminds you how difficult it is for some people to find love who are desperate to be loved. The Pacino character openly admits his love for the Pfeiffer character. She shuns him because, years before she met him, she was in a physically abusive relationship, and she was still afraid of being loved because it might lead to another physically abusive relationship. He is persistent in his quest to gain her love. She is persistent in refusing to give that love back to him. Eventually she understands that all he wants to do is to cherish her. The movie ends with her acknowledging the fact that he loves her, and she is willing, finally, to love him back.

Jack turned off the television. I don't think he had any idea why I got up, put my arms around him, and kissed his lips for several seconds.

"What did I do right?" he asked.

"You married me."

"I had no choice. I couldn't live without you."

"We have an hour before the kids get home."

"Jess, are you propositioning me?"

"No. I'm telling you to make love to me." I felt a desire for Jack that was missing for so long. I kept thinking about how patient he'd been with me. It made me desire him even more, and I hurried him upstairs. Jack went into the bathroom to wash. I looked for something sexy to put on for him, although I realized it would be off moments after I got into bed. I turned down the covers and got into the bathroom the moment Jack got into bed. Little did Jack know I had a handful of laxatives stashed in my hand as I went into the bathroom. When I finished, I turned off the bathroom light, then I turned the bedroom light off. Not only did the bedroom lights go out, so did mine. All of a sudden, I saw stars and blacked out. Thank goodness the floor was carpeted.

Jack was holding me in his arms when I opened my eyes.

"Jess, I'm taking you to the emergency room."

"No, Jack. I know what this is. If they have a bed for me, you're taking me back to Springdale tomorrow."

* * *

It was exactly 9:00 in the morning on Sunday when I called Springdale. Deborah answered. She told me that Dr. Barrow was not in, but she could make the arrangements for my reentry. "Jess, I'm sorry things worked out this way. You know the routine. Get your bags and come on in. We'll do all we can to help you," she said in a compassionate tone. It gave me some solace after these several days of torture. Someone cares if I live or die besides my husband and kids.

Within two hours, my bags were packed, Jack delivered the kids to their friends' houses, and we were on the road. The radio was off, and there was little or no conversation between Jack and me. I was disgusted with myself. I hated myself. I despised the fact that I was going to be away from the kids again, but I knew it had to be this way. We were already on the road for an hour and a half when we hit a wall of traffic just past the 8A Exit off the Jersey Turnpike. The proverbial parking lot of traffic before us pushed my stress level to an intolerable level. Jack turned on the radio. I immediately turned if off. "Jack, you knew there would be traffic here. You should have gotten off and taken the back roads the rest of the way."

"But, Jess, I . . ."

Whatever Jack was going to say didn't matter. The car was at a standstill, so Jack had the chance to look deeply into my eyes. He remained quiet. I didn't. "Jack, why don't you ever say anything about my condition? Didn't you know what I was doing all last week?"

"Jess, except for yesterday, I had no idea that anything was wrong. I thought you had it all under control."

"Well, I didn't. I still don't. If I did, we wouldn't be in this car."

Jack knew it was safer and easier to remain silent. Instead of the normal twenty minutes, it took us another hour to get to the hospital. I was exasperated. When Jack turned off the car in the parking lot, I just got out and headed into the hospital without waiting for him. He followed behind with my bag and knew to meet me in Dr. Barrow's waiting room. Dr. Barrow had just opened his door to see me when Jack walked in and sat down in the waiting-room chair. I looked at Jack, then I turned to enter Dr. Barrow's office. It was Dr. Barrow who requested we meet alone this time.

Dr. Barrow opened the conversation as soon as we sat down. "Jess, I'm terribly sorry about this situation. It's the first time a patient was released to a therapist who didn't take that patient's insurance coverage. From now on, we'll make certain outpatient care is covered by the patient's insurance before release. Please forgive us. It won't happen again to you or any other patient."

"Dr. Barrow, it's just my kind of luck to go through that kind of crap."

"Jess, you left here at about 105 pounds. What is your weight now?"

"Right back to where it was when I first sat in this chair. The depression is back worse than ever, and so is the suicidal ideation."

"Do you want to be helped?"

"That's why I'm here. I hate this place. I hate the fact that I'm away from my kids, but I'm here because I know you care and you might be able to help me. Last week was a week of hell. First I had to deal with that moron of a therapist and his bimbo receptionist. Then I learned Thatcher wouldn't be back for two weeks. Then I found out my daughter was cutting again. I needed relief. I purged my brains out and took bottles of laxatives."

"Jess, I'll lay my cards on the table. There are going to be bad times in everyone's life. We can't use those bad times as an excuse to return to an eating disorder."

"I'm not giving you excuses," I said in an almost convincing tone. "I'm giving you the facts. The therapist didn't care. He made me wait over an hour after my scheduled appointment. He didn't even have the courtesy to see me to apologize for the mistake. He let his bimbo do the dirty work. Dr. Thatcher was a joke. He was out of town. He was probably gallivanting around the country to promote his book. No one cared about what happened to me, so neither did I."

"Jess, I care."

"Yeah."

"You could have called me for help."

"I didn't call you because I didn't want to be here."

"But you are here."

"And hating every minute of it."

"Jess, how many people do you know who tried to quit smoking?"

"Quite a few."

"Do you know someone who stopped for a couple of days or weeks and then started again?"

"Yes."

"Why do you think they went through the emotional pain of withdrawal, then started up again?"

"One person got upset because she had a flat tire, and the only thing she felt would calm her down was a cigarette."

"Do you think the cigarette improved the flat tire situation or the emotional stress?"

"No. It was a crutch for bad times. But . . ." I didn't want to say anything further.

"But what, Jess?"

"So you think I went back to purging and laxatives as an emotional crutch when I reentered real life outside the bubble?"

"Don't you?"

"No!" I paused. It felt like I had just lied to him. I knew when I left the hospital that I felt unstable and should have told him I wasn't ready to leave. "OK, say, for argument's sake, that's what it was. What am I supposed to do about that?"

"Good question."

"Give me a good answer."

"Change your lifestyle."

"What does that mean?"

"That's what we'll work on while you're here. We'll give you tools, mental and emotional tools, to help you. It's a form of behavioral psychology. It's the same technique used to help people quit smoking. If you're in a habit of purging when no one's around after a meal, make sure you have a meal with your husband. But first, let him know you have the desire to purge after a meal. Let him, and his company, be a change. Communicate your situation with him. It's not for him to police you, but for him to help you. Do you understand the difference?"

"We hardly ever talk about my eating disorder."

"Then make that the first behavioral change. Include him in your secret world. Make the secrets go away. After all, an eating disorder is often called 'the secret disorder.' You'll need to get your disorder out in the open, instead of locking it up in secret, deceiving, and self-destructive behaviors."

"You don't hold back, do you?"

"Jess, I'm here to help you, not hold your hand and tell unrealistic, sympathetic lies."

Dr. Barrow and I exited his office over an hour later. Jack was still in the waiting room. I wondered, if the situation were reversed, would I be so patient? Probably not, I thought to myself.

Jack stood as I approached him and stopped inches before him. I looked into his eyes and started to cry. "Jack, please forgive me," I said, although I knew that Deborah and Dr. Barrow were in earshot of everything I said. I didn't care.

"Jess, you were just upset about the traffic."

"That's not what I'm talking about. I was wrong to leave here. I wasn't ready. I had to get out, at all costs. As a result, I hurt you, Megan, and Jason. I'm sorry."

"Listen, Jess, the only thing to think about now is getting you back on the right track. I'll take care of the kids. You take all the time you need. Do the right thing here, and learn how to do the right thing when you get out. That's all I want."

"Jack, I'll try."

"OK. Give me a hug." I embraced Jack for several seconds.

Jack kissed my lips and turned to Dr. Barrow, "Take good care of my girl."

"We'll do our best," Dr. Barrow said as he shook Jack's hand.

Jack stared into my eyes, touched my cheek, turned, and left. I stepped over to the doorway, watched him wait for the elevator and get on, then I turned back to Dr. Barrow when I saw the doors close. I sighed and said under my breath, "Well, here we go again."

Dr. Barrow picked up my bag. "Jess, I'll show you to your room."

Perhaps it was fitting that Dr. Barrow took me to the same room and same bed I had occupied the previous time. I saw a younger person's clothes and things on the other bed, which indicated my old roommate was gone. I thought about Claire, my space cadet, for a few seconds and silently wished her luck. Then an attendant came in. I placed all of my things on the bed for him to inspect. Strangely, I wasn't as annoyed this time when he searched my property. If I hadn't messed up so miserably the week before, he wouldn't be doing this now, and I'd be home with my family, so I felt it was my own fault that I had to be put through this humiliation again.

The admission nonsense was finally out of the way. Dr. Barrow extended his hand to me. I shook his hand and felt an extraordinarily kind feeling pass in our touch. "Jess, forget about whatever happened before. This is a fresh start. I know you can make it work."

"Thanks. I'll try to push my choice point in a positive direction. I want forward, not back, not status quo." Dr. Barrow put his other hand on top of mine, and perhaps it was my imagination, but I felt another surge of positive energy.

When Dr. Barrow and the attendant were gone, I sat on my bed alone and, as usual, started to cry. That lasted for about twenty minutes until my new roommate entered and paused at the door.

"Sorry. I'll leave you alone if I'm bothering you."

She appeared to be in her mid-twenties, about five foot three, with beautiful blonde hair and an extremely attractive face. Of course, she was very thin.

"Don't be silly. I always go nuts on check-in day."

"Yeah. Me, too. This is my second inpatient."

"Same for me. No, wait. This is my third."

"Well, let's hope it is the last for both of us. I'm Cindy, bulimia."

"Jess, anorexia and bulimia."

"Are you from Jersey?"

"No. Long Island."

"I live close to here in Freehold, New Jersey."

"You're lucky."

"How's that?"

"Your family can get here more than once a week."

"Some might consider that lucky, but you don't know my domineering mother. It seems like I can't get rid of her."

Cindy sat next to me that night at dinner. When they put my meal in front of me I picked up my fork, paused, and then I scanned the room. It appeared that I was the oldest one in the room. It freaked me out. I put down my fork and pushed my chair away from the table. Cindy noticed my apprehension.

"Jess, are you OK?"

"Fine, Cindy. You got a guy at home?"

"Yeah. We're unofficially engaged."

"What does that mean?"

"He's saving up money to get me a ring. He's great. He helped to motivate me into here. He said, 'Cind, I love you. I want you to be healthy. It's your head and heart I love.' Wasn't that sweet?"

"Yeah. My husband's also a great guy."

"Any kids?"

"Two."

Cindy saw a matron take a step toward us and said, "Food police approaching."

I actually chuckled when Cindy used the "food police" expression. For a moment, it felt like Kylie was with me again. I moved my chair back toward the table, picked up my fork, stuffed my mouth with my first bite, then the second, third, and fourth. It was time to break the cycle again. It was time to move away from self-destruction and get on the road to recovery.

* * *

Two days later, I was in Dr. Barrow's office for my first review. The meeting was simple and short because we both knew I wasn't ready to be discharged.

Shortly after the morning therapy session, Cindy and I were back in the room. Cindy was trying to nap. I was thinking about the patient from the session that morning. She probably had a gorgeous face, but I could tell that her disorder had robbed her of some of her beauty. She was five foot six and down to about 85 pounds, which made her look emaciated. She was physically weak and had difficulty talking because she had damaged her esophagus from excessive purging.

I heard someone approaching the room with heavy footsteps. I knew it wasn't an attendant because most of them wore rubber soles and heels. It also sounded like the woman was wearing high heels, something none of the patients wore. Suddenly I heard from the doorway, "Cindy, are you there?"

The woman was in her mid-forties, tall, extremely well groomed, and dressed perfectly. It was obvious that it took a bunch of money to get her looking so good. The woman just stood at the foot of Cindy's bed.

Cindy was still a little groggy as she sat up and said, "Hi, Mom."

"Cindy, you look terrible. Why the hell don't you put on any makeup? Didn't you have time to brush your hair this morning?" A guy about twenty-five, good looking, nice brown hair, and with a physique that was no stranger to a gym, walked in sheepishly behind her. He just approached Cindy and gave her a small kiss on her lips. "Hey, beautiful."

"Beautiful?" her mother said to admonish him. "Son, are you out of your mind? It looks like she lost 10 pounds since last week."

Ironically, Cindy had put on several pounds since last week, a major accomplishment for someone in this unit. Then Cindy's words, "domineering mother," came back to me. I felt sorry for Cindy, and I thought about my own mother, who had never said a word to me about my weight situation in the last twenty years. I didn't know which was worse: a mother like Cindy's, who pushes her beyond reason, or a mother like mine, who seems like she doesn't care or know enough to say a word at all. Then I thought to myself, "Somewhere in the middle is the mother who knows how to say something constructive to help her daughter, rather than ignore her daughter or try to beat her daughter's psyche into hell."

Cindy's eyes caught me looking at her. I think she understood every word of sympathy my eyes could express silently.

Ten minutes later her mother and fiancé were gone, but the damage her mother caused had remained. I went over to Cindy, hugged her, and said, "Cindy, take it from an old lady like me. You're a good and beautiful kid. Don't let her crap be your problem. Just do what you have to do."

* * *

Eight days and four review sessions later, Dr. Barrow teetered on releasing me. I convinced him I wasn't ready yet. Unlike last time, I wasn't going to delude myself. I wasn't going to let go of the bubble's insulated comfort zone until I felt like I had a chance to survive outside the bubble.

Two days later, Friday, February 27, I was back in Dr. Barrow's office. Nineteen of the thirty days allotted by the insurance company were expended. We had a decision to make. The next logical step would be the "intensive outpatient program," which would eat up my remaining days of coverage for the year. And, since this was the end of February, it would be an extremely long time before I could be hospitalized again if I fell heavily back into my disorder.

The intensive outpatient program, known to the eating disorder world as the IOP, is like partial hospitalization. It means I'd return to Springdale multiple days a week. It starts out at three days a week. I'd have my breakfast and my lunch at the hospital, and I'd attend therapy groups in between the meals. After that, they would slowly wean me down from three full days to two full days, and then it goes down to half days. The entire IOP lasts about two months. After that, I'd start seeing my own therapist, and I'd continue seeing Dr. Thatcher for my medication.

Dr. Barrow also told me that the IOP includes meetings with one of the hospital's nutritionists. Hearing Dr. Barrow explain the role of the nutritionist reminded me of the wacko nutritionist I once saw, but Dr. Barrow explained how the nutritionist at Springdale specializes with patients like me, and that she wouldn't set unrealistic goals just to shove food down my mouth.

Unlike two days before, I felt confident that I was ready to leave for the right reasons. I had put on a few more pounds, my mind was welcoming recovery, and I felt like I was ready for the next step. Dr. Barrow, on the other hand, was tentative about discharging me.

"Jess, the last time we discussed your release, you convinced me to hold you here. What's changed in the last two days?"

"My attitude."

"How so?"

"Dr. Barrow, the last time I got out, I wasn't entirely forthcoming with you. I wanted out, but for the wrong reasons. This time, I feel stronger. The last two days have given me enough strength to face life outside the bubble. I'm looking forward to the IOP. Most importantly, I want to finish the IOP and continue with the proper therapist. I'll go over the list of doctors you suggest, give you a name this afternoon, and we can make sure the therapist is covered by my insurance company. This time, I think I'm ready to start recovery in the real world. My depression is subsiding. The new medication seems to be working."

"In your mind, Jess, what is recovery?"

"Getting rid of ideation. Getting my weight to a safe level with the help of the IOP meals, following the nutritionist's guidance, and participating in the IOP therapy sessions. Over the past eleven days, with your help, I've broken the cycle again."

"Jess, what else does recovery mean to you?"

"Seeing my kids grow up. I don't want to die. My course down the slow, suicidal path guided by this disorder has to stop."

I think what got to me the most during my extensive three-hour discharge interview with Dr. Barrow was the realization that I'm in a life-threatening situation. Astoundingly, the insurance company's position is, "If you don't get cured within thirty days, tough." The insurance company would have no qualms about dropping me like a hot potato and saying it's nothing personal, just business.

Dr. Barrow took a deep breath as though my life depended on his decision. Actually, it did. If Dr. Barrow didn't think I was ready for discharge, I would have to stay at Springdale, and each additional day under inpatient care would diminish the time I would have for the IOP and decrease my chances at recovery.

"Jess, the IOP won't be easy. First, you'll have to commute here from Long Island several times a week. That will cause stress."

"Dr. Barrow, you're saying I'll find excuses to relapse again."

"Exactly."

"I guess the word 'excuses' will be something good for me to bring up in the therapy sessions."

"Good idea." Dr. Barrow took off his glasses and rubbed his eyes. I felt like the foreman of the jury was about to read the verdict. "Jess . . ."

"Yes . . ."

Although it must have been only two or three seconds, it felt like hours until Dr. Barrow said, "Call your husband to pick you up tomorrow."

"Thank you, Dr. Barrow."

"Jess, for your sake, I hope we're both making the right decision."

"I think we are," I said with some hope and some conviction. Actually, there was probably 90 percent hope and 10 percent conviction in what I said.

"Here is a list of therapists in the New York area. Once you give me a name, I'll call to make sure the doctor is covered by your insurance company."

"Sounds good."

* * *

Minutes after I was out of Dr. Barrow's office, I was back in my room. I got on my bed and scanned the names of the therapists. There must have been hundreds of names, with at least one hundred from the New York City and Long Island area. Since it was Friday, I felt a certain amount of stress to find a doctor so Dr. Barrow could call and check out the insurance situation before the close of business. I felt frustrated, and I think it showed on my face as Cindy walked into the room.

"So? How did it go?"

"I get paroled tomorrow."

"That's a good thing. Isn't it?"

"It is if I can find a therapist in the next hour or two. There are so many names. It's like picking out a doctor from hundreds of names in the Yellow Pages."

"What are you going to do?"

"I don't know. I just hope I get lucky."

"Anything I can do?"

"Know any good prayers?"

"Sorry, Jess. I'm not that type."

"Yeah. Neither am I."

"How about if I just leave you alone to do what you have to do?"

"Thanks, Cindy."

Twenty minutes went by with no results. I felt the pressure mount. Suddenly I had an idea. Why not call Dr. Thatcher's office with the hope he would be in, and that he could recommend someone. I got on the phone, forgetting it was Friday, the day 99 percent of doctors aren't in their office. I dialed Dr. Thatcher's number. It rang once, twice, a third time, and then, just when I thought I would get his answering machine, I heard him say, "Dr. Thatcher."

"Dr. Thatcher, this is Jess Gordon."

"Hello, Jess. What can I do for you?"

"Dr. Thatcher, you have no idea how happy I am you picked up. I'm getting discharged from Springdale Hospital tomorrow. I need the name of a therapist to work with. Do you have any suggestions?"

"Well, my first suggestion would be my co-author, Noel R. Marcus, Ph.D. He has an office not far from your home. His specialty is eating disorders."

It was like karma had taken over a possible negative situation. My frustration was immediately resolved. Dr. Thatcher went on about why Dr. Marcus would be good for me, and I took the time to check for his name in Dr. Barrow's list. There it was. I recognized the address and realized he was within five miles of my home.

"Dr. Thatcher, thank you so much for your help. Dr. Marcus sounds like the right doctor for me."

"Jess, I'll call him and let him know I'm referring you. I'll expect to see you in my office shortly. Just call my assistant on Monday to schedule an appointment."

"Absolutely. Thanks again, Dr. Thatcher."

"You're welcome."

I was back in Dr. Barrow's office within minutes of that conversation. He tried calling Dr. Marcus, but all he got was the answering service. Dr. Barrow didn't give up. He immediately picked up the phone again and called my insurance company. He told them my name and other identification information, and then he asked the company if Dr. Marcus would be covered by my insurance policy. The situation seemed so right for me. I wanted an immediate and positive answer so badly, which made the few seconds I had to wait feel like an eternity until Dr. Barrow said, "Uh, huh," and shook his head to give me a sign that everything was OK. I took a deep breath and felt like I had just taken one giant step onto the recovery road. I knew there were thousands of steps ahead of me, but the first step on any journey is always the most important. Without it, you go nowhere.

"Jess, call Dr. Marcus with my phone and leave your contact information."

"Thanks, Dr. Barrow." I called immediately, left a message, and asked for a return call on Tuesday because I knew I'd be in the IOP program on Monday. There was a huge smile on my face when I left Dr. Barrow's office. Deborah noticed. "You look happy, Jess."

"I am."

"Jess, if at any time you need my help before or after the IOP, I'm here for you."

I approached Deborah and hugged her. I think I did that because I felt so guilty about being so wrong about her when I first saw her. "Deborah, you're very sweet. Just give me a smile whenever you see me." I knew Deborah had no idea what I meant about the smile. I just hoped she knew I had good thoughts about her.

Cindy was back in the room by the time I returned. My smile still hadn't vanished. "Wow, Jess! I never saw you smile that much. Come to think of it, I don't remember ever seeing you smile."

"Things worked out with the therapist."

"Fantastic. I'm really happy for you."

"After therapy tonight, I'll pack and get ready for tomorrow's ride home. With luck, after the IOP, I'll never see this place or any other place like it for the rest of my life. Jeez, I better call Jack."

Cindy sat on her bed and just looked at me. I saw something painful in her eyes. "What's wrong, kid?"

"Well . . . nothing."

"Don't give me that."

"I don't want to bring you down."

"What do you mean?"

"Jess, I wish you luck."

"Kid, spit it out."

"Forget it, Jess."

The pain in Cindy's eyes was still there. I couldn't let it go, the same way I wouldn't let it go if I saw that kind of pain in Megan's eyes. "C'mon, kid, what's on your mind? People like us are like sisters in this place. Sit next to me. Let's talk."

Cindy slowly rose, walked over to my bed, sat down, and stared out the window several seconds before she turned to me and said, "Jess, what do you think our chances are?"

"You mean, about us going into recovery and not dying from this crap?"

"Yeah."

"Good question. My best answer is fifty-fifty."

"Those aren't very good odds."

"Let's face it, Cindy. An eating disorder is not like a headache. You don't just take two aspirins and make it disappear. This is your second inpatient. This is my third. I was in recovery over ten years after my first bout with this stuff. During that time, I never thought there would be a second hospitalization, much less a third go-round. God, I hate being here."

"Yeah."

"But if I weren't here now, I think I would have died in a month."

"Seriously?"

"Absolutely. Either the eating disorder would kill me, or my ideation would turn into action."

"Do you still . . ."

Cindy couldn't finish her sentence, but I knew exactly what she wanted to ask. "Yeah, ideation and I are no strangers. It hasn't gone away. Neither has this disorder. While I was walking back to the room from Dr. Barrow's office, I thought about two things. First, I thought about my secret stash of laxatives. I asked myself if I could resist them this time."

"What do you think?"

"The only thing I can say without lying to you is that I'll have to face that situation when I'm home tomorrow. I mean, I'm like a junkie getting out of rehab knowing I've got a fix back at home. I'm not sure whether this junkie will resist those pills and flush them down the toilet, or give in to them."

"What was the second thing?"

"Will I purge after dinner tomorrow?"

"And . . ."

"Same answer."

"Not a very good one. Is it?"

"Chin up, kid." I put my arm around Cindy. "Don't give up. We ain't dead yet."

* * *

I called Jack before the evening therapy session and let him know to pick me up at 10:00. Cindy sat next to me at therapy that night. I often caught her looking at me, but I avoided her eyes so I could avoid talking with her about my feelings and my upcoming discharge. Nothing that was said during that therapy session sunk in. I was too deep into my private thoughts, and I'd had enough of ingesting other people's problems. I had too many problems of my own to deal with, and I was too aware of the additional situations I'd have to face after I walked through the front door of my house.

Once I got back to the room, I packed my things except for my toothbrush and an outfit for the morning. My plan for tomorrow was to finish breakfast, sign my discharge paper, get outside, and have a cigarette or two while waiting for Jack to get to the hospital.

Cindy and I were already in bed at lights-out time. "Cindy . . ."

"Yeah, Jess."

"I know I'll be seeing you again tomorrow, but I left my address and phone number for you. If you ever need me, don't be afraid to call or write." Cindy and I said nothing else. Hours later, I was still up. I noticed the clock read 3:00 as I felt myself start to doze off. When I opened my eyes, the clock read 3:50. I never fell back to sleep.

By 9:10, I had packed my last few things. Cindy sat silently on her bed watching me. She was kind enough not to break into my thoughts. When I snapped the case shut, I put on my coat and turned to her. "Listen, kid, thanks for being my friend here. I was serious about you contacting me."

"Thanks, Jess. I wish you luck."

"You too, kid," I said as I hugged her. "Well, here I go again."

Cindy walked me to the elevator. We hugged each other for several seconds as though we'd never see each other again, even though we both knew we'd see each other tomorrow at my first IOP breakfast. The elevator door opened, I got in, pushed the first-floor button, and watched the door close as Cindy waved goodbye.

I got outside at 9:20. It was sunny and cold. There was still some snow left from a few days before. I lit a cigarette and looked around at the grounds. All that I could think of was the IOP, finishing it, and never seeing this place again. When I lit my second cigarette at 9:35 I promised myself to do all I could do in the IOP and at home to stay the hell away from this place.

At 9:50 I saw Jack start up the driveway just as I lit my third cigarette. I stamped it out and tossed a mint into my mouth. Jack saw me at the entrance and drove the car to where I was standing. He got out without turning off the engine, gave me a huge hug, kissed me, and helped me get my bag into the trunk.

"How you doing, Jess?"

"Better than the last time."

"Good. Let me know what I can do to help."

"Sure, Jack."

As Jack drove down the driveway and out onto the road, it felt a little weird to know that I'd get back into the car tomorrow and return here to start the IOP.

At first I didn't realize that the radio was on. I think Jack purposely made sure the radio was off Megan's stations and tuned into one of those easy-listening stations for the ride home. I was exhausted from not having slept the night before, so I kissed Jack's cheek and told him I was going to take a nap.

"Pleasant dreams, Jess. It's going to be great to have you home again."

I closed my eyes and heard nothing until Jack reached our house, stopped the car on the driveway, kissed me, and said, "Welcome home."

The kids weren't home when we walked in. Jack took my suitcase upstairs to the bedroom, then he told me he was going out to get Megan and Jason.

I was alone. When I went to put my underwear away, I saw the laxatives in their hiding place. I thought about what Cindy and I discussed. I picked them up, caressed them, and said, "My friends, you've got to go." I must have dumped over three hundred pills into the toilet at one time. When I flushed, I suddenly got scared that they would clog the toilet and cause a flood. Thank goodness, they swirled around and vanished. It felt like part of me was actually giving in to Dr. Barrow's advice to change my behavior. It felt like I took my second step toward recovery, and it almost felt good.

The kids were glad to see me when they got home. This time, Megan even felt comfortable enough to hug me and kiss my cheek. Jason was his usual lovable and carefree self. He hugged me tight and kissed my face at least a dozen times.

Once again, Jack ordered in some Chinese food. After dinner, I remembered Dr. Barrow's advice again: change my pattern. The kids left the table before Jack and I got up. I think Jack was shocked when I said, "Let's leave the dishes and go out for a walk."

"Jess, it's cold out there. Are you sure?"

"Yeah. Let's get out for an hour." Little did Jack know my motivation. In an hour, purging would have little or no effect.

As I fell asleep in Jack's arms that night, I felt pretty good about myself. I felt like I had increased my chances at making it into recovery because I had disposed of the laxatives, and because I hadn't purged my dinner. The last thing I thought to myself before falling asleep was, "How long will this continue?"

* * *

I got up at 4:15 a.m. on Monday because I wanted to be out of the house by 5:30 to get to Springdale by 7:00, which was breakfast time. I showered and dressed quietly so I wouldn't wake Jack and the kids, then I went downstairs to get a cup of coffee to take outside so I could have a cigarette or two. At 5:25 I went upstairs to wash my face and brush my teeth. Jack's alarm went off. I only had time to give him a goodbye kiss and hear him wish me luck.

It felt strange driving alone to Springdale. Jack had driven me there on my two previous trips. The other oddity I had to contend with was the fact that I'd leave the hospital later that day. I wasn't used to those feelings, but I had a hunch I'd get used to them after my first few IOP sessions, which were scheduled for Monday, Wednesday, and Friday.

It was a few minutes after 7:00 when I entered the dining room, saw Cindy, and sat down next to her.

"Hi, Jess. How did it go last night?"

"Better than expected. The laxatives are gone and I didn't purge."

"Nice going. Keep it up."

"I'll try, kid. What about you? How are you doing?"

"It felt strange not having you here last night. I had difficulty sleeping."

"How did it go at therapy last night?"

"The truth is, I never heard a word they said. My mind was preoccupied with my review meeting this morning with Dr. Barrow. I see him after breakfast."

"That's great. I hope you two decide you're ready to get out of this hellhole."

"You got that right. I think I'm ready."

"Don't rush it. I had to worry about the medical insurance covering my stay here, but I don't think your mother is worried about the expenses here. Remember what your guy said, 'It's your head and heart I love.' And one other word of advice from an old lady: I saw your mother in action when she visited you. Don't let her get to you and kill your chance at recovery. Live your life the way you want to, not the way she wants you to. Get married, love your guy as much as he loves you, and live your lives making important decisions as a team."

"We're thinking of moving to California."

"The further away, the better. I found peace in my life ten years ago when my bipolar brother moved from New York to live with my parents in Florida. A year ago, at age fifty-seven, he moved to Oregon to be on his own for the first time in his life. Believe me, kid, distance does make a difference."

When Cindy and I finished breakfast, I went to therapy, and she went to see Dr. Barrow. All during the session, my mind kept thinking about Cindy and hoping she'd be discharged tomorrow. I also thought about how lucky I was to have her as a friend during my stay at Springdale.

Therapy ended at 11:30. I went back to the dining room at noon. I sat down and kept an empty place next to me for Cindy. I felt a little nervous before I finally saw Cindy come in with a huge grin on her face. Before she sat down, she hugged me and said, "Jess, I'm out of here tomorrow. My IOP starts Thursday. I'll be doing Thursday, Saturday and Tuesday. This is phenomenal!"

"Fantastic, kid. You're gonna make it."

"I'm going to give it a shot. I don't want to be away from Bobby any more. I really love him as much as he loves me."

It suddenly dawned on me that this would be my last meal with Cindy and, perhaps, the last time I'd ever see her or speak with her. When we said goodbye after lunch, I silently hoped that if I ever saw Cindy again, it wouldn't be in this place.

* * *

There was a euphoric feeling running through me as I started the car for the drive home. It didn't last very long. Driving from Long Island to New Jersey at 5:30 a.m. was a piece of cake. Driving from New Jersey to Long Island at midday is a horror. First I hit parking-lot type traffic struggling to get from Exit 8 to Exit 8A on the Jersey Turnpike. I cruised along for a while until I hit the approach to the Outerbridge Crossing. My next traffic nightmare hit on Route 440, which is wrongfully named the Staten Island Expressway, the road that leads you to the Verrazano Bridge. Next there was a minor accident on the Belt Parkway, but every idiot had to stop to check out what had happened. To make matters worse, I ran out of cigarettes.

The same trip that took me about ninety minutes in the morning took me over three hours in the afternoon. I was totally stressed out when I walked into the house. I immediately went upstairs, got into comfortable clothes, and laid down for an hour. I was too wired to fall asleep, but at least the rest reenergized me enough to prepare dinner.

I was in the kitchen at about 4:50 when the phone rang. I was hesitant to pick it up because I thought it was one of Megan's friends. I wasn't in the mood to talk with anyone or to write down a long message. At first, I started to walk away from the phone and ignore it completely, but instead I checked the caller ID. Surprisingly, I saw it was my parents' phone number. I got nervous immediately because my parents and I don't talk that frequently, usually about once every six to eight weeks, and I had just spoken to them the week after my first stay at Springdale. On the third phone ring, I decided not to answer. I was still too stressed out from the afternoon's ride home and felt I couldn't deal with any situation I would have to face with my folks, so I took the cowardly way out and let the phone ring a fourth time, knowing the answering machine would take their message. After the beep I heard, "Jess, it's Mom. Give me a call as soon as you hear this. I'm afraid I've got some bad news."

My first instinct was to think my father died, but that didn't make sense because he's been in relatively good health. My mind starting racing into all negative possibilities, which only caused me more pressure. Instead of calling, I grabbed a cigarette and a coat and headed outside. "Of all days, I don't need that kind of message," I thought to myself. By the time I finished two cigarettes, I had built up enough courage to call my mother.

I dialed the number and heard my father's voice almost immediately. "Hi, Dad. I got Mom's message. What happened?"

"Hold on, Jess."

It bothered me that my father didn't answer my question and that I had to wait for my mother to get on the phone.

"How are you, Jess?"

"I'm fine, Mom. What's the problem?"

"I have terrible news."

"Mom, what's the problem?"

"It's Mitch."

"What about him? Did he get arrested?"

"No." Her answer was followed by silence, which only increased my anxiety.

"Mom, what happened?"

"The police came here." Again, a long pause.

"And . . ."

"Your brother is gone."

"Gone where?"

"He's passed on."

"What are you talking about?" Her words were clear, but they didn't register because of my state of mind. "Mom, what happened to Mitch?"

"Your brother died today."

"Died? What are you talking about?"

"He was alone in his apartment. A friend of his found his body."

Suddenly, the realization of what she was talking about hit me like a thunderbolt of mixed emotions. "What was the cause of death?"

"We don't know?"

"Was he sick?"

"No."

"Were there any signs of foul play?"

"No."

"Are you arranging an autopsy?"

"No."

"Why not?"

"What killed him doesn't matter, and your father and I don't want to know. The fact of the matter is he's gone, and we're arranging for the body to be sent back to New York for the funeral on Saturday."

My first thought was that Saturday was a day I could attend the funeral because I wouldn't have to be at the IOP. My second thought was how I talked about Mitch just days before with Cindy and said, "Distance makes a difference." Well, now the greatest of all distances existed between the two of us. I hadn't spoken to Mitch in over a year. I never had a chance to say goodbye.

"Mom, how are you and Dad doing?"

"We understand he's gone, but we can't believe it. Jess, no matter what you thought of your brother . . ."

"Mom, my concern right now is about you and Dad. I'm sorry this happened. Let me know what I can do for you."

"Thank you, Jess. We'll call you again tomorrow to let you know the plans."

"OK." She hung up, and I listened to the dial tone for several seconds before I put the phone back onto its cradle. I paused because I couldn't think clearly. I got my cigarettes and coat and headed back outside. I was glad Jack and the kids weren't home yet. I needed to come to grips with the fact that my brother was dead. "What did he die from? What don't they want to know?" I asked myself. Then it hit me. Except for his mental ailments, he was never sick. I'll never be sure, but since he had been on drugs since he was a teenager, my instincts told me it was an overdose. That was the only reason that made any sense. My folks had always infantalized him because of his condition. Perhaps they needed to. They held tight reins on him. But since he moved to Oregon, he was free to do and move about as he pleased. Perhaps he just made the wrong friends out there. Perhaps they were drug addicts. I'll never know. I had no resolution to my feelings when I went back into the kitchen. Jack and the kids got home a few minutes before dinner was ready. We started the meal by me telling everyone that Mitch was gone. The kids showed almost no emotion. One of their last memories of him was his wild-man antics in the car down in Florida. Jack came over to console me with a hug.

"Jess, I'm sorry. What can I do for you?"

"I can't think of anything. I still can't believe he's gone. He was only fifty-eight."

"What happened?"

"My folks don't know."

Jack went back to his chair. For a few seconds, we just looked into each other's eyes. I felt like I knew exactly what was on Jack's mind, and my mind. I think we both remembered all of the Mitch horror stories we lived through over the years and thought, "No more tales of terror and incomprehensible aggravation."

The four of us finished our meal quietly. Unlike the previous night, I was in no mood for a walk with Jack. I was desperate for psychological relief.

Megan asked if she could go over to a friend's house for a while. I told her not to be home too late. Jason asked if Jack could help him with some homework. I told Jack I would take care of the kitchen myself and the two left the kitchen. As soon as I heard them upstairs in Jason's room, I left everything as it was and headed for the downstairs bathroom. Without any guilt at all, I locked the door, lifted the toilet seat, got on my knees, shoved my finger down my throat, and purged every ounce of food in my stomach. I knew it was one step backward, but I didn't care. The high I felt from purging calmed me like a fix would calm a junkie. I thought of Mitch and said to myself, "Mitch, I guess we were both cursed with a deadly addiction."

* * *

The next morning I got my return call from Dr. Marcus at about 9:30. I thanked him for returning my call, explained my status, and made a 10:00 a.m. appointment with him for the first Monday in May, two months away, when my IOP would be complete. I liked his voice. It was calm. He spoke in a very matter-of-fact and pragmatic fashion, and I liked it. I had a feeling he'd work out. I looked forward to finishing the IOP and meeting him, with the belief he might have a chance at helping me.

I spent the rest of the day drinking coffee, going outside for cigarettes, and vegetating in bed until it was time to prepare dinner.

Jason was the first to get home. His friend's mother dropped him off at the house. Megan arrived shortly after, and Jack got home at the regular time. No one had much to say during the meal. Again, Jason asked if Jack could help him with some homework, and Megan asked if she could go to a friend's house. I told Megan to wait for an hour until her father and I got back from a walk.

* * *

There were two more trips to the IOP before Saturday's funeral. My folks, Jack, the kids, and I made up the entire funeral party. The clergyman gave a typical euphemistic sermon before Mitch's body was laid to rest. Afterwards my folks came back to our house. They spent time with Jack and me and practically ignored the kids. At first this made me angry. Then I remembered how they ignored me until I reached adulthood, so I didn't get on their case about how they treated my kids. They were too old to change their ways. Nothing I could do or say would have any impact. I swallowed my anger, spoke courteously with them, then Jack and I drove them to the airport for them to return home. They had accomplished their goal in New York, and I wondered when I'd see them again.

Monday's IOP session and all the other sessions that followed seemed like they became routine missions. I never got used to the misery the traffic caused me on the way home, but I knew that I had no choice about the situation. Each session I attended made me feel that much closer to my first session with Dr. Marcus.

In some ways, the IOP was successful. It got me into a pattern of eating three meals a day, two at the IOP and one at home, and I managed to get my weight back up to about 109. I felt like that was an accomplishment. I felt like I still had a good chance for recovery, although I was still purging whenever I felt it was necessary to achieve some emotional relief. The good thing was that the purging was cut down from my pre-Springdale days of three or four times a day, down to two or three times a week. Perhaps that doesn't sound like much, but for me, that was a minor miracle.

* * *

Perhaps it was the sunshine on that first Monday in May, or perhaps it was the knowledge that I was about to meet Dr. Marcus, that gave me a slightly elevated feeling. Yes, I was nervous. That was nothing new because I was always nervous before meeting a doctor for the first time. Yet, because I had spoken with him on the phone and was pleased with what he said, I was slightly less nervous than usual. Jack's early alarm woke me, and I had my first cup of coffee with him before he left the house. I got Jason ready for school, but then I had a hard time getting Megan ready. Getting her ready in the morning had become a painful ritual. Most teenage girls are fussy about what they wear to school, but Megan went beyond fussy into neurotic, spending hours trying on one outfit after another until only an argument and screaming got her dressed and out of the house. I had spoken with Dr. Thatcher about it at her last appointment. He said it was an indication of OCD tendencies and that we had to monitor her. He put her on medication, but none of them seemed to help her. The only good thing about her attitude that morning was that it diverted my thoughts about my appointment. Before I had a chance to start looping about my therapy session, I was already out of the house and driving there.

I parked my car in a small public parking lot outside his office at 9:40. It was a pleasure not to have to drive a long distance to Dr. Marcus' office, which had a small waiting room and a pleasant, young, and attractive receptionist. "Can I help you?"

"Yes, I'm Mrs. Jess Gordon."

"Is this is your first visit?"

"Yes."

"May I have your insurance card?"

"Yes."

Although I had confirmed that Dr. Marcus took my insurance, I still felt some trepidation when I handed her my card. In turn, she handed me a clipboard with the standard privacy-invading questionnaire, plus a pen, which was not attached to the clipboard. It made me smile. I guess they felt I wouldn't steal the pen. "Mrs. Gordon, please fill this out and sign the consent forms."

"I don't mind the consent forms, but do I have to answer all of these questions?"

"Well, I can ask Dr. Marcus about it, but it would facilitate your first appointment if Dr. Marcus had your background in front of him when you go into his office."

"Sorry, dear. Don't bother asking him about it. It's just that I've filled out too many of these in the past few years. One more won't make a difference. I'll take care of it."

"Thank you, Mrs. Gordon. In the meantime, I'll copy your insurance card for our records and I'll call to confirm your coverage."

So far, the experience was pleasant. Unlike the last rude and nasty experience I had with a private therapist's receptionist, her immediate attention to me made me feel good. I sat down and started the arduous task of answering the multitude of questions. Within five minutes, the receptionist called me back to the window, handed me back my card, and said everything was fine with my insurance coverage. That also made me feel good.

It was 10:10 when I finished the questionnaire and handed it to the receptionist, who immediately got up to take it to Dr. Marcus. At 10:14, Dr. Marcus opened the door to the office corridor. "Mrs. Gordon?"

"Yes."

"Nice to meet you."

We shook hands. "Nice to meet you, too."

"Right this way."

"Thanks."

Dr. Marcus looked like he was in his late forties. He had extremely dark and slicked-back hair, a pleasant smile, and stood about five foot ten. He was well built. I think it would have bothered me if he was overweight, and I would have gone nuts if he was obese. An obese doctor, in my mind, could never relate to my issues. I noticed his left ear was pierced. Either he used to wear a stud, or he still wears one, but not in the office. In my mind, his pierced ear made him a regular person who maintained a professional attitude. In general, his appearance set me at ease.

Dr. Marcus held the door opened and indicated which way to go. The hallway was filled with at least six doors that stretched left and right. Dr. Marcus' office was the last room on the right. I sat down on a large black chair. Dr. Marcus closed the door behind him and sat at his desk. He reviewed the questionnaire a few moments and simply commented, "Uh, huh," several times, then he put the questionnaire on his desk and faced me. "Mrs. Gordon . . ."

"Jess."

"Jess, how can I help you?"

"Well, I recently did an inpatient stay at Springdale Hospital in New Jersey, and I just finished their intensive outpatient care program."

"I'm very familiar with both programs."

Hearing him say those words put me at ease. I felt like everything we were about to discuss would be territory he had discussed many times before with his other patients. That meant he was experienced with my situation, which was another positive sign about him.

"Jess, I see that you've gone through periods of deep depression and ideation. How would you rate yourself on those conditions now?"

"The medication Dr. Barrow prescribed seems to be working. I still have bouts of depression and occasional ideation, but not as often and not as severe as before I went through the Springdale program."

"I see. What's your status with your eating disorder? I see you've gone through an extended period of anorexia and bulimia."

"Well, now I'm eating three meals a day, and my purging has subsided considerably. It's down from three or four times a day to a few times a week."

"Uh, huh. I see your height is five foot five, and you list your current weight at 109 pounds. How do you feel about that?"

"Very good. When I entered Springdale, I was down to about 88."

"How did you feel about your inpatient stay at Springdale?"

"Which time?"

"Let's start with the first time."

"I didn't want to be there."

"And you went because . . . ?"

"I wanted to break the cycle. The only way I could do it was to enter the bubble. I mean, I needed that kind of totally protective and supportive environment, but it's not reality. You live under the eyes of the food police. They lock the bathrooms so you can't purge. They sit on top of you to make sure you're eating your meal. I was not allowed to chew gum or shake my foot because it burns calories. I started eating without purging. I didn't have a choice. There was no option. I said to myself, 'OK. I know I have no choice about eating this meal. I'm going to eat it.' It's easy to be in recovery there. But, as soon as I got out . . . it's like . . . How do I deal with it once I'm out of that environment, nobody is watching me, nobody is home, and the stress piles on? Purging is easy at home. It's a part of my routine, especially when I don't have to sneak away from Jack, my husband, or the kids. It's my way of living. It's very secretive."

"Well, you know it's called 'the secret disorder.' That's its nickname."

"Yes. I've heard that."

"Why do you fear giving up purging?"

"I'm afraid of gaining weight. I have an unbelievable fear of gaining weight. The lower I go, the lower I want to go. Frankly, it's terrifying. Even though I'm thin, I look in the mirror and still see this fat person looking back at me. I'm afraid that if I gave up purging, I would balloon up to who knows what weight. What can I say? It's a part of my personality."

"Are you comfortable with it?"

"Yes. I think I have it under control. It's amazing that I'm purging so much less now than a few weeks ago. I won't get fat. I won't let myself get that much out of control."

"Uh, huh. Jess, why do you think you were discharged from Springdale only to have to reenter a week later?"

"I convinced Dr. Barrow I was ready to be discharged. OK, maybe I wasn't ready. Maybe I just wanted to get back to my family and it was too soon."

"Anything else?"

"Yes. I thought I had a therapist set up for outside support. It turned out he didn't take my medical coverage. I guess I just freaked a little bit. However, when I was discharged the second time, I felt I was ready, and the IOP helped to support me while living in the real world. I'm really doing so much better than before."

"Jess, what stands out in your mind the most during your inpatient or IOP therapy sessions?"

"Not that much, except for one thing. I was the one on the carpet during one of the group therapy sessions. Unusually so, Dr. Barrow was not the facilitator; it was one of the other doctors. I explained how I had reduced my purging from several times a day to only two or three times a week. The doctor's comment was, 'Don't beat yourself up, just try to continue to reduce the frequency. I know and you know you can do better.' I felt that he was almost giving me permission or encouraging me to purge."

"You realize, of course, that until you stop purging entirely, you'll be preventing yourself from entering a tentative recovery phase."

"Yeah, I guess so, but I do feel different and better. I'm eating regularly again."

"That's good, Jess. Eating regularly is critical. Let me explain something about your metabolism. When you starve yourself through restriction and purging, your metabolism slows. So, therefore, the brain, the controlling organ of the body, says, 'No! You're not going to kill me.' It compensates by slowing the metabolism. When you start eating more regularly and normally, the metabolism picks up and compensates, to a large degree, as a result of the increase in caloric intake. That is a concept that most of my ED patients . . ."

"Excuse me, Dr. Marcus, what does 'ED' mean?"

"Sorry, ED is short for eating disorders. As I was saying, that is a concept that most of my ED patients have a tremendous difficulty believing. They'll read it on the Internet, they'll read it in books, but they have a very difficult time actually believing that it's going to work. Once my patients get it and they prove it to themselves, their outlook and prognosis improve."

"I see."

"I also believe, since we both know that we're never going to weigh the same all week long, that you should look at your weight within a range. So, once you get the range concept, and that the body will increase the metabolism, not decrease it, if you eat more regularly, your possibility for recovery increases. Another thing to consider is exercise. You can't over-exercise. Over-exercising and becoming hypergymnasic make the body slow down even more. Again, it's the brain. It's going to say, 'No, you're not killing me. You can kill everything up to your neck, but when it goes beyond that point, I'm holding back.'"

"I see."

"Jess, I'd like to ask a simple and basic question: Do you want to go into recovery?"

"Actually . . ." I stopped for a moment, not because I had to decide if I wanted recovery–I did–but to decide whether I was already on the way there. Dr. Marcus never took his eyes off me as I thought. His eyes were intense, so I thought hard about what I was about to say. "Listen, in my opinion, I think I've already started a partial recovery. I've put on over 20 pounds. Perhaps another pound or two would be OK, but I don't want to put on much more weight than that. I'm eating three meals a day. I'm not passing out now. I'm off the diet pills and laxatives again. I just purge a little. It's under control."

"Is it?"

"I think so."

"Uh, huh. Jess, how do you think your eating disorder started?"

"I don't know."

"Was it a reaction to someone else's opinion of your physical condition? For example, did some call you chubby?"

"No. My first experience started by accident because I thought I'd look better in my wedding dress if I lost a couple of pounds."

"Were you going through an unusual amount of stress at that time?"

"Just the opposite. It was probably one of the happiest times of my life. I've heard so many stories where one set of parents or the other causes a great deal of stress before the marriage, but that wasn't the case with us. Neither of our parents did or said anything negative about our forthcoming marriage. Everything was wonderful. I just wanted to lose a few pounds to look better in my dress."

"On a scale of one to ten, with ten being the best score, how would you rate your relationship with your husband?"

"At least a nine. Probably a ten. I can't imagine being with anyone else."

"I see. Were there any other factors that you can remember about how your ED started?"

"The best way to describe it would be to say that after I started losing weight, I suddenly heard people say positive things about me, like, 'Oh, you look so good. You have such control. You have such discipline. I wish I could lose weight.' Suddenly my old clothes felt different on me. A lot of my stuff became too large, which made me feel good and made me continue in that weight loss pattern. In addition, I could wear trim-fitting, stylish clothes that I could never wear before. I even looked great in a bathing suit. It was one of the first times in my life that I felt so good about myself, and I thought I was doing the right thing."

"Did you ever have a time when you thought you were doing something excessively or in a perfectionistic fashion?"

"Yes. I distinctly remember a time when I lived through what I called 'the perfect little girl' period. My parents were never the nurturing type. They didn't know how to relate to children. The only positive comments I got were from my teachers, and that only happened when I performed like the perfect little girl. You know, every homework in on time, the highest grades on tests, and that sort of stuff."

"Uh, huh."

Dr. Marcus spent the last few minutes of our first session reiterating some of the points about metabolism and eating regularly, and that I should avoid over-exercising, which had no meaning to me since I almost never exercised. Before I knew it, the session was over. Dr. Marcus asked me if I wished to continue seeing him, and about the frequency of appointments.

"Dr. Marcus, throughout the session, I felt comfortable with you. Yes, I definitely want to continue. Do you think we can meet once a week?"

Dr. Marcus opened his appointment book. "How about this time and day on a weekly basis?"

"That sounds good. Dr. Marcus." I wasn't sure if I needed to ask about what was on my mind, but I felt compelled to share my thoughts with him. "I feel like I'm in a much improved condition at this point. I think future sessions with you will keep me on this track."

"Jess, you're on the right track, but I feel you still have much more to accomplish before you can consider yourself in any form of recovery. I'm not satisfied with your current weight. You need a higher range. You need to be in a range where the loss of a few pounds doesn't put you into a danger zone. You're not there yet. I also think you should consider working with a nutritionist. If you don't have one in mind, I can suggest a very qualified colleague. Also, I'd like to contact Dr. Thatcher to review some of your background. Is that OK with you?"

"Sure."

Dr. Marcus stood and extended his hand. I took that movement as the official end of our first session. I rose, shook his hand, and said, "Next week."

"If there's an emergency, call at any time."

"Thanks."

Dr. Marcus escorted me to the exit door. I left his office and searched my handbag for my cigarettes and lighter as I descended the stairs. I lit up as soon as I got outside. I was in no rush to get anywhere. I just stood in the parking lot and felt glad that he was my new doctor. I felt like he knew his business. It did, however, piss me off a little to think he wanted me to gain more weight than I had in mind, but I didn't get too anxious about it. I just relaxed for a while. After that session, I felt I deserved it. Usually, I would run immediately to do anything I needed to, but not that day. I stopped to savor the moment. I stopped to enjoy my freedom from Springdale and the IOP sessions. Perhaps it was because the sun was unusually warm for that time of year and it felt good on my face. When I got to my car, instead of getting in and running like a chicken without a head, I leaned against the car with my face up to the sun, and I finished the first of two cigarettes before I drove away to do my errands. It felt like the first vacation I had in a very long time, and it felt great.

It was 3:30 by the time I got home. I called my folks to see how they were doing. Both of them were still in disbelief that Mitch was gone. As soon as I got off the phone with them, I put them out of my mind. Perhaps it was selfish, but the only thing I thought about was myself. I felt I had earned that right.

The kids and Jack got home at their regular times. Dinner that night was pleasant and, again, I told Megan to stay in the house with Jason until Jack and I got home from our walk.

"What's up with these walks, Mom?"

"The weather is beautiful, and it gives me some special time with your father." The truth about me avoiding purging during that hour was nothing that Megan needed to know. Besides, the weather was extremely conducive for a walk. Actually, something else was changing. I was beginning to have affectionate feelings toward Jack. Those feelings and passionate desires for him were missing since before I started the inpatient and IOP sessions. It felt good to want to be close with my husband again. It felt good to be in love again.

Jack and I walked aimlessly around our neighborhood for an hour. For the first few minutes, we walked separately. Then I took his arm, and I felt like we were two lovers who were just starting to date and couldn't let go of each other. By the time we got home and the efficient time for purging was gone, I felt good about myself. As Jack and I approached the house, there was one thought that came to me: "Why didn't Jack ask me about my meeting with Dr. Marcus?" My answer to myself was, "Jack doesn't ask. I don't tell. Or, perhaps he was just being polite, and he was waiting for me to broach the subject." Then I heard Dr. Barrow's and Dr. Marcus' words ringing my ears, "An eating disorder is nicknamed the secret disorder."

We stopped outside the house, and I kissed Jack on the lips. He was a little surprised, but he went with the kiss in a long and affectionate manner. When our lips separated, I asked myself, "Is Jack's don't-ask-don't-tell situation a positive or negative situation for me?" I had no answer. Then I thought, "Purging is a secret I won't divulge to Jack. It's a safe haven for when I need psychological relief, even at the cost of not progressing 100 percent into recovery."

We opened the door, and Megan flew out of the house to be with her friends. Jason came over and asked Jack if he would help him with something that was troubling him with his homework. I chuckled. Jack asked me what I was laughing about. "Nothing special," was my response. Actually, I laughed at the recognition that I was out of Springdale, under the proper doctor's care, and happy about surviving in the real world.

I sent my two favorite boys upstairs to get their work done, then I went back into the kitchen to finish cleaning up. For a moment, I almost felt like a "normal" person living in a "normal" family way. I felt a sense of accomplishment. I felt like I was already in recovery, no matter how much Dr. Marcus believed that I hadn't reached that point yet. I felt good about my life and myself, and I seduced my husband when we got into bed later that night. The longer we held each other, the more I enjoyed those feelings that were missing for so long. That night, I slept without nightmares. I woke the next morning and had a small breakfast without purging.

* * *

My second appointment with Dr. Marcus was on Monday, May 12, 2003. I parked my car at 9:40, had a cigarette, and walked into his waiting room at 9:57. There was soft rock playing. I didn't remember hearing the music at my last appointment, but that didn't surprise me. The last time I was there, I was too focused on the questionnaire and meeting Dr. Marcus, so nothing else had a chance at penetrating my conscious thoughts. I approached the receptionist. She opened her glass window, I handed her my medical co-payment, and she told me it would be a few minutes. What I realized that day was that all of my appointments would begin ten minutes after the hour, and end on the hour.

There were a few magazines available, but none of them interested me. Actually, I was a little eager and enthusiastic about starting the session, which I had looked forward to for the entire previous week.

Dr. Marcus opened the door at exactly 10:10. "Hi, Jess."

"Hi." This time he didn't have to tell me which way to go. I headed into his office and got comfortable in the large black chair. Dr. Marcus closed the door, sat down, reviewed some notes in my folder, turned to me, and said, "How are you?"

"Pretty good would be an accurate statement."

"Good. How are you doing with your weight?"

"My range is 109-111."

"That's about where you were last week."

"Yeah. Dr. Marcus, I've got a question for you."

"OK."

"Aren't you going to weigh me?"

"Do you want me to?"

"Not really. I'll tell you my real weight."

"That's what I thought. Jess, when it comes my ED patients and the scale, I always say, 'I won't weigh you unless you make me weigh you. If you make me, I will. But, if you are honest, we'll keep you off the scale and it doesn't matter.' Also, I find that most of my ED patients don't lie to me. If I forcibly weigh you, I become a sinister and threatening figure. That's not what I'm here for. I'm here to help you."

"Thanks, Dr. Marcus."

"That's OK. Now, what about the purging?"

"It's about the same."

"Any thoughts about giving it up?"

"I thought about it, but I feel OK about the infrequent times I'm doing it now, versus the numerous times I did it before Springdale."

"Uh, huh."

"Give me some time, Dr. Marcus. I'm happy with myself that I'm maintaining a three-meal-a-day program."

"I spoke with Dr. Thatcher a few days ago." Dr. Marcus paused to review his notes. "I told him that you presented yourself well, that you're cooperative, verbal, you come across as an intelligent woman, and you're definitely willing to go into detail. I understand you have an appointment with him next week."

"Yes, I need a prescription renewal."

"What about the depression and ideation?"

"It comes and goes, but nothing as severe as the way it was a few months back. I think this new antidepressant is working."

"Very good. More than likely, it's a combination of the medication and stopping the malnutrition, which is a major factor with depression." Dr. Marcus paused, checked his folder again, looked at me, and said, "Jess, today I'd like to explain a few things."

That moment pleased me. It was as though Dr. Marcus had taken the time to prepare a game plan for me. He had done his homework to help me and reviewed it before he spoke.

"First, we'll talk about the tools we have to help you and, second, the 'Twelve-Step Program,' which I've modified toward people with eating disorders, rather than drug or alcohol problems."

"Very good."

"Let's start with breaking the routine. This means behavior modifications. It helps if you get out of the house, exercise in moderation, and spend more time with your family. Of course, I'd like you to continue on your present course of three meals a day, and I strongly recommend seeing a nutritionist."

"Do you think the nutritionist is covered by my medical plan?"

"We can check it out for you."

"Do you have someone to recommend?"

"Yes, Joan Dupont. I've known her for years."

"I'll take her number and contact her."

"That's good.

"Jess, in addition, distractions are good for you. That means finding activities outside the house that interest you. I'd also like you to start journaling your activities."

"Actually, I was thinking about taking classes."

"Very good. If you have a dog, take it for a walk instead of sitting at home."

"It's funny that you mention that. I don't have a dog. Instead, I take my husband for a walk after dinner."

"That's the idea. We'll get involved with relaxation techniques. Sometimes I'll work with biofeedback. It teaches relaxation, which is quantitative, so there's no guesswork. Biofeedback gives us numbers that can be monitored, just like taking a person's temperature. It helps with impulse control because this is a pure impulsive disorder. In other words, you feel it and you do it. There's no thought filtering. You just go with the impulse and do it. ED is an addiction. It's an addictive disorder as much as heroin and cocaine or other illegal drugs are addictive disorders."

Suddenly I zoned out on the next few words Dr. Marcus said and focused on memories of Mitch, and that drugs probably caused his death. Dr. Marcus probably noticed my spacy condition because he paused until my eyes met his again. "Jess, are you OK?"

"Fine, Dr. Marcus. I'm with you."

"Good. OK, let's go through some of the highlights of the 'Twelve-Step Program.' You admit you are powerless over ED. You take a moral inventory of yourself. You acknowledge, and then look for ways to remove your shortcomings. You list those people who have been harmed by your ED, and you look for a way to amend and resolve those relationships. You put these practices into your daily life. Lastly, for now, and I'm quoting the AA program, is 'learning how to live in the gray area that we are working on in recovery– learning to live in balance between the extremes.' Jess, understand that these steps are taken over the course of time. It took a long time for you to get into the condition that caused your inpatient stays. It'll take time to get out of that mode and into recovery."

LITTLE OR NO EFFECT

Hearing what Dr. Marcus said, and the way he said it so convincingly, made me pause. "Dr. Marcus, I'm glad I'm here."

"That's good, Jess. Is the same time good for you next week?"

"Yes." I looked at my watch and realized the session was over. Dr. Marcus handed me his card with the date and time of our next session. He also gave me Joan Dupont's contact information. It was startling to see that the time went so quickly. Dr. Marcus stood, shook my hand, and escorted me to the exit.

"Take care, Jess."

"See you next week."

I was in no rush that afternoon. I had no errands to run. I only had to be home when the kids got back from school. I lit a cigarette, leaned against the car, and pointed my face up to the sun. It was becoming a habit, and one that I enjoyed. It surprised me that Dr. Marcus hadn't gone into my past yet. I assumed he had to lay the groundwork on present needs before he went into that direction. Most of all, I felt confident that he was the right doctor for me. That was a great feeling.

I felt lucky, and it had been a long time since I had felt that way. So often, finding a new doctor is hit and miss. You never know if he's going to be good before you meet him. You don't know if he is going to have a background in what you need to help you with your special problem. Well, that's not the way I felt about Dr. Marcus. He was right for me, and the nutritionist he recommended turned out to be right also. She wasn't like the quack I once saw. Joan understood eating disorders and set me up with meal plans that were aimed to help me gain weight slowly. After I met her, the words "reasonable, understanding, and knowledgeable" came to my mind, and I continued to feel that way as the months passed.

Each time I saw Dr. Marcus, he asked me about my purging, and each time I could see the disappointment in his face when I told him I hadn't stopped, only kept the frequency to a minimum. However, he did smile each time I told him my weight range inched up a pound or two. Between Dr. Marcus, Joan, and Dr. Thatcher, who I only saw infrequently because he was usually travelling around to be on television doing interviews, I felt like I had a fantastic support team guiding me through my journey into a recovery. My depression wasn't anything like it used to be, and bouts with ideation became fewer and further between episodes.

I tried to adhere to Dr. Marcus' advice about getting out of the house. Jack and I continued taking walks together after dinner. At first, they were a means to prevent purging, but then I found them a great way to get closer to my husband. We had time to talk again. We held hands as we walked. In many ways, I think the two of us felt like newlyweds do shortly after they're married. We made love more often. Many times on our walks, Jack would see me stare into his eyes. He'd ask me what was on my mind. I always had the same answer, "I can't believe how lucky I was the night we met. I can't imagine my life without you." Jack always had the same response. Wherever we were, no matter who was around us, he'd kiss my lips, and I got turned on every time he did that.

Besides the walks, I signed up for art classes at our local community college. They were courses set up for adults. At first, I enjoyed them. People oftentimes tried to make friends with me, but I didn't want socialization. That bothered me. I didn't want people to invite me to their house for coffee and cake, and there was no way in hell I wanted to entertain those strangers in my home. After several classes, as the work progressed, I felt artistically inadequate and, rather than enjoying them, they caused me stress. Stress was the last thing I needed in my life, so I gave them up without regret.

Several times that summer, people from Jack's hospital invited us over for a barbecue. I remember when his bosses invited us for the Fourth of July weekend, but we made up an excuse to get out of it. Fortunately, Jack didn't have a problem with it. Neither of us was a real social butterfly.

A few times, I thought about my old job. I took a leave of absence before I entered Springdale. My old bosses knew about my condition and never put pressure on me to return unless I felt physically and mentally strong enough for the workload, but that never happened. They remained supportive even when I told them I wouldn't be returning and that I was going on disability. I guess they really appreciated all those years I worked hard and conscientiously for them, and this was their way of paying me back. Occasionally someone from work would call to see how I was getting along. Each time someone called, I stayed on the phone for a few short minutes, then made up some excuse about why I had to get off. It was another form of socialization that I couldn't deal with.

There were so many happy memories I had from the summer of 2003. Jack had some time off, so we got away to a lodge for a week. The four of us living so close together in a single room made me feel incredibly great, especially when I remembered how I missed them all that time I was away in Springdale. At the end of the week, there was a smile on my face throughout the entire two-hour ride home.

In September, the kids returned to school. That meant I was alone in the house during the day. I was proud of myself that I still managed to keep my purging to a minimum, even though I had the opportunity and privacy to purge at any given moment. By October, I was able to report to Dr. Marcus that my weight range neared 116-119 pounds. He and Joan were both pleased that I continued making progress, but Dr. Marcus kept reminding me that I was at a minimally safe weight range. He kept saying that any setback could throw me back into the danger zone, and I thought I hit my first setback in late September, the sixth-month anniversary of Mitch's death.

I never experienced guilt over my love-hate feelings toward Mitch. I never forgot all those unexpected and wild tirades I experienced. I never let go of the memory of his barbaric and animalistic eyes when he ran naked around the house with that huge knife and tried to kill my friend and me. As the saying goes, I forgave, but I never forgot. Yet, on the sixth-month anniversary of his death, a sudden depression gripped me, and it affected my eating disorder. I couldn't eat for two or three days, and I didn't care. I felt sorry for my folks. I felt ashamed at my accusation of him dying from a drug overdose. I felt frustrated at never having found out the truth about his death because my parents ruled out any possibility of an autopsy. I kept repeating to myself, "How sad that this was his life, and that it was cut so short." Although I had wished him dead several times when we were kids, he didn't deserve to die. Dr. Marcus and I discussed my thoughts and feelings about Mitch's death. Dr. Marcus told me I had a natural delayed reaction and that I was still going through the grieving process. His main concern was that it was affecting my eating habits, and he reiterated that I had to be concerned about my weight range. "Jess, any minor weight loss is a concern when your cushion is insufficient." Shortly after that session with Dr. Marcus, I started eating normally again. I put back the few pounds I had lost and maintained my minimal purging schedule. Over the next few sessions, Dr. Marcus asked me how I felt about my ED, and I responded, "I think I'm in recovery." Dr. Marcus always retorted, "Jess, at best, it's a partial recovery, and that won't change until you stop purging."

Other situations caused slight setbacks. However, there was nothing dramatic enough for me to restrict or change my purging frequency. Megan was always a source of consternation, but I guess I was used to my problems with her. My depression had abated, and my suicidal ideation was less frequent. As Thanksgiving approached, overall, I thought I was in fairly good shape and that my future prognosis looked good. I was wrong. In fact, I was almost dead wrong.

About a week and a half before Thanksgiving, I came down with a cold, which quickly felt more like another upper respiratory infection. After having suffered through so many, along with asthma attacks, I thought my self-diagnosis was accurate. I considered going to the doctor but postponed making an appointment, with the hopes that all my symptoms would subside if I cut my smoking down to a pack a day, got some bed rest, drank plenty of liquids, and took a few cold tablets. My symptoms didn't subside. They got worse. All I kept thinking about was the dozens of times Dr. Marcus told me to stop smoking because it was just another form of self-destructive behavior, but I ignored him and refused to stop. By the fourth day of my initial symptoms, I could hardly get myself out of bed. My muscles ached like I had the flu. I ran a fever. At times, I suddenly had teeth-chattering chills along with fast, shallow breathing and a rapid heartbeat. The rapid heartbeat made me think of all the times I passed out from malnutrition, but I knew that wasn't the case this time because I had been eating. By the afternoon, I was nauseated and had to vomit. As weak as I felt, I chuckled because it was the first time in decades that I had thrown up when it wasn't a result of purging. But the thing that scared me most of all was coughing and spitting the phlegm into a tissue. There was blood, which was the final straw that convinced me I couldn't doctor myself back to health and that these symptoms were serious enough to warrant an immediate medical evaluation. I called Jack to leave work early and told him he should take me to the emergency room at his hospital.

Emergency rooms and I were no strangers, but this time I wasn't there because of my eating disorder. They got me into a bed in the ER in about an hour. Jack took care of all the medical insurance paperwork. A half an hour later, I saw Dr. Rivera, who instructed a nurse to draw blood and to get me in for chest X-rays. The nurse was a pleasant-looking woman with a good bedside manner. She took some additional medical history and paid special attention to the fact that I smoke, suffer from asthma, and had frequent upper respiratory infections. When she finished getting my information, she told me it would be several minutes before I got into the X-ray room because there were a few patients ahead of me. I didn't mind. I was glad I was in the hospital to get this problem checked out. Coughing up blood scared the hell out of me. I laid there with my eyes closed until I heard footsteps approach me and stop at my bed. I opened my eyes to see Dr. Fisher, a relatively good-looking man in his mid-thirties. He had treated me a year before, which was just before I entered Springdale and when I was at my last year's lowest weight. "It's Jess. Isn't it?"

"Yes. Hello, Dr. Fisher."

"What seems to be the problem?"

I told him my symptoms. He took my pulse, checked my eyes, and listened to my heart and lungs.

"How long have you felt like this?"

"A few days."

"Have you ever had pneumonia before?"

"No."

Dr. Fisher checked my chart. "Good, Dr. Rivera will be treating you. You're in excellent hands."

"Good to know. I feel like crap."

"Give it a week or two and you'll be out and about like normal."

"Thanks. I've had my fill of hospitals."

"Jess, even though you're not feeling well, you look terrific. I see you gained some weight. It looks great on you."

"Uh, huh."

"Gotta go, Jess. You'll be fine."

"Yeah."

As he turned his back and walked away I said to myself, "Oh, my God. He thinks I'm fat. I must look like a big cow now." As weak as I was, I could have killed him for saying that to me. Suddenly I felt a psychological click go off in my head. It was as though he had put a virtual gun to my head and pulled the trigger.

Just then the nurse returned. She and an attendant wheeled me into the X-ray room. They got their pictures, then returned me to the main room. Dr. Rivera returned a few minutes later. He confirmed Dr. Fisher's informal diagnosis. It was pneumonia. He told me he was going to check me in immediately and to expect to stay at the hospital about a week, depending upon how I reacted to the antibiotics. I wound up staying there for five days and hated every minute of it, especially as I started getting stronger.

Throughout my stay, I had no appetite. I wasn't restricting, per se, I just couldn't eat because I felt so weak and ill, and it didn't bother me in the least. I entered the hospital at 115 and left weighing 105. When the nurse told me how much I weighed, I never considered any of Dr. Marcus' warnings about my safe weight range. I laughed at how easy it was to lose weight without trying, and without purging once during my entire inpatient stay. I remember saying to myself, "Wow! This is unbelievable. I didn't even have to work at it. I'm losing weight without doing anything."

The next time I saw Dr. Marcus he was flabbergasted. "It's inconceivable that they didn't monitor your weight, only your pulmonary functions. They know your history. And Jess, you took advantage of the situation."

"How so?"

"You took it as a license not to eat."

Throughout that entire session, Dr. Marcus was extremely blunt. I guess he had good cause because of the major setback in my weight. I felt like a little schoolgirl being scolded by her teacher. And, like a little girl, I didn't listen to half the things he said to me.

"Jess, you're close to dangerous territory. It's called the slippery slope. Once you're on that, you're in big trouble. Putting the brakes on ice is very difficult. We both know that. Drive on ice and hit the brakes, and you know you're going into a spin. Think of it like this: It's directional. If you're going in the right direction, I don't care how slow it is, there's no problem. If you're going in the wrong direction, there is no such thing as slow because of the slippery slope. It's to the point that if someone is out of range of the low end by a pound, I'll always say straight out, 'It concerns me.' Well, that's where you are now. Those were ten pounds you couldn't afford to lose."

"It's not a biggie. I can handle this. Between you and Joan, everything will be fine."

"Uh, huh. That's what you think?"

"Sure."

"When do you see Dr. Thatcher again?"

"I don't know. I called for an appointment, but they told me I'd have to wait for him to get back into town before I can get a firm date. That's starting to piss me off. What good is he if he's not around?"

"And what about Joan?"

"Next week."

"Does she know what's happened to you?"

"I told her I was in the hospital."

"Does she know about your weight loss?"

"No. I figured I'd tell her when I see her."

"So, losing 10 pounds didn't seem that significant to you."

"It wasn't."

"I see. Jess, until further notice, I want to start seeing you twice a week. I can book you in at 10:00 on Tuesday and Thursday."

"Well . . ."

"What I just said wasn't exactly a suggestion."

"Oh."

"Be careful, Jess. Be very careful."

"OK, Dr. Marcus. I'll see you on Tuesday."

The moment I left Dr. Marcus' office and hit the outside air, I lit a cigarette. I felt a little pissed at how he admonished me. I'm his patient, not his little kid. Instead of heading straight home as planned, I decided to go to Eckert's to pick up a few feminine items for Megan and me. After I found what I needed, I took a walk over to the area where they had their laxatives and threw ten boxes into my cart. The teenage girl at the cash register looked at the boxes and gave me a puzzled look.

"Anything wrong?" I asked.

"No, ma'am. Will that be charge or cash?"

At first I reached for my charge card, then I decided to pay cash so Jack wouldn't see the purchase on our statement and ask me about it. Two minutes after I got into the house, all but twenty laxatives were stashed away. I popped the twenty into my mouth, took a gulp of water, and they flew down my throat. I hadn't taken any in months, but you don't forget how to do something like that.

Later that night after dinner I suggested that Jack help Jason with some of his homework. Jason hadn't asked for help, but he was always happy to have Jack's company. As soon as Jason, Megan, and Jack were out of the kitchen, I left everything where it stood and went to the downstairs bathroom. I locked the door, got on my knees in front of the toilet, stuck my finger down my throat, and threw up every ounce of food that entered my body. When I got up to start my mouth-washing routine, I felt like I was about to pass out, so I held on to the vanity to prevent myself from falling. It was extremely difficult getting up the stairs. I gripped the banister firmly to keep myself from falling. Once upstairs, I got my lighter and cigarettes and stayed outside until I finished two. The cigarettes, my purging, and the fact that I hadn't fully recovered made my brains take off for outer space. That night, everything I had accomplished at Springdale, the IOP program, and the multitude of hours with Dr. Marcus and Joan vanished. I heard Dr. Marcus' voice in my head say, "The slippery slope," and I didn't care. I told myself, "I can handle this. I like the weight I'm at. I don't give a damn what anyone says. I'm happy where I am, and I'm not changing for anyone."

* * *

By the end of the week I began to restrict more. I was back to purging three or four times a day and popping at least twenty laxatives a day, and I didn't care. It didn't even bother me when I saw Dr. Marcus and admitted, like a defiant schoolgirl, that my weight dropped a pound or two. There was no reason to lie. If I did, I knew Dr. Marcus would know it, and he would simply put me on the scale to check if I lied to him. The only thing I didn't revert back to were diet pills because I remember Dr. Thatcher telling me they would give me a stroke or heart attack. As for my depression, I didn't have any. In fact, for the remainder of November and through Christmas, I

LITTLE OR NO EFFECT

felt like I was on a high. My clothes got big on me, and it made me feel good about myself, regardless of what Dr. Marcus and Joan thought. By the week after New Year's Eve, I broke the triple-digit weight range. For the first day or two, it felt phenomenal. Jack even commented that I seemed to be in an extra-cheery mood. Two or three days later, when I reached 95 pounds, he asked, "What happened to that cheery wife of mine? You seem down in the mouth."

Jack was right, although he seemed clueless about what I was doing, and he didn't ask any more questions. To me, it seemed like the antidepressant stopped working. My depression escalated on a daily basis along with my suicidal ideation frequency. I was in an uncontrollable slide down Dr. Marcus' slippery slope, and I didn't care.

* * *

Chapter Nine

Russian Roulette with a Blade

My session with Dr. Marcus on February 5, 2004, started in the usual fashion with him asking me my weight.

"My range is 94-96."

"Jess, that low weight is unacceptable."

"Dr. Marcus, I'm not concerned with my weight."

"You should be."

"But I'm not."

"Uh, huh." Dr. Marcus paused, checked his notes, and turned back to me with an intense look like I had never seen before on his face. "Jess, let's try something here."

Dr. Marcus had an ominous look before he started hitting me with a rapid series of statements that I had to respond to. The first statement seemed simple and obvious to answer.

"You have no appetite."

"Right."

"You're suffering from insomnia."

"Yes."

"You have no energy. You're feeling fatigued."

"Right."

"You have low self-esteem."

"Correct."

"Poor concentration."

"Right."

"You have difficulty making simple decisions."

"Yes."

"You have a feeling of hopelessness."

"Yes."

"Jess, how would you respond to this: 'I don't want to actively kill myself, but if I don't wake up tomorrow, that would be ideal.'"

"I'd agree with that."

"Jess, what I described are the criteria to diagnose depression."

"So what if I'm depressed."

"Jess, based on your responses, you need to go inpatient."

"No way."

"Your ED makes you a danger to yourself."

"I don't see it that way. I just think my antidepressant needs to be changed or the dosage is insufficient. And if Dr. Thatcher were ever around, I'd be OK."

"Your malnutrition would cause any antidepressant to fail."

"It was working, then it stopped."

"It stopped because you are restricting, purging, and abusing laxatives. The medication isn't in your system long enough to be effective."

"I don't see it that way."

"Perhaps you should."

During the next thirty minutes, Dr. Marcus tried to make me understand the seriousness of my condition. Every word fell on deaf ears. He accused me of being in denial of my health status. I let him know, in no uncertain terms, that I was aware of my condition, but I was not willing to do anything about it. The final minutes of the session were devoted to Dr. Marcus trying to convince me to go inpatient, and me repeatedly refusing to accept his advice. The session ended in silence as he wrote some remarks in my chart and then wrote something on the back of one of his business cards. When he finished, Dr. Marcus turned toward me, looked hard into my eyes, and startled me. "Jess, I understand your condition. I want you to promise me something. If you're about to do anything dangerous to yourself, you'll call me."

"What?"

"Do you promise me you'll call?"

"OK, I'll call."

"Jess, you're a smart woman. I think you understand me. If things get out of control, don't hesitate to call. You can reach me 24/7 with the number on the back of the card." Dr. Marcus handed me his card and I took it.

"Sure, Dr. Marcus," I said with no intention of ever listening to his instructions. I rose, left his office without saying another word to him, and headed to the exit in the waiting room. I usually waved goodbye to the receptionist with a smile on my face as I left Dr. Marcus' office. That day, there was no smile on my face as I walked silently passed her. I didn't mean to be rude. I just wasn't in the mood for small talk or pleasantries after what I'd heard from Dr. Marcus. The moment I hit the cold outdoors, I lit the first of two cigarettes. I coughed frequently because I still hadn't gotten over the full effects of the pneumonia.

After dinner that night, I half expected Jack to ask me about how my session went with Dr. Marcus. He never brought up the subject. Neither did I. Instead, I waited for the earliest opportunity to get downstairs to the bathroom so I could puke my guts up.

The next four Tuesday and Thursday sessions with Dr. Marcus were almost identical to the session I had on February 5. He pushed me to go inpatient. Each time, I flat-out refused. On Tuesday, February 23, I woke expecting to have another verbal fencing dual with Dr. Marcus about me going inpatient, but something was different that day. It started by me seeing 88 pounds on the scale. Part of me was ecstatic about the low number. Jack and the kids were out of the house when I went downstairs to have my coffee and cigarettes. For the past several days, it had become increasingly difficult to find the energy, or the desire, to get out of bed. I was listless and felt useless. Nothing motivated me to do anything. By 8:30, I was dressed and ready to leave. But since the drive was less than ten minutes, I put on a sweater and went outside in the twelve-degree weather to have another cup of coffee and a few cigarettes. By 8:32, halfway into my first cigarette, I started experiencing an uncontrollable amount of anxiety. Beads of sweat started to drip down my face. My legs felt like they were about to buckle under me. Part of me wanted to just fall down unconscious and freeze to death. It would have been a painless and clean way to exit this world. Unfortunately, I didn't.

Ten minutes later I gathered my coat, purse, and keys, and got into my car. As I started the engine, I could hear Dr. Marcus' voice admonish me, "If you're about to do anything dangerous . . ." Any person in her right mind would have realized she was in no condition to drive. If she were to drive anywhere in that condition, she would have headed straight to an emergency room. I didn't. I headed for Dr. Marcus' office, although I knew I'd get there an hour early.

From the moment I hit the gas pedal, there was trouble. The car was parked on the driveway. Fortunately, it was several feet away from the garage door. I thought I put the car in reverse to back out onto the street. I was wrong. The car was in drive. I was lucky enough to notice I was going in the wrong direction and lucky enough to stop the car an inch or two away from the garage door. My nerves went out of control, and I paused to light a cigarette before putting the car into reverse and backing out onto the street. I never did see the car fast approaching my driveway. Luckily, the guy saw me, honked, and slammed on his brakes. He got out of his car, cursed me like I was never cursed out before, then got back into his car and drove off. I turned onto the street and slowly drove toward the stop sign at the end of the block. Cars passed heavily from the left and right. I stood my ground impatiently and waited for all traffic to clear before I proceeded. Two blocks later I drove through an intersection but never noticed the stop sign. Fortunately, the car approaching from my left noticed my stupidity and swerved to narrowly avoid me. For the remainder of the few-minute ride, I drove between five and ten miles per hour because I didn't trust myself. It was a miracle that I got to Dr. Marcus' office alive.

The receptionist greeted me with a polite smile and a surprised look. "Good morning, Mrs. Gordon. It's almost nine, but your appointment isn't until ten."

"Sorry, but I have to see Dr. Marcus immediately."

"Is this an emergency?"

"Yes."

"OK. Have a seat." The receptionist immediately picked up the phone to contact Dr. Marcus. All I could hear her say was, "Yes, Dr. Marcus. She said it was an emergency."

I was pacing the small waiting room floor when Dr. Marcus opened the door leading to the office area.

"Dr. Marcus, I have to see you now."

"Jess, I'm with a patient. What's wrong?"

"I've never felt this bad in my life."

"OK. Come in. You can wait for me in another office."

Dr. Marcus took me into one of the empty offices, told me to sit, and put on a tape with soothing ocean sounds.

"Jess, I'm sorry, but I have to finish this appointment. Don't leave here. If you leave, I'll call the police. Do you understand me?"

"Yes." At that point, I started shaking uncontrollably. Never before had I felt such strong desires for death.

"Jess, would you rather I leave the door open or closed?"

"Open. I feel like I'm suffocating."

"OK. Jess, I'm serious. If you take one step out of this complex I'm calling 911. It's for your own protection."

I replied harshly. "I got the idea."

Dr. Marcus went back to his patient. At first, I paced the small room, then I felt too weak to stand. Although there was a large comfortable cushioned chair, I decided to just sit down on the floor to wait.

I felt desperate for immediate help so I turned to the one person who could empathize with my feelings and offer me comfort, solace and strength as I waited impatiently for Dr. Marcus to return. I got my cell phone, pointed to her name in my directory, and waited anxiously for a connection. The phone rang twice before a male voice responded.

"Hello."

"Hi, Dave," I said in no mood for social chitchat. "This is Jess. Is Kylie home?"

"Hi, Jess. It's been a long time."

"I know. I haven't been well. I don't mean to be impolite, but can I speak with Kylie? It's important."

"I'm sorry, Jess. I guess you didn't hear."

"Hear what?"

"About Kylie," Dave said with an unusual and ominous tone. "She . . ."

"Dave, what's wrong?"

"Kylie . . . she . . . she died last month."

There was silence on both ends of the phone for several seconds until I got the courage to ask, "What happened?"

"Eight months ago she had a miscarriage. She blamed herself, but it wasn't her fault. She fell into a deep depression, and she reverted to her disorder. She kept dropping unbelievable amounts of weight. I got her to see a few doctors, but she didn't respond to the therapy or the medications. Jess, she lost all will to live. It was as though she starved herself to death and no one could stop her. She mentioned your name often and hoped you were doing OK."

Dave paused. I could hear he had started to cry. I felt like I would choke from the lump of sadness in my throat. All I could utter was, "Dave, I'm so sorry. If I had known . . . Dave, I'll miss her. She was one of my very few friends. I'm so sorry. So sorry. Take care."

"You, too, Jess. Send my regards to Jack."

"Sure." I flipped off the phone and wanted to scream out my pain, anger, and frustration, but I couldn't. All I could do was to sit there in an emotional stupor as tears welled up in my eyes and down my face.

I was still on the floor, shaking, crying, and sweating, when Dr. Marcus finally returned. He extended his hands to help me up. As I rose he said, "I called your husband. He's in the waiting room. I'm going to see you both now."

Jack had never met Dr. Marcus. Jack didn't know what was going on with me, but that was about to change. I did not attempt to fix my unkempt look or wipe the sweat or tears from my face as I walked into Dr. Marcus' office and sat in my regular place. Jack walked in a few seconds later. His face was paler than usual, and there was a flabbergasted expression on his face. "Jess, what's wrong?"

"Mr. Gordon . . ."

"Call me Jack."

Dr. Marcus extended his hand to shake Jack's hand. "Thanks for coming right over."

"Yeah, I mean, I knew your name as soon as we got on the phone."

"Jack, Jess is in serious trouble. She needs to go inpatient."

"I'm not going inpatient!" I blurted out.

"Wait a second, Jess. Dr. Marcus, what's going on here?"

"Jess is distraught and shaking as a result of uncontrolled emotional instability. She's also suffering from extreme suicidal ideation."

"What? Everything was fine this morning."

"Jack, Jess hid the severity of her problems from you, and you've closed your eyes to them. Forgive me for being so blunt, but the three of us need to get on the same page immediately. You two need to improve communications. From everything I've learned from Jess, you two practice a don't ask, don't tell policy. That has to stop. Now. In addition to Jess' emotional problems, she's allowed herself, no, she's forced herself to a life-threatening weight level. Probably unbeknownst to you, for the past several months, since her bout with pneumonia, Jess has been restricting, purging, and abusing laxatives."

"Jess, I thought you got over all of that."

I snapped at Jack, "Obviously, I didn't. And maybe, if you ever talked with me about this crap, you'd know better."

Jack took a few seconds before saying anything. "Jess, after all these years with this stuff, nothing has changed. Has it?"

"Yeah, it's changed. It's gone from bad to worse!"

"Why?"

"I don't know and I don't care. I'm living through depression that you don't see. Jack, when it comes to my habit and my addiction to a self-destructive lifestyle, you're deaf, dumb, and blind. All you do is live in your little self-delusional world. You think your wife is perfect. I'm not. Except for what it would do to the kids, I don't give a damn if I wake up tomorrow or not."

There was an incredulous look on Jack's face. He had never seen me in this condition, and it was an unbelievable shock to his system. He stood as though he wanted to pace the room but there was no room to move about. Jack looked lost, dumbfounded, and astonished at the revelations just thrust upon him.

"Dr. Marcus, what do we do?" Jack asked, with a look of helplessness.

Dr. Marcus looked at Jack, paused, then looked into my eyes as he said, "Jess needs to go inpatient."

"Damn it, Dr. Marcus. I told you. I'm not going inpatient."

"Jess, you're in a condition whereby you may not have a choice."

"It's always been my choice to enter the hospital voluntarily."

"But you've never been as sick as you are now."

"I can handle this."

"Not this time. Jess, here it is in a nutshell. Either you agree to go inpatient, or I get on the phone to Dr. Thatcher, inform him of your condition, and have his diagnosis of you confirmed by a second physician's opinion. It's called the 'Two PC' law. It stands for 'two-physician certificate.' In New York, it means that if a patient refuses treatment, but two physicians diagnose circumstances that indicate a patient requires treatment to ensure the patient's preservation of life, prevention of suicide, or protection of innocent third parties, they can override your refusal for treatment."

"You're saying they can put me in a psych ward against my will."

"For a physician to provide care against a patient's will, he or she must show a reasonable belief the patient would harm himself or others. If a person is a threat to self or others, a patient may be transported without consent. Yes, Jess you can be committed to a psych unit, regardless of what you say."

"Dr. Marcus, you're making too much of all this. It's not a biggie. I can turn this around on my own."

"Sorry, Jess. I don't think so. With most ED patients I've seen, they continue along their merry way until there is a crisis like blood when they throw up, rectal bleeding, or symptoms of a heart attack. That gets their attention. And if the symptoms temporarily go away, it's forgotten. There is always tremendous denial."

"I'm not in denial."

"There is a difference between being aware of your problem and doing something about it."

"I told you. I can handle this on my own."

"Jess, not one of my hundreds of ED patients has turned it around on their own."

"Then I'll be the first." Deep down inside I knew I needed help and that there wasn't a molecule of truth in what I just said, but Dr. Marcus was pissing me off. His reaction to that statement was unusual. He finally lost his patience with me.

"Jess, I've been called all kind of nicknames by my patients. They've called me 'Dr. Blunt' and 'Dr. Don't Waste My Time.' But they keep coming back. Jess, listen to me and understand me. You're no longer manageable on an outpatient basis with me. Either you go inpatient, voluntarily, or I'll refer your case to another doctor."

"Are you saying you'd stop seeing me?"

"That's exactly what I'm saying."

"You're threatening me?"

"No. Just opening your eyes to your limited options. Listen, Jess, under the circumstances, if you were to pass out, and if Jack were to take you to an emergency room, he could inform the physician of today's events. He could have that physician call me to confirm what has happened today. In a minute, that physician would cover himself with a second physician's opinion. Within minutes, you'd be committed involuntarily. You don't want to go that route."

"No, I don't. But I don't want to leave my kids again."

"Jess, do you trust me?" Dr. Marcus asked.

Part of me wanted to respond in an obnoxious fashion again, but I maintained my social control and simply responded, "Yes."

"Jack, you better drive Jess home. There should be someone with her at all times."

Jack looked at me, then responded to Dr. Marcus, "I'll take a few days off."

Dr. Marcus gave me that deep and grim look again. "Jess, please understand that you need help that I cannot provide at this time. You've got to go inpatient. Go home. Think about it. Call me later, or call me tomorrow to let me know what you decide. I'll take action based on what you decide."

"Dr. Marcus . . ." I wanted to tell Dr. Marcus to get off my back, but didn't. "OK, Dr. Marcus. I'll call you."

Jack and I left. When we got downstairs I let Jack know that my car was on a two-hour meter. Jack put enough coins in the meter to get the time up to the full two hours, then he told me he'd get a friend to get the car home for us.

I pulled my pack of cigarettes out of my coat and lit one. Jack looked at the cigarette with disdain, but didn't say a word about it. He hugged me and said, "Jess, I'm sorry I've let you down. I've never been this scared before."

As Jack drove us home, I was still silently refusing the idea of going inpatient, but I didn't know how to break that news to him or to Dr. Marcus. That night Jack ordered in some food and we ate together. He and I didn't talk much. The kids felt the tension between us and broke the silence with Megan saying how she was fed up with school, and Jason telling us how well he did on a recent test. Jack didn't leave me when the kids finished dinner and went up to their rooms. His irritating presence meant I didn't have an opportunity to purge. He took notice of the pissed-off look on my face but didn't comment. Actually, we hardly said a word to each other until we got into bed. At first, Jack seemed cold to me and stayed on his side of the bed. He was on his back just staring up at the ceiling for several minutes. I was on my side facing away from him. Then, all of a sudden, Jack came over to my side of the bed and held me. "Jess, you know I love you more than anything else in the world. I love the kids, too. Like you, I'll do anything to protect them. It's time this stopped."

"Jack, it's not like a light switch that I can turn on and off."

"I know that."

"So, what are you saying?"

"Go inpatient."

"No."

"Jess, I didn't want to say this, but I guess I have to. I have to say this to protect you against yourself, and to protect the kids."

"Jack, what are you talking about?"

"Jess, go inpatient or I'll leave you and take the kids."

I sat up, feeling angry at the fact that Jack actually had the nerve to threaten me like that. "You're out of your mind!"

"No. Meeting with Dr. Marcus today opened my eyes. He knows what he's talking about. He's ready to call Dr. Thatcher to have you committed. Don't you understand? You have no choice."

"Sure. You go from 'Mr. Silent' to 'Mr. Threatening, Big-Mouth, Know-It-All.'"

"Jess, I know you don't mean that."

"The hell I don't."

Instead of Jack getting out of bed and walking away from me, he sat up and put his arm around me. It was like he was a boxer fighting for his life, only it was my life he was fighting for, and he wasn't going down for the count. "Jess, if you won't go inpatient for your own health, do it for the kids. I'd rather see you go away from us for a short time, then watch the kids live the rest of their lives without a mother."

Until that moment, there was no way Jack could have said anything to convince me to go inpatient to help myself. Absolutely nothing would have made an iota of a difference. However, as soon as he mentioned the kids growing up without a mother, the cemetery scene of Jack, Megan, and Jason standing over my grave consoling each other flashed into my memory again. "Jack . . ."

"What?"

"Do you know you can be a lovable pain in the ass?"

"You get what you give. Does calling me a pain in the ass mean you'll go back to Springdale?"

"No. I could never face Dr. Barrow and that staff knowing how much I let them down. Their disappointment and my humiliation would be intolerable. There was that other place, Queensland Hospital, in Pennsylvania."

"Thanks, Jess," Jack said before he kissed me on the cheek several times. "I'll call the hospital and Dr. Marcus tomorrow."

"OK." For a moment, I felt relief. Jack finally did something to eliminate my secret and self-destructive lifestyle. There was no guarantee that I'd go into recovery, but returning to the hospital at least opened the door for that possibility.

* * *

As usual, Jack was true to his word. He called Dr. Marcus first thing the next morning and let him know I finally gave in to the inpatient situation. Dr. Marcus gave him the telephone number for Queensland Hospital, and Jack called the hospital as soon as he got off the phone with Dr. Marcus. Unlike with Springdale, I couldn't check myself in the next day. They told Jack they would admit me as soon as a bed became available. That annoyed me, and I let Jack know about it. He calmed me by saying that it must be a good place if so many people go there.

Purging became difficult with Jack around me so often. Consequently, I reluctantly put on a few pounds while I waited an intolerable amount of time for Queensland to call. Neither my depression nor suicidal ideation diminished. However, each time my ideation tried to take control of me, I used the picture of my family in the cemetery standing over my coffin. Strangely enough, that helped me get over those moments.

It was two weeks between Jack's original call to Queensland and the time they finally called to say a bed was available. Jack arranged for the kids to stay with friends for the day and drove me to the hospital.

At the end of the journey, he'll hand me over to the professionals he hopes will save my life. The truth is, they can't save me. The only person who can save me is me.

This time, as he has done in the past, Jack will sign the insurance forms and ask me to sign the self-admitting inpatient consent forms. Once again, he'll carry my small suitcase to the elevator door that will take me up to my voluntary prison walls. He'll kiss me goodbye. I'll go up the elevator, sit on my bed, and cry for two hours as I've always done in the past. I'll chastise and condemn myself for having gotten myself into this situation, then I'll cry again because of the guilt and worthlessness I feel inside.

I don't want to go where I'm going. I don't believe I need to go where I'm going. I feel fine. I don't belong in a hospital sharing a room with a perfect stranger and being told what to eat, how to behave, and how to exist over the next several weeks. I can take care of myself.

We're minutes away from the hospital. Though it's freezing outside, my window is open to help me from choking on the suffocating anxiety, anguish, and the feelings of failure stuck in my throat. I know this routine all too well. I hate it. I hate myself for putting myself into this potentially deadly and self-inflicted condition. I'm a mother about to abandon my children, again.

God, please, let this be the last journey of this kind, or let me just die and finally find peace in your sanctuary.

* * *

Jack parked the car and took me inside. We were directed up to the doctor's office where, again, I filled out another one of those obnoxious forms as Jack filled out the insurance papers. Shortly after we finished, I was introduced to Dr. Jenkins, who was in charge of the unit. Dr. Jenkins was a nice-looking man in his mid- to late forties. I was glad to see him wearing a wedding ring. That meant I didn't have a young runaround playboy for a doctor. Dr. Jenkins was formerly from Springdale, so when he introduced the program to us, it sounded like the same routine I had become accustomed to. As usual, the bathrooms were locked after meals. Their therapy sessions were held as group meetings, with one patient in the hot seat in each session. Dr. Jenkins kept asking me if I had any questions. I didn't. All of this nonsense had become too familiar.

The meeting took only ten minutes, then the three of us got up and headed toward the bank of elevators. Jack put my suitcase on the floor and hugged me firmly. I didn't want to let go of Jack.

"Your wife is in good hands, Mr. Gordon," said Dr. Jenkins as the elevator arrived. He stepped in and held the door open for me. I let go of Jack, went into the elevator, and looked out at Jack. The last thing I saw were Jack's eyes welling up. I started crying.

Dr. Jenkins escorted me to my room. As usual, an attendant came into the room to search my bag and purse. After finding no prohibited items, they left me alone. There were two beds and minimal furniture. The all-too-common strainer was over the sinkhole. The bed nearest the window was empty. The bed against the wall had clothing on it. From their appearance, they belonged to a very young woman.

I climbed onto my bed and continued crying and feeling guilty. I know I put myself into this position, but that didn't take away any of the feelings of sadness and anger at being away from my kids. Two hours later, I was still crying when my nineteen-year-old roommate entered.

"Hi," she said shyly.

"Hi."

"Do you want me to leave?" she said with a childlike politeness.

"No. I want to leave."

"Yeah. I know that feeling. Is this your first time?"

"No. I'm a vet. I lost track of how many times I've been hospitalized. When did you check in?"

"Three days ago."

"I wish you luck."

"Yeah, you too."

An elderly female nurse weighing close to 250 pounds knocked at our open door. "Mrs. Gordon?"

"Yes."

"Dr. Jenkins wants to see you. You need to do an entry physical."

"Yeah, sure."

Before I left the room, I extended my hand to my roommate. "Call me Jess."

"My name is Rose."

"My name is Gertrude," said the nurse. "And Dr. Jenkins is waiting."

The way she said that made me feel like the Gestapo gave me an order. I looked at her, ready to slam her verbally, but then I held my tongue, knowing I'd have to deal with her during the length of my stay. "I'm right behind you, nurse Gertrude."

Nurse Gertrude walked a few steps ahead of me. I noticed something about her and I couldn't help chuckling out loud.

"Something funny?" she asked.

"Not really." Actually, I had just noticed her ass. I couldn't remember seeing such a big ass on a woman.

Nurse Gertrude stayed with Dr. Jenkins during my physical. I was surprised to see the balance scale hit 93 pounds. Those meals Jack forced me to keep down without the ability to purge made a difference. I smiled to think my weight was 88 at the infamous session with Dr. Marcus, and that I had 5 pounds less to gain at Queensland.

After my physical they let me walk back to my room alone. I paused to stare out the window. Unlike Springdale's foresty-looking grounds, Queensland's view offered nothing but cold cement sidewalks, tar-covered roads, and a parking lot topped with gravel. It was the parking lot that caught my attention. I saw a young boy who resembled Jason get out of a car and approach the hospital, probably to visit his mother. A huge surge of depression took over me. I started crying again and badgered myself silently. "What kind of mother am I?" I answered myself immediately. "I'm a total failure as a mother."

I couldn't stand the feeling. I realized that it was over three hours since Jack left me at the hospital and that he was probably home. I ran up to my room, got a handful of change, and charged for the public telephone. I called Jack. He picked up almost immediately, "Jack, get back here and take me home."

"You're kidding. Right?"

"I've never been more serious."

"Jess, be a good little girl."

"Don't you patronize me!" I blasted into the phone.

"Do what the doctors and nurses tell you to do," Jack said calmly. "The kids and I are about to have dinner. I suggest you do the same. I love you, Jess. That's why I'm staying here, and you're staying there."

"Jack Gordon," I screamed.

"Yes, Mrs. Gordon . . ." Jack said quietly.

"You really can be a pain in the ass."

"Thank you, sweetheart. I know that means you love me."

"Put Jason on the phone."

"As you wish."

Talking with Jason and Megan calmed my nerves.

That night I fell asleep crying into my pillow so Rose wouldn't hear me.

* * *

Everything about my stay at Queensland seemed identical to my stay at Springdale, only Dr. Jenkins was less patient and tougher with me than Dr. Barrow. At each of our first two-day exit interviews, he saw right through me. I kept telling him I was ready to leave. He just grinned and said, "Perhaps at our next session, Jess." After ten sessions and after putting on several pounds, he finally agreed that I was ready to get the hell out of there. He set up my IOP with a new place called Fernwood. Of course, I made sure they took my medical insurance before I left the hospital. The good thing about Fernwood was that it was located in New York City. That meant I could get there by the Long Island Railroad, instead of driving sixty miles each way over the course of the next few weeks.

I would like to report that I was a changed woman as Jack drove me home, but I wasn't. I was already questioning if I'd go back to purging and my laxatives. Yes, I had gained weight, but I didn't kick my mental addiction to my eating disorder. That's not something you can easily do in twenty days. I also thought about my laxatives. Would I have the courage to flush them down the toilet as I did the last time? I didn't have to answer that question. After we got home, I checked for them in my secret hiding place. I found the boxes. They were all empty. There was a small handwritten note attached to one of them, "Jess, I'll no longer be blind to our problem."

Part of me wanted to kill him. Part of me was glad that he was finally involved in taking care of me.

* * *

Once again, I was out of the bubble and back into the real world, having to deal with a great deal of stress and a hectic medical routine. I was set to see Dr. Thatcher once a month to renew my medication, which he had changed since the last time I saw him. I was scheduled to see Dr. Marcus on Tuesdays and Thursdays, which Jack and I had to pay for out of pocket until Fernwood was completed, and I saw Joan on Thursday after my session with Dr. Marcus. Fernwood was set for up Monday, Wednesday, and Friday. More than anything else, besides the therapy, they felt their function was to stuff huge amounts of food into my face. I got there for breakfast. I attended therapy, had lunch, attended therapy a second time, and then I headed for home just before rush hour.

Jack attended my first session with Dr. Marcus, who was glad to hear that my range was up from 87-89, to 108-109. Of course, he reminded me that I still had a long way to go for my safe weight situation, but at least I was, as he said, "in the right direction on the slippery slope."

Fernwood was a relatively new establishment and, compared to the IOP staff at Springdale, most of the people working there were rookies. Dr. Marcus knew I never lied to him, but he was incredulous when I told him a story about one of the therapy sessions. It happened during the second week. The Fernwood therapist and I were setting goals for me. I told the therapist that I went back to purging into the porcelain goddess. The therapist said my goal should be to cut down on my purging frequency. I told Dr. Marcus that I thought the therapist was out of his mind. I told Dr. Marcus that the therapist should have told me that my goal should be to cut out purging entirely, not to cut down on it. From that point on, I felt like the therapist had condoned my purging, and I had little faith that I would accomplish much during my attendance there.

* * *

I went into Springdale in February 2003 and finished Queensland and Fernwood by the end of March 2004. By New Year's Day of 2005, my weight was back up to 115. No matter how many times Dr. Marcus chided me about the 115 range, I wasn't going to let it get any higher.

As the months passed uneventfully on toward the end of spring, I would occasionally reflect about that time. I always arrived at the same sad and aggravating conclusion: I had put my family and myself through such hell, and all I managed to accomplish was to get back to where I was. I was still purging a few times a week, but not to reduce my weight. I knew that would cause me more stress from Dr. Marcus. He was a tough and no-nonsense guy, but I had faith in how he treated me and tried to guide me. No, purging was more of my means toward emotional stability. Whenever I felt too full after a meal or I was stressed, depressed, or totally without emotion, I purged, and both Jack and Dr. Marcus knew about it. Neither was pleased with what I did, but neither of them had a choice.

* * *

May 30, 2005, marked another turning point. It was Memorial Day. Jack was home from work and the kids had the day off from school. Most families celebrate the day by getting together with family or friends. Not our family. Jack had been invited to his boss' house, but Jack let me politely refuse the invitation. I was still uncomfortable in "food" situations. I was always concerned that people would force food in my direction, and I always hated the unpleasant feeling of having to make up excuses as to why I wasn't eating, or wasn't eating enough. Besides, Jack and I were the always the type to isolate ourselves from social functions and enjoyed our own private company much more. Homebodies, that's how I would describe our life.

Well, home was the last place for pleasantness that day. Jack was up late the night before to watch one of his favorite movies, so I let him sleep late. Jason and Megan were up around six thirty. I made breakfast for them and kept them company with my coffee. After breakfast, Jason was scheduled to go to one of his friends' houses for the day. Megan and I were supposed to go to the store to pick up her dress for her sweet sixteen party, which was scheduled for Sunday, June 12. Jason went up to his room when he finished eating. Megan, still in her pajamas, stayed with me because I wanted to talk with her. I noticed something different about her over the past week and needed to find out what was going on. As had happened in the past, it was news I didn't want to know. Within minutes of the start of our private talk, I found out that Megan had cut school for the past two weeks. When I asked her why, all she said was, "I had to."

"Megan, sweetheart, can you give me a little more to go on?"

"Which part don't you understand, Mom?"

At first, I wanted to start going nuts on her, but I refrained and tried a different tactic. "Megan, do you think you need a medication adjustment? Is your depression getting to you again?"

"Mom, I can't stand that place. I hate my classes. I hate my teachers. All the kids make fun of me. I can't take it anymore."

"I'll call Dr. Thatcher today and leave a message that we need to see him immediately."

"Mom, there's no magic pill for what's wrong with me."

"Megan, what else can I do?"

"I don't know," she yelled at me, venting every ounce of frustration she must have pent up over the past weeks or months.

"Honey, why didn't you say something to me sooner?"

"Because I don't know what's happening to me. Things other kids can do in a few seconds take me an hour. A few weeks ago, we had to change classes. It took thirty minutes for me to get my books together. It was a miracle that the room I had to leave was empty. I just couldn't move any faster. By the time I got to the next class, the teacher sent me to the office for discipline. It wasn't my fault. I just couldn't do anything differently. I'm never going back there, Mom. Never. Never. Never. Never!" she screamed.

Megan was hysterical. All I could do was hug her and try to comfort her. A few seconds later, Jack came into the kitchen as Megan started crying. She broke out of my arms, ran past Jack, pounced up the stairs to her room, and slammed her door.

Jack was a little shocked at what he witnessed and still rubbing the sleep from his eyes when he kissed me good morning. "What was that all about?"

"Jack, we have a problem."

"Now what?"

"I just found out that Megan cut school for the last two weeks."

Jack was astonished. At first, all he could do was get himself a cup of coffee. He sat down with me and simply said, "Never a dull moment. What's wrong?"

"Megan needs to see Dr. Thatcher as soon as possible."

"What is it? Her antidepressant?"

"I'm not sure, but I think it's more than that. You've seen how it can take her hours to get ready for school in the morning."

"Yeah."

"I'll spell it out, Jack. OCD. Obsessive-compulsive disorder. When I was in-patient, I saw dozens of women with the same condition. It took one woman fifteen minutes just to get her chair right before she sat down for the meal. The food police thought she was trying to avoid eating and took away her privileges. I remember one therapy session when a young girl said it took her thirty minutes to set her alarm before going to sleep and thought it was normal until her college roommate told her she was crazy."

"What do we do?"

"You call Dr. Thatcher for an emergency appointment. Then you call the school. Tell them that we are aware that she hasn't been attending classes, and that's she's under a doctor's care. We can't send her back there feeling this way."

"Anything else?"

"Yeah, I better go up there to let her know we're behind her."

"Thanks, Jess."

"Jack, we have a major problem here," I said before I left the kitchen and headed upstairs. I knocked on Megan's door. She didn't answer. I opened the door slightly and stuck my head in. "Can I come in?"

"You're not sending me to school tomorrow, Mom."

"You're right," I said as I approached Megan, joined her on her bed and hugged her.

"I'm lucky to have a mom like you."

I looked into Megan's eyes and started laughing.

"What's so funny, Mom?"

"I guess that could be debated." Megan understood exactly what I meant and started laughing with me. "Honey, listen, your father and I are behind you. You have a problem. We'll get you into Dr. Thatcher as soon as possible to start working on it."

"Mom, there's one more thing I want."

"What's that?"

"Please cancel my party."

"What?"

"Please, Mom. Please. I never want to see those kids again."

The first thought that came to mind was the small fortune of money Jack and I would lose by canceling her party. I quickly shoved that thought out of my head and thought only of Megan's welfare. "OK, honey. Whatever you want."

* * *

Jack got in touch with school the next day. They let him know that they were about to send a truant officer after Megan. However, since he let them know she was under a doctor's care, they changed their tune and asked that we keep in touch with them. Jack also called Dr. Thatcher. Luckily, he was in town and willing to see Megan that afternoon.

Jack offered to leave work early so he could join Megan and me at Dr. Thatcher's office. I thanked him for his offer and told him it wasn't necessary.

It shocked me that Dr. Thatcher's office was empty. Usually, whenever I had an appointment, I'd have to wait thirty to sixty minutes before seeing him. He started by talking with the two of us and asking Megan a myriad of questions. All he kept doing was nodding at Megan's answers. Rarely did he comment on anything she said. Finally, after forty-five minutes, he said, "Megan, I'd like to have a few minutes with your mom."

"Sure."

Megan left the room.

"How are you doing, Jess?"

"I'm holding my own."

"Are you satisfied with your antidepressant medication?"

"Pretty much."

"Jess . . ."

I didn't like the way he paused and braced myself for bad news.

"Jess, Megan has every symptom of obsessive-compulsive disorder."

I just shook my head in agreement.

"You and your husband are in for a rough time."

"How so?"

"I'll prescribe a medication for Megan. However, you have to know that OCD medications are started on a low dosage to monitor possible negative side effects. If the medication works and there are little or no side effects, I'll gradually increase the dosage. If the side effects become too much of a problem, I have to take her off the medication, wait a week or longer, then I'll try a different medication."

"That sounds very time consuming."

"That's the point. Eventually, we'll find the right medication and the right dosage."

"I see."

"Megan will also need to see Dr. Marcus. His behavioral method of therapy is just what Megan needs. He can teach her breathing exercises to reduce her anxiety. He can do biofeedback with her. He can also work on those things that frighten her and help her learn to cope with those things."

"You should know that Megan refuses to go to school. We notified them that she's under your care."

"I'll write a note saying that she won't return this year. In fact, until we get the medication set, and until Dr. Marcus is satisfied that she's made progress with the therapy, I doubt she'll return in September. We have to take a wait-and-see position. Again, the therapy will take time. Dr. Marcus will have to teach Megan to react differently to certain bodily sensations that trigger her panic attacks and anxiety. This doesn't happen quickly."

"Jack said it perfectly yesterday. There's never a dull moment."

"Jess, I'm concerned about you."

"That makes two of us."

"You shouldn't use Megan's problems as an excuse."

"I'll try not to."

Dr. Thatcher wrote the prescription and a note to Megan's school. I put my glasses on so I could read his school note. Yes, I had reached that point of my life that glasses became necessary to read anything. Otherwise, I was virtually blind to anything close to me.

"Jess, watch her closely after she starts the medication. If you see anything negatively unusual, contact me."

"OK."

"I'll call Dr. Marcus today and let him know what happened here today."

"Thanks. How often to you want to see Megan?"

"Until we get the medication right, once a week."

"Will you be around?" Those words just popped out of my mouth, I guess I expressed my building frustration over his unreliable scheduling with my own appointments. He looked at me like he knew what I was talking about.

"I'll be here, for both of you."

"Can I get that in writing? Just kidding. Just kidding." I started to laugh.

"Keep laughing kid," Dr. Thatcher said. "You, your husband, and Megan are in for an extremely bumpy ride."

We shook hands goodbye, then I got Megan and headed home. By the time we got home, there was already a message from Dr. Marcus saying we had an appointment for the next day at 4:30. Usually, Dr. Marcus' last appointment was at 4:00. That meant he was extending his help in a most unusual and good way.

* * *

Nothing prepares a parent to deal with their sick child. When one of your kids has a cold or fever, we're all taught to give them aspirin or Tylenol, give them plenty of liquids, and give them lots of hugs and kisses for support through their uncomfortable feelings. But Megan didn't have a cold or fever, which goes away in a few days. Megan had OCD, which is something that never goes away. She just takes medicine that attempts to deal with the symptoms. After several months, there was no progress. Dr. Thatcher tried at least a half a dozen medications at various dosage levels. Nothing was working. Megan only complained about the indescribable side effects she suffered through, and all I could do was sit there and lie to her that everything would soon be fine.

After all that time, I began to feel jealous of Jack. Each weekday, he was lucky enough to get dressed, get out, get to work, and come home several hours later. He didn't have to deal with Megan's mood swings, which were as unpredictable as a menopausal woman's hot flashes. At first, I didn't let anything get to me. My temperament remained stable. It had to. I had to care for Megan. After all that time of medication experiments with Dr. Thatcher and behavioral counseling sessions with Dr. Marcus, I saw little to no progress. I guess that's what got to me. If I had seen a hint or an inkling of progress, perhaps I wouldn't have reverted. But there was no progress, and I, like a junkie, fell back into the comfortable ED hole.

I remember that it was at a session at the end of August when I told Dr. Marcus that my weight felt uncomfortable. I was still at 115. "Dr. Marcus, I just want to get down to 111. I know if I get down to 111, I'll feel better about myself and my weight."

Dr. Marcus wasn't happy at all and told me to forget the idea. I remember him saying, "It's not going to be enough. You're going to want to go further."

"But, Dr. Marcus . . ."

"Jess, it's not safe."

"But, Dr. Marcus . . ."

"I won't condone this thinking. It's wrong, and it's dangerous."

"I'm not talking about going down to 85 pounds."

"Jess, you're how old? Forty-five?"

"Yes. Thanks for reminding me."

"I'll bring back the word 'denial.' I bring up an expression, 'the immortality-of-youth complex.'"

"What are you talking about?"

"You think you're immune to medical problems. So far, you've been extremely lucky. You haven't had kidney failure. You've escaped cardiac irregularities, renal failure, blood clots, rectal bleeding, or other organ failures. You think it won't happen to you. It happens to other people, and you've seen it personally. Yes, you've had an electrolyte imbalance that put you into the emergency room a few times. You had times you've suffered through memory and concentration problems, which were typical of dehydration and starvation. You walked away from all those problems thinking it was nothing to worry about because you were able to function the next day. Well, you have to understand that your luck can run out."

"Dr. Marcus, I can handle this. It's just a few pounds."

"Jess, it's medically defined as being passively suicidal."

"I haven't dealt with any major suicidal ideation for weeks, almost months."

"Jess, you're sitting here asking my permission to go down a slippery slope. You're operating on what you think. What you're thinking is distorted, so you think it's OK."

"Dr. Marcus, it's just a few pounds. Get over it."

"No, it's just another excuse for self-destructive behavior. You can lie to yourself, but you can't lie to me."

"Dr. Marcus, it's not a big deal. I'm OK."

* * *

Some people say, "If I only knew then what I know now, things would have been different." Well, I was never like most people. I knew everything before I got involved with my self-destruction, but I didn't listen to other people's warnings, and I didn't listen to that tiny voice of reason in my head. Nothing and no one could get through to me to reverse where I was headed, and I didn't care.

Everything Dr. Marcus said to me at my last session, and the sessions that followed, made sense to everyone–except me. As Dr. Marcus predicted, I wasn't satisfied with myself, or my weight, when I reached 111. At that point, I let Dr. Marcus know I wanted to drop 3 more pounds. Again, he spewed out the warnings. Again, I told him I could handle it. When I got to 105, it still wasn't enough for me. I was full blast back into purging and restricting behind Jack's back. I also went back to abusing laxatives, only this time I hid them carefully enough for him not to find them.

Dr. Thatcher's prediction of Megan not returning to school by September turned out to be accurate. She was home constantly. The good thing was that by late September, Dr. Thatcher had found a medication that worked minimally. It was an improvement, but nowhere close to where any of us were satisfied. Actually, the minimal abatement of the symptoms only lasted a few weeks. By mid-October, we were back to square one with her medication experiments. It was unbelievably frustrating to know that I was doing everything possible to help her, but she was still suffering from enormous anxiety over what her future life would be like. She constantly repeated one question. "Mom, do you think some guy would ever want to marry a sick girl like me?"

"Honey, when the time is right, you'll find the right guy like I did." As her mother, I endured and absorbed every trace of her anguish as I lived through my own self-induced hell.

The closest moment I had toward feeling happy or satisfied came when I got on the scale and it read 99 pounds. I felt like an accomplished person although, when I looked at myself in the mirror, I saw a huge person staring back at me. Actually, I almost bragged about my weight to Dr. Marcus, "See, Dr. Marcus, I can handle this."

Dr. Marcus just shook his head and said, once again, "Jess, you know where this is headed."

Actually, although Dr. Marcus was referring to another inpatient stay, I had no clue where this new situation was headed. I was certain of only one thing. I needed emotional release from the stress, but I couldn't find it.

* * *

November passed uneventfully. My sessions and Megan's sessions with Dr. Thatcher were almost useless. I was still seeing Joan, my nutritionist, but all I did with her was give her lip service. There was no way I was going to follow her food plan. Dr. Marcus, on the other hand, kept coming at me to improve myself and do something that would reverse my direction on the slippery slope.

"Jess, I'm glad your weight has stabilized, but you understand that you're in extremely dangerous territory. You can't break the cycle or reverse this current negative pattern on your own."

Of course, Dr. Marcus was right, but I refused to listen to him. I tried to explain my point of view to him, but all Dr. Marcus would do was to warn me about the need to go inpatient again. He was not surprised when I refused.

"Dr. Marcus . . ."

"Go on, Jess."

Ordinarily I was unafraid to say anything to Dr. Marcus. At that moment, however, I was concerned about what I was about to say and chose each word carefully. "Dr. Marcus, my depression and suicidal ideation are on the increase."

"Jess, you know the deal. The medication isn't staying in your system long enough to work properly."

"Right." I paused again. There was something I had to talk about, but the subject would probably make Dr. Marcus think I'm crazy.

"Jess, you look like there's something you want to say to me."

"You're right. There is." I paused again. "Dr. Marcus . . . I hear a voice in my head."

"What does the voice say?"

"It says, 'Don't eat that. It will make you fat.' Or, 'If you eat, purge it. Get that food out of you.'"

"And you do what the voice tells you. Don't you?"

"Yes." I was scared to tell Dr. Marcus about other things the voice was telling me to do because I knew that one day I was going to listen to the voice, even when it went beyond the topic of food and into other self-destructive behavior.

"Jess," Dr. Marcus said calmly but emphatically, "you need to go inpatient."

"No, thank you. My weight is OK." A normal person would have felt remorse about returning to that near-death weight. I didn't. Remorse was the last feeling I could think about.

Every action I had taken in the past few months was fine in my mind. Like I said, "If I knew then what I know now, things would have been different." Actually, that wasn't right in my case. I knew what I was about to do, and I didn't care. I had to do it. I had no choice. The consequences didn't matter.

* * *

Saturday was the day I always looked forward to because Jack was home, and he usually came up with some event he and the two kids could share, which left me alone to my own thoughts. It also meant I didn't have a doctor's appointment or places to run to.

The day started with me making breakfast for everyone, except myself. My breakfast lately consisted of a cup of coffee and a cigarette. By this time, since Megan was always home, my smoking was no longer a big secret that forced me to smoke outside. Now, once the kids or Jack were out of the kitchen, I could sit back and light up casually. Breakfast was always followed by a shower that lasted almost a half an hour because I would just stand there and let the hot water and high pressure massage my neck and shoulders.

I went upstairs, got undressed, put on a CD of "Rhapsody in Blue," set it to repeat, and got the things I needed for the shower–a washcloth, a towel, and a utensil I used to scrape the dead skin from the heel of my foot. I thought I felt relatively calm that morning, then I heard that voice again: "Do it, Jess. Do it. You'll see how it makes you feel better. Do it, Jess. Do it. Feel the pleasure."

There was no explaining it. I made a conscious decision to give in to the voice, regardless of the outcome. Without hesitation, I reached for the skin scraper, opened it, and took out the double-edged razor. I looked at my arm. Without my glasses, it was fuzzy, but I could make out the blue line from a vein. I paused, then I heard that crazed voice inside my head again, "Do it, Jess. Do it. Feel the pleasure." The only way I could stop the voice was to cut myself. I lowered the razor to the side of the blue vein line and cut myself the length of about a quarter of an inch. I wanted to scream from the pain but held it in for fear that a neighbor might hear it and call the police.

There was little blood, but enough for me to watch it run down my arm and into the draining water below. The sight of the blood calmed me. I welcomed the physical and emotional pain. I felt like I deserved it, but I was still rational enough to say to myself, "What am I doing? Oh, my God!"

The cold weather made it easy to hide what I had done to myself. My long-sleeved sweatshirt and long-sleeved pajamas were enough to hide the small bandage on my arm. I had another secret from Jack and the kids, and I didn't care.

For about a week I stopped hearing the voice. I thought it was gone forever. I was wrong. I was alone again the next Saturday. Just before I got into the shower, I heard the voice again. "Do it again. You tested the waters. You enjoyed it. Do it again. Feel the pleasure."

I gave into the voice again. I went over the same cut as last week, only I made the cut a little longer and a little deeper. A great deal more blood flowed down my forearm and into the bubbly, draining water. I stood for several minutes with the water running down my head and arm. The pain and the sight of my bloody arm and the bloody swirling water gave me a high like I had never felt before. At first I let the blood flow freely, then I held my hand over the cut to try to stop the bleeding. After several minutes, the bleeding subsided, but not the high. It seemed like that continued for hours.

After Jack and the kids got home, Jack saw me with a smile on my face.

"What are you in such a good mood about?"

"Nothing much. It was just a relaxing day."

"Glad to hear it."

I smiled again at Jack, then I thought to myself, "I have to tell Dr. Marcus what I'm doing. It's going to be one hellava session this Tuesday."

* * *

While sitting in Dr. Marcus' waiting room I debated whether or not to mention any of the cutting to him. Even when he escorted me into his office, the debate continued.

"How are things going, Jess?"

"OK."

"How are you doing with your weight?"

"Holding at the 99-100 range."

"That's not good, but at least you're stable."

"Dr. Marcus . . ."

"I saw it in your face, Jess. There's something you have to tell me."

"Yes."

"Do you remember when I told you about hearing voices?"

"Yes. Is that still happening?"

"Sometimes."

"Besides the food subject, what else are you hearing?"

It was time to take a deep breath. "Well . . . ah . . ." All of a sudden I felt I was wrong to bring up that subject and cowardly backed away from the full truth. "The voice is telling me to cut myself."

"Uh, huh. And how do you feel about that?"

"I feel like giving in to the voice."

"Do you think these thoughts are a result of Megan's history with cutting?"

It was interesting to hear that question because the thought never entered my mind. "No, Megan has nothing to do with it. I'm sure of that."

"Jess, you're Catholic. Aren't you?"

"I was born Catholic, but never really practiced."

"You've been under tremendous stress for several months now. Do you feel perhaps your religion is playing into this situation?"

"How so?"

"From the sacrament: I shed my blood for Christ."

"That never came to mind. No. If I'm going to shed my blood for anyone, it will be for me."

"And what do you think that will do for you?"

"I remember one of the young girls talking about it at Springdale . . ."

"And . . ."

"She said that cutting, purging, and restricting gave her an emotional release. It was her way to regulate and control her emotions. She said she did it when she felt no emotions at all, or when she was too sad, too anxious, or too overwhelmed. Dr. Marcus, there are times I just need to release my emotions or just get them under control."

"Jess, don't start. Once you start there is no turning back."

"I guess you've had a few patients in this chair who have done it. Haven't you?"

"Too many. Learn from them. Don't start."

"OK, Dr. Marcus, you made your point. How do you think things are going with Megan now?" I was interested in finding out the answer to that question, but more interested in changing the subject so Dr. Marcus wouldn't catch me at my lie. It was the first time I actually lied to him, and I, like a little girl, was very glad I got away with it.

"Well, Dr. Thatcher and I spoke the other day. He's eliminated certain medications, but he still thinks he has to hone in on the right medication for Megan. The good news is that she's responding to my therapy. I feel she's a little more relaxed lately."

"Do you think that's just because she's removed the pressure of school?"

"That's a part of it. She enjoys your company."

"And I enjoy her company. She's a great kid, but I'll be happier when she's on the right medication and right dosage. In the long run, I think she'll be better off back in school and leading a somewhat normal life."

After that day, several sessions with Dr. Marcus passed with me being able to keep my secret. I just couldn't find the courage to admit the truth to him. I was afraid of the consequences I might face if he learned the truth, and the truth was that my cutting frequency was increasing. It was my little secret, and no one knew about it. The first person who almost caught me was Jason. One day I had my sleeves rolled up while doing the dishes. He noticed the bandage on my forearm.

"What happened to you, Mommy?"

I felt lower than a worm because I had to lie to my son. "Oh, Mommy was clumsy and cut herself, honey. It's nothing."

That was the end of the conversation. He was too innocent to think of the actual reason why I had my arm bandaged. Two weeks later, however, he noticed new cuts on my arm.

"Did you cut yourself again, Mommy?"

This time Megan was standing next to Jason as he asked the question.

"Yeah," said Megan. "Mommy cut herself."

I could tell from the look in Megan's eyes that she knew exactly what I had done. Silently, Megan just turned and went upstairs to her room. Jason went into the den to watch television. I turned off the water and went up to see Megan.

I knocked before entering her room.

"C'mon in, Mom."

"I think we need to talk."

"It's OK, Mom."

"No. I think we need to talk."

"Go ahead."

I didn't know what to say. I expected her to blow up in my face. She didn't. I expected to hear, "You told me hundreds of times not to cut myself, now you're doing it. You have to be the biggest hypocrite in the world!" To my great surprise and relief, that's not what she said. I paused and just looked into her eyes.

"Mom," she said quietly. "I understand. I hope you get better."

I couldn't say anything. All I could do was hug her. "Megan, I love you."

"I love you, too, Mom. I wish you luck. It's a tough habit to kick. I guess we have something else in common."

"What's that, Megan?"

"We're both cutups."

I couldn't help but laugh.

"Mom, we have to go down as the craziest mother-daughter team in history."

The two of us laughed hysterically. Jason ran upstairs to see what was so funny. He stood in the doorway and asked, "What's the joke?"

"It's a girl thing," Megan blurted out.

* * *

Jack and I spent New Year's Eve at home alone watching the ball drop. Jason and Megan both spent the night at their friends' homes. I had nothing to celebrate. For a brief moment, I had a realistic thought: I paused to wonder if I'd live to see the next New Year's celebration.

Unbeknownst to Jack, Dr. Marcus, or anyone else, my cutting frequency jumped from once a week to three or four times a week. It got to the point that I would put a tourniquet on my arm to make my vein pop out, then, being half blind and without my glasses, I tried to cut myself along the vein. A quarter of an inch in the wrong direction would have meant a mistake that could have taken my life. I could have bled to death in the shower with no one around to call for an ambulance or assistance. Each incision got deeper, causing more pain and greater blood flow. Each time I hurt myself, I felt emotional relief for a few hours, then the depression, the malaise, and the suicidal ideation all returned stronger and worse than ever.

My laxative abuse was back to where it was during my worst times. I'd usually pop fifty pills an evening and pay the price with the pain from the dehydration and stomach cramps the next morning. I was also purging two to four times a day, although there wasn't much food to purge because my restriction was rampant. My weight dropped from the 99-100 range down to the 93-94 range. I was on a fast and out-of-control slide down Dr. Marcus' slope, and I didn't care. Delusions of immortality ran rampant through my distorted consciousness.

On Tuesday morning, February 14, 2006, Valentine's Day, I got a special present, but it wasn't from Jack or the kids. It was more like a gift from God. Megan was in her room upstairs and I was in the downstairs bathroom. First, after a bowel movement, I wiped myself and saw blood in my stool. It was the first time anything like that ever happened to me, and it scared the hell out of me. I flushed the toilet as if to make all the badness disappear, then I stuck my face into the porcelain goddess to purge. Blood spewed from my mouth. I freaked and thought I was moments away from death.

An hour later I was in Dr. Marcus' office for my regular Tuesday morning appointment.

Dr. Marcus started with his usual question about my weight.

"It's at 93-94."

"Jess . . ."

"Dr. Marcus. I won't go."

"I'll say it again, if there's a crisis in your life, you create an excuse that maintains your destructive behavior. You make all kinds of excuses for feeling fat, and then you compensate for that with the eating disorder."

"So?"

"So, I'm concerned that you'll find an excuse to say, 'Let me get away from all of this. I've had enough.' Jess . . ." Dr. Marcus paused. It was as though a sixth sense hit him that something else was wrong. Without any warning, Dr. Marcus said, "Jess, you can tell me the truth, or you can roll up your sleeves."

Ironically how things changed on the day of love. Only now, I was about to get a heavy dose of tough love and threats.

"You're right, Dr. Marcus. I've been cutting."

Without saying another word to me, Dr. Marcus picked up his telephone, called Jack, and told him to drop everything and get to his office without explaining why. Jack arrived fifteen minutes later. By that time I had blurted out what had happened that morning, and the techniques I was using to cut myself.

Dr. Marcus held back no punches when Jack joined us. "Jack, I appreciate that you came here. It was important, otherwise I wouldn't have called you. Until now, Jess has been passively suicidal. That's what an eating disorder is, a form of passive suicide. Things have changed. Jess, roll up your sleeves."

"Dr. Marcus . . ."

"Jess . . ."

I rolled up one sleeve. Jack gasped at the sight of the cut marks. I rolled up the other sleeve and exposed many more healing wounds.

"Jess, you have to be out of your mind."

"You're not far from the truth."

"Jesus! Isn't it tough enough with Megan doing that crap?"

"Jack, I know you're upset. I'm sorry."

Jack looked desperately at Dr. Marcus, "Now what?"

Dr. Marcus looked at me and paused before asking, "Jess, what would it feel like if you bled out and your kids find you dead in the bathroom?"

I had no answer.

Jack came back at me. "What do you get out of that crap?"

"The more blood I see, the better I feel. The more pain I feel, the more I hurt myself, the better I feel."

Dr. Marcus knew what he had to do. "Jess, I'll give you two choices. Either Jack takes you to the hospital, or you see a psychiatrist today."

"I've been to psychiatrists. What's different about this one?"

"His specialty is suicide prevention."

"I'm not going inpatient. I'm not going to start with another doctor."

"Jess, with the marks on your arms, I can have Dr. Thatcher here within the hour. He, with the signature of another doctor, can have you committed to the Long Island Medical Center Psychiatric Ward before sundown."

"I'm not going to that hellhole."

"Jess, we're not negotiating."

"Who's this new doctor?"

"He works out of South Side Medical Center. I've known him for several years."

"OK, I'll see him."

"Smart choice."

Dr. Marcus found his number in his phone book, picked up the telephone, and got right through to Dr. Jeffrey Stevens. It was 10:50. The two of them set up an appointment for 2:00 that afternoon.

I was expecting Dr. Marcus to read me another riot act. He didn't. He turned to Jack. "I suggest you stay home with Jess for the next few days to make sure Jess doesn't hurt herself."

"Absolutely."

"Jess," Dr. Marcus said in a fatherly way, "promise me that if you have thoughts of harming yourself, you'll immediately take yourself to the hospital, or have someone take you."

"Sure. No problem."

"Next, promise us that before you cut yourself, you'll tell somebody."

"That's ridiculous. I'd rather not cut myself."

"Exactly."

"Listen, I don't know if promising anything will do any good. I'll try."

Jack and I left Dr. Marcus' office with me feeling like a little kid being taken out of the principal's office by her parent after she was just suspended. You know that feeling of guilt when you've been found out doing something wrong. Only I hadn't cut classes, I had cut myself, and gotten caught.

* * *

Jack and I headed for our cars. I led the way as he followed me home. Once inside the kitchen, we both had a cup of coffee without saying a word to each other. I tried to avoid Jack's criticizing eyes by smoking several cigarettes before we left for Dr. Stevens' office.

Although the drive from our house to Dr. Stevens' office was only a thirty-minute ride up the Cross Island and east on the Grand Central, Jack and I left an hour before the appointment. It's a good thing we did. South Side Medical Center is a vast complex with dozens of buildings spread out over several acres. We had to ask a few people directions before we found Dr. Stevens' building.

When we got up to Dr. Stevens' waiting room, there was one other woman sitting there flipping calmly through a magazine. Immediately, I thought she was another patient and that I'd have to wait for her to see the doctor before I got into see him. I started toward the door to leave. Jack gently took my hand and said, "We're here, and we're in this together."

"You know, you're a pain . . ."

"I know. It's part of my lovable character." Jack led me to the receptionist's window. "Mrs. Gordon to see Dr. Stevens."

The receptionist, a pleasant-looking woman in her mid-forties, put together two clipboards and handed them to Jack because she saw that I was ignoring her. The first clipboard was filled with insurance forms, the second was the personal history questionnaire.

"Here are two pens, Mr. Gordon. You or your wife will have to fill these out."

"Thanks." Jack took both clipboards and handed me the one with the questionnaire as we sat down. I noticed the clock opposite us on the wall read 1:50.

Jack filled out the usual insurance papers. That day, I just didn't give a damn and never bothered to fill out more than my name, address, and phone number on the obnoxious personal information form. The rest of my history was just going to have to wait until the doctor and I met.

At 2:25 I was anxious and pissed off that I was still sitting in the waiting room. I turned to Jack and asked, "What kind of schmuck would leave a suicidal patient wait like this?"

"Jess . . ."

The door leading into the office complex suddenly opened and a twelve-year-old girl exited, glanced over at me, and hugged the other woman in the waiting room. At first I asked myself, "What kind of problems can a twelve-year-old girl have that would require a psychiatrist?" Then I remembered being in the same situation with Megan when she was twelve.

Jack squeezed my hand. "How ya doin'?"

I gave Jack an annoyed look.

"Uh, huh," Jack said, but he wouldn't let go of my hand.

A tall man with white hair, glasses, and a full salt-and-pepper beard opened the office complex entrance. "Mrs. Gordon."

"Yes."

"I'm Dr. Stevens."

"Call me, Jess," I said as I handed him the two clipboards.

"Very good." He handed the insurance clipboard to his receptionist.

Jack stood and kissed my cheek.

"Yeah. A kiss for luck and I'm on my way."

"Mrs. Gordon, join me, please."

"Right."

Dr. Stevens led me to his office, which had several diplomas and medical citations all over one wall above his desk. "Well, at least the guy is educated," I thought to myself.

Dr. Stevens looked at my virtually empty questionnaire, put it on his desk and said, "These things can be a nuisance."

I was a little taken back by that comment. I expected him to be annoyed with me.

"Mrs. Gordon . . ."

"Jess."

"Jess, Dr. Marcus gave me some of your background on the phone. He said he'll forward notes about you later today. I understand that you're also under Dr. Thatcher's care."

"Yeah. I've been seeing him for a few years."

"He's a well-known physician with a very good reputation."

"Yeah."

"Jess, how can I help you?"

That question threw me. If he spoke with Dr. Marcus, and if he knew I was suicidal, then why did he ask it? With a bit of annoyance in my voice, I said, "Well, maybe you can do something that might make me want to live."

"That's what I'm here for. Right now, what do you think is keeping you alive?"

"The thought of my kids standing at my grave."

"How many kids do you have?"

"Two."

"And how's your relationship with your husband?"

"He's the best guy in the world. Frankly, I don't know how he tolerates me."

"I guess he loves you very much."

"Either that, or he's masochistic and he should be your next patient today."

"Sorry, you're my last patient for the day. He'll have to make an appointment for tomorrow."

Dr. Stevens smiled, then I smiled. "What do you know? He's a doctor with a sense of humor," I commented to myself. I paused before I could say another word. I knew he was just trying to get me to talk and relax. At that point, I looked into his large brown eyes and got down to the reason I was sitting in his office. "Dr. Stevens, I've been in and out of hospitals, psychiatrists' offices, and therapists offices for decades. Nothing is working. I feel hopeless. I feel worthless. I feel like death is the only way out of my misery." I paused again. "Everything's been tried, and failed."

"Well, perhaps you and I can try something different. Jess, you're here because . . . ?"

"If I didn't agree to see you, Dr. Marcus and Dr. Thatcher were going to throw me into a psych ward."

"I see."

"Once again, I've reached my choice point."

"Choice point?"

"A doctor taught me that expression. There are three points to a choice point triangle. First, your symptoms increase and your health quickly decreases, possibly leading to death. Second, you maintain your status quo, which might also lead to death, only in a slower fashion. Third, you do something to save your life."

"Well, let's see what's behind curtain number three that can save your life."

For about the next hour, the two of us went into an abridged and gruesome version of my entire history. Frequently, certain things I said managed to make him raise his bushy salt and pepper eyebrows. I found that fascinating, since I thought at his age he had heard it all.

At the end of the session, Dr. Stevens gave me the same speech about his plans for my medication. I thought I was listening to Dr. Thatcher all over again, especially when he said he would have to try different medications at different dosages, and that it was a time-consuming situation.

"Jess, I have three medications in mind. Of course, we'll have to try one at a time and watch how you react to each one. You may show negative side effects, or you may feel that the medications don't properly treat your condition." Dr. Stevens reached behind his desk and pulled out a five-inch-thick book to look up each medication. "Let's give this one a chance," he said as he wrote out a prescription and handed it to me. "I'll see you again next week. You can arrange for an appointment with my receptionist."

We shook hands as he said, "Jess, I'm here for you. You have an entire team of qualified medical professionals behind you. We won't give up. Stay with us."

Jack smiled when he saw me again. After we got into the car, I was a little surprised when he asked, "How did it go?" So frequently before, Jack didn't ask questions about my therapy sessions. The change pleased me.

During the drive home, and even later that night, I kept thinking about Dr. Stevens' final words that afternoon, "Stay with us." I thought to myself, "Did he mean stay with the team, or did he mean don't kill myself?"

* * *

My life had never been a fairytale type of story. No. I had always lived a horror story. After four months and failures with the first three medications Dr. Stevens tried, I felt like this was just another chapter in my hideous existence.

"Jess," Dr. Stevens started at what appeared to be a session like all the rest, "you've been a wonderful patient."

"Thanks."

"Dr. Marcus and I spoke earlier this morning. I'm glad your weight is remaining stable."

"Yeah, there's something about getting involuntarily committed to a psych ward that motivates me to cooperate."

"I'm going to try a relatively new medication today. It's called topiramate. It's sold as Topamax. I'll start you at 25 milligrams a day and, hopefully, build you up to the full 400 milligrams a day. At first, you may have difficulty concentrating."

"That's nothing new."

"It may cause drowsiness, dizziness or coordination problems. Most of the side effects are usually mild. Just let me know about anything out of the ordinary, and don't wait for your next appointment if you suffer any extreme discomfort."

"Got it. What's special about this one?"

"Would you like the clinical answer or a nonprofessional, blunt answer?"

"Let's go with blunt."

"Here it is in a nutshell: On the street they call it the 'I don't give a damn medication.'"

"Excuse me?"

"Seriously, that's what it's called. It flattens out the thinking. It makes what you think of now as a big issue, such as your weight, seem like a less important issue. Basically, it's a chemical brain reorganizer."

"OK. My brains are scrambled eggs anyway. Let's give it a shot."

When I left Dr. Stevens' office and went to have the prescription filled, I didn't think there was much of a chance for success, but I went along with his game plan.

After two weeks of taking Topamax, the side effects he warned me about never seemed to appear, or they never reached a point that bothered me. Slowly, over the next several weeks, he kept increasing the dosage. To my great astonishment, I slowly started feeling less apprehensive, less anxious, less depressed, and less concerned about matters that used to seem like big issues.

Throughout that time, I continued my sessions with Dr. Marcus. Even he commented that he saw improvement. My sessions with Joan also showed results. The new food plan she prescribed started putting back some of the weight I lost. Ever so slowly, I inched my way up to a safe range. What I found so remarkable was that I didn't mind. I had to buy new and larger clothes, and even that didn't upset me. And what surprised me most was that I didn't mind Jack looking at my new and larger body when I was naked and he made love to me. Yeah, even that part of my life improved.

* * *

Chapter Ten
The Final Word

As usual, I got to Dr. Marcus' office a few minutes before ten, knowing that I wouldn't see him until ten minutes after ten. The whole morning I kept asking myself, "What will we talk about?" but I had no answer. I felt different. I felt feelings and emotions that were new or, at least, I couldn't remember the last time I felt those feelings. What was most strange is that emotions were swelling up inside me and they didn't bother me as they did in the past. Yes, in the past, when I felt too many emotions, I controlled them by restricting, purging, and cutting. In those few minutes of waiting, however, I relished them as a kid enjoying treats in a candy shop. It felt good. I felt alive. I felt invigorated with a sense of renewal.

Dr. Marcus opened the waiting room door to escort me to his office. We sat down. He looked at the last session's notes, then looked at me and asked his usual opening question about my weight.

"My range is 134-135." Yes, I finally reached the range Dr. Marcus thought was healthy.

"How do you feel about that?"

"Different."

"How so?"

"It doesn't bother me. I feel comfortable with myself."

There was a broad smile on Dr. Marcus' face. It was as if I said the right thing and that all of his work wasn't in vain. It's as though I validated his existence as a doctor, and both of us were glad about it.

"Jess, what else feels different?"

"Well, I remember all of those hospital therapy sessions. So often the doctor would ask the patients about themselves and their relationship with their mirror."

"And how would you describe your relationship?"

"I can sum it up in three words–the mirror lied."

"Did it?"

"Yes."

"What makes you say that?"

"Because I was the mirror."

"Interesting," Dr. Marcus said as he sat back in his chair. "Tell me more."

"I remember when I was down to less than 90 pounds. I'd look in the mirror and all I saw was a fat, ugly, disgusting cow. But the mirror is an inanimate glass object. All I was doing was projecting my negative self-image into the mirror. In return, my sickness, my ED, provided me with a distorted projection to prolong my sickness."

"Fascinating."

"I'm not fat now. I wasn't fat then. On and off, for over twenty years, I deluded myself. It's time for that to stop. It's time for me to stop blaming myself for my father having an affair when I was five. It's time for me to stop blaming myself for my brother's bipolar disorder and the negative actions I suffered because of what he did to me. It's time for me to stop thinking I was raped at fifteen because of anything I did. It's time to stop blaming myself because my daughter cut herself. It's time to stop blaming myself for my daughter's OCD. It's time to stop letting my feelings and emotions control my existence in such a negative way that I throw myself into a depressed state. It's time I stop my slow suicide by abusing my body through malnutrition and self-inflicted mutilation. It's time I stop my passive or aggressive suicidal ideation and actions. It's time to say I want to live, and not just because I want to see my kids grow up. Don't get me wrong. I hope one day to see my future grandchildren. I've got the best and most unbelievable husband in the world. It's time to get back to enjoying my life with him. It's time to say,

'The mirror lied. I have an eating disorder.' A year ago, I never would have agreed to this weight. I would have said you were crazy to even suggest it."

Dr. Marcus laughed. "Jess, that's exactly what you said to me."

I smiled. "Yeah. I guess I did. Sorry."

"That's OK. That's what I'm here for. Jess, you have woman's body now, and it's perfectly normal."

"Dr. Marcus, I was a resistant patient. You were the pain-in-the-ass doctor who kept on charging forward to help me."

"Thank you."

"Anytime."

"What do you hope for?"

"Good question. I hope for recovery."

"You're right. You've only taken the first few steps. But you haven't taken these types of steps in many years."

"Dr. Marcus, I've only been like this for four or five months. I understand there is the danger that I can revert with the first excuse."

"Right."

"From now on, recovery means living one meal at a time, and one day at a time."

"Jess, what do you think will have to happen for you to acknowledge recovery?"

"One day, and it won't be soon, I'll sit down and eat a meal without thinking. I'll just eat what's in front of me and enjoy it–like a normal person."

When my session was over, I made it a point to smile and wave goodbye to the receptionist.

She waved back, smiled, and said, "Have a good day, Mrs. Gordon."

"Thanks, hon, you, too. It's gorgeous outside."

* * *

I walked out into the warm, sun-filled parking lot feeling like a new person. As I lit my cigarette I said to myself, "I'm not a new person. I'm that happy and in-love person that I was just before I married Jack."

I inhaled deeply and let out the smoke. I got into my car, drove home, had lunch with Megan, and went up to the study to continue writing my journal. I felt an inner glow to understand that I thought about purging as I ascended the steps up to the study, but threw the thought out of my head.

The first words I typed for the day were, "ED is an addictive and deadly source of pain, suffering and death, seeking tens of thousands of future casualties. People with anorexia or bulimia have a mentally debilitating affliction which will kill them unless they get help. There is no such thing as a cure. There is only recovery, which lasts from moment to moment, and day to day. Moreover, no recovery is guaranteed or permanent."

I looked at what I typed and understood that I had learned all that the hard way. I started typing again: "As with recovering drug addicts, alcoholics, or smokers, one slip and a recovering eating-disorder person reverts into an eating-disorder victim. Anorexia and bulimia are mind disorders that are guaranteed to kill the spirit and body. Time and therapy are the two major weapons to fight eating disorders. Sometimes they work. Sometimes they fail. The only guaranteed way to stop an eating disorder is by never letting it start."

I picked up my several-hundred-page journal and reread my opening sentence. "There are two types of people with eating disorders: those who live and those who die."

It hurt to think that only months ago, I was almost one of those who died. I was unbelievably happy to relish in the fact that I was still alive. I started to cry without knowing that Jason just entered the room.

"Mommy, what's wrong?"

"Everything is good, sweetheart. These are tears of happiness." I gave Jason a big hug and kiss, patted him on the tush, and said, "I love you. Go out and enjoy."

I wiped the tears from my eyes, turned back to my keyboard and typed my journal's final words for the day, "To those in recovery, stay there. To those who seek help, may you find a good therapist who knows how to help you. To those in denial of their eating disorder problem, heaven help you."

* * *

About the Authors

MARC A. ZIMMER, Ph.D., holds a Doctorate in Psychology and is a Diplomate in Clinical Social Work. For over three decades he has been the Director of Biofeedback and Psychotherapy Development in Valley Stream, New York, where he specializes in the treatment of eating disorders and stress-related problems. Both he and his staff provide individual, family, and marital counseling, as well as biofeedback training. Using sophisticated instrumentation, Dr. Zimmer and his staff teach patients safe and painless ways to recognize subtle physiological changes that signal stress, and how to use these techniques to reduce the stress in everyday situations. What is special about Dr. Zimmer's treatment of eating disorders is his combined psychotherapy and biofeedback program, which is specifically tailored to patients with these problems. Dr. Zimmer is a consultant and lecturer to various organizations, and author of numerous articles in professional and educational journals. Dr. Zimmer is the co-author of *Dying to Be Thin: Understanding and Defeating Anorexia Nervosa and Bulimia–A Practical, Lifesaving Guide.*

N.R. Mitgang has written for book and magazine publications, the stage, television, and electronic media for the past thirty-five years. His writing credits include: playwright/lyricist, *BOJANGLES* (The AMAS Repertory Theatre, New York); co-author, *Mr. Bojangles* (Jim Haskins and N.R. Mitgang,

William Morrow); writer, *I Knew the Man Bojangles* (WNBC-TV, New York–nominated for an Emmy, Best Director); co-creator/publisher, *Well ... There You Go Again! The Humor That Shaped America* (N.R. Mitgang and Malcolm Kushner, Mitgang/Kushner Inc.–CD-ROM encyclopedia of President Ronald Reagan). He was an editor for Grosset & Dunlap and Director of Electronic Publishing for Facts On File. Mitgang has also served as a consultant or historical contributor to A&E's *Biography*, The Smithsonian Institution, The New York City Archives and, The National Archives.

* * *

Eating Disorders:

Are You at Risk?

The intent of this section is not to act as a substitute for experienced and professional medical and psychological assistance. On the contrary. This section is intended to highlight the red flags that can act as a wake-up call and, if it is necessary, perhaps this section will help convince you or a loved one to seek experienced and professional assistance.

If you score above the danger zone on this Eating Disorders Assessment and if you fail to take action, you are putting your life on a "slippery slope" toward danger. That may sound harsh, but please understand that an eating disorder (ED) can be detrimental to your health or even life threatening.

Our intent is to help you or someone you care about. People can reverse their negative course. We hope we can guide you onto a path toward a positive and lifesaving regimen. We want you to eat to live.

Anyone who even thinks she or he has an ED knows that eating to live sounds like an easy action, but we understand that it isn't easy. There is hope. You, like so many others, can learn to eat to live and regain a balanced and healthy lifestyle.

Remember, ED does not discriminate. Anyone can be an ED victim.

* * *

Eating Disorder Assessment

1. Are you at least five foot three, weigh less than 105 pounds, and you look in the mirror and see a fat person?
   (~~Yes~~ / No)

2. Have you learned to suppress your hunger as a means of losing weight?
   (Yes / ~~No~~)

3. Have you labeled healthy foods as safe or unsafe to eat?
   (Yes / ~~No~~)

4. Do you take laxatives or diet pills beyond their recommended dosage?
   (Yes / ~~No~~)

5. Do you over-exercise without the proper nutritional requirements?
   (~~Yes~~ / No)

6. Do you empathize with underweight people?
   (Yes / ~~No~~)

7. Have you ever purposely thrown up a meal because you felt too full?
   (~~Yes~~ / No)

8. Have you lost 20 to 30 pounds in the last thirty to sixty days by restricting food intake or by other unhealthy means?
(**Yes** / No)

9. Do you often intentionally and inappropriately skip meals in a continued effort to lose weight?
(Yes / **No**)

10. Do you obsess about your weight because you think your body is not perfect?
(Yes / **No**)

11. Does your mother (aunt, grandmother, sister) have an ED, and you need to compete with her for a thinner figure?
(Yes / **No**)

12. Do family and friends frequently urge you to gain weight?
(**Yes** / No)

13. Do you isolate yourself because you fear social or family gatherings where food will be served?
(Yes / **No**)

14. Does your weight cause you sufficient depression that you suffer from suicidal ideation?
(Yes / **No**)

15. Are others' attitudes toward you predicated on your weight?
(**Yes** / No)

16. Have you seen a picture of an emaciated person and wished you were that thin?
(Yes / **No**)

17. Have you ever binged and purged and felt the relief of an "emotional high?"
(Yes / **No**)

18. Do you cut yourself as a form of punishment or reward based on your weight?
(**Yes** / No)

19. Do you weigh less than 140 pounds and make conscious attempts to lose up to 50 pounds?
(Yes / **No**)

20. Does your doctor tell you to gain weight, and you do everything you can not to gain weight?
    (Yes / No)

21. Has a therapist or doctor ever asked about your dietary habits, and you lied to hide the truth?
    (Yes / No)

22. Are you extremely thin or underweight and have felt heart palpitations, suffered from dizziness or blackouts, or been diagnosed with kidney or other medical problems?
    (Yes / No)

23. Has your menstrual cycle been disrupted for a prolonged period of time based on inappropriate eating?
    (Yes / No)

24. Have people told you, "You look emaciated," and it made you feel proud of yourself?
    (Yes / No)

25. Do you think you have an ED?
    (Yes / No)

* * *

Eating Disorder Assessment Scoring

I f you answered yes to one or more of the previous questions, you should consider seeking professional and experienced medical and psychological assistance. We are not confirming that you have an ED. We are suggesting you might be at risk.

* * *

Eating Disorders:

What To Do When You Have One

A norexia and bulimia, and other forms of eating disorders, are disorders of the mind or psyche, and they are dangerous. Current medical knowledge says that an ED is not caused by a virus. Some doctors believe it may be genetic, but this is not a proven fact.

More often, this disorder has deep-seated affiliations with depression, a poor self-image, obsessive-compulsive behavior, and other psychological causes.

The following steps are based on thousands of sessions and years of cognitive behavior therapy (CBT) practice specializing in ED. Other people have reversed their "slippery slope." It is possible for you to do the same.

In plain and simple English, we will try to suggest the steps you should take to put yourself, or a loved one, on the road to a lasting recovery.

STEP 1.

Seek the help of a competent and experienced psychologist, psychiatrist, social worker, or other mental health professional. The word "experienced" is extremely important because too often, doctors attempt to treat this problem with little or no experience. Someone who has not treated hundreds or thousands of ED patients can sometimes do more harm than good.

STEP 2.

If you answered "yes" to several of the previous questions, it's time you said something to yourself: "I have an eating disorder." ED, like alcoholism and gambling problems, cannot be treated unless you admit you have a problem.

STEP 3.

Start a daily food intake diary to bring to your doctor.

STEP 4.

Use the same intake diary to discuss your eating habits with a nutritionist.

STEP 5.

Discuss your problem and your plan with a person you love and/or trust. A support group or person is extremely helpful, and your conversations will start to remove the cloud of secrecy caused by your ED.

STEP 6.

Understand that your ED affects not only you, but all those you love and care for. Food deprivation, or bingeing and purging, often causes social isolation. Understand that you can go to parties, enjoy yourself, have something to eat, and still have a good time without the fear of weight gain.

STEP 7.

Be brave, honest, and realistic in setting goals for yourself.

STEP 8.

Deal with facts, not fears (re: food, calories, and clothes).

STEP 9.

After getting medical clearance, exercise moderately, not excessively.

STEP 10.

Discontinue comparing yourself to others, as you will always lose this destructive game.

STEP 11.

Do not keep clothes in your possession that are too small, as that will create a setback scenario and prevent further progress.

STEP 12.

Have the professionals that you are in treatment with communicate with each other for a comprehensive treatment plan.

STEP 13.

Engage in activities that add to your ego and self-perception. Do not avoid situations out of fear or apprehension.

STEP 14.

Learn to express your emotions and feelings. Do not stuff them. Take the "risk" to gain the benefits.

STEP 15.

Gain patience and understanding that recovery is a process, not an event.

STEP 16.

Focus on "direction," not the numbers on the scale. Use the unforgiving scale appropriately, not excessively.

STEP 17.

Fear can be used to mobilize and motivate, and not prevent or distract. Confront your fears.

STEP 18.

Learn to trust certain individuals and gain better discretionary skills.

STEP 19.

Ensure that recreation and "fun" are incorporated into your life.

STEP 20.

Strive to be reasonable—not "perfect."

* * *

Food Intake Diary

If you would like a free copy of this spreadsheet, send your request via e-mail to:

ZimmerMitgang@AOL.com.

Please put FOOD INTAKE DIARY in the subject line.

FOOD INTAKE DIARY

		Date	Time	Emotional State	Food Consumed
Day					
Day					
Day					
Day					
Day					
Day					
Day